Bernie Sanders's Democratic Socialism

Nicolas Gachon

Bernie Sanders's Democratic Socialism

Holding Utopia Accountable

Nicolas Gachon
American History and Politics
Université Paul Valéry
Montpellier, France

ISBN 978-3-030-69660-3   ISBN 978-3-030-69661-0   (eBook)
https://doi.org/10.1007/978-3-030-69661-0

This Palgrave Macmillan imprint is published by the registered company Springer Nature Switzerland AG
The registered company address is: Gewerbestrasse 11, 6330 Cham, Switzerland

To Nathalie, Emilie, Charlotte and Sébastien

Acknowledgments

This volume owes a great deal to the generosity of friends, family, and colleagues. I am particularly grateful to Françoise Coste who has provided me with sustained encouragement and advice with this work. I am also indebted to Nathalie Dessens, Monica Michlin, Hélène Quanquin, Antoine Coppolani, and François Vergniolle de Chantal for their comments.

I would like to thank Palgrave Macmillan, especially Rebecca Roberts for her trust in the concept of this book. Thanks are extended to Palgrave Macmillan's anonymous reviewers for the balanced and helpful assessments of the original manuscript.

INTRODUCTION

Heather Gautney, a senior policy advisor on Bernie Sanders's 2020 presidential campaign and a professor of sociology at Fordham University in New York, recounts in *Crashing the Party: From the Bernie Sanders Campaign to a Progressive Movement* that one of the first things she had ever read about Bernie Sanders when she was hired to work in his office was that he carried a Eugene Debs keychain in his pocket.[1] Sanders's fidelity to Eugene V. Debs, the legendary socialist, the founding member of the Industrial Workers of the World, the five-time candidate of the Socialist Party of America for president of the United States who received almost a million votes[2] as a third-party candidate running from prison in 1920[3] is unquestionable. Sanders spent most of his career studying and

---

[1] Heather Gautney, *Crashing the Party: From the Bernie Sanders Campaign to a Progressive Movement*, New York, Verso, 2018, p. 14. The title of Gautney's book is also a reminder of: Ralph Nader, *Crashing the Party: Taking on the Corporate Government in an Age of* Surrender, New York, St. Martin's Press, 2002.

[2] Eugene Debs received 919,490 votes (3.43% of the popular vote). "U.S. President National Vote," November 2, 1920, *Our Campaigns*, https://www.ourcampaigns.com/RaceDetail.html?RaceID=1952.

[3] Eugene Debs was charged and convicted under the *Espionage Act* of 1917. He was incarcerated in Atlanta, Georgia, on April 13, 1919, following the Supreme Court's affirmance of his conviction.

emulating his political hero, to the point that, "looking backward,"[4] Debs may almost be regarded as a sort of Bernie Sanders of the 1920s. In 1979, Sanders wrote and produced *Eugene V. Debs: Trade Unionist, Socialist, Revolutionary, 1855–1926*.[5] The recording served as the background to an unsophisticated thirty-minute narrative throughout which Sanders's distinctive voice is heard, and certainly remains the most vivid expression of his fascination for Eugene Debs. The documentary was released in 1979, only two years before Sanders was elected to the mayor's office of Burlington, Vermont. Sanders was subsequently elected to the U.S. House of Representatives by Vermont's at-large congressional district in November 1990, then to the U.S. Senate in November 2006, and he ran twice for the presidential nomination in 2016 and in 2020.

Over time, many questioned whether Bernie Sanders's steadfast insistence that he was a socialist, a self-described "democratic" socialist, could ever be politically viable and make him electable in a country like the United States where the majority of people share positive images of business, entrepreneurs, and free enterprise. Where did Senator Sanders actually stand? Was he to be regarded as a social democrat? As a welfare-state liberal? What, exactly, was democratic socialism supposed to mean in the twenty-first-century United States? The values Sanders so consistently sought to embody and to promote over the years seemed anything but politically "bankable" in mainstream America. However, perceptions of Bernie Sanders changed dramatically after he launched his campaign for the White House on April 19, 2015, and indicated that he would run for the Democrats' 2016 presidential nomination. Sanders had caucused with Congressional Democrats before but had never been a registered Democrat himself, and he was still proclaiming to be a democratic socialist while running for the Democratic nomination. Hillary Clinton's first contender in the 2016 Democratic race, therefore, a 74-year-old socialist and former hippie from Vermont raging against wealth stagnation and the power of banks and corporations, was a most unlikely presidential candidate. Clinton's nomination seemed inevitable. It was "her turn," Heather Gautney wrote, "because the historic nomination of the first black president should

---

[4] *Looking Backward* is the title of Edward Bellamy's 1886 utopian novel. See *infra*, p. 46.

[5] Sanders, *Eugene V. Debs: Trade Unionist, Socialist, Revolutionary, 1855–1926*, New York, Folkways Records, 1979.

be followed by the equally historic nomination of the first female president, as though that had been an implicit understanding on which the party united around Obama."[6] Sanders, however, was not only challenging Clinton's established dominance over the Democratic primary, he was also a threatening reminder of why grassroots Democrats might be suspicious of the former first lady, a reminder that Hillary Clinton was a polarizing figure, an elite member of the establishment who was running her campaign on a "TOGIW" (The Other Guy Is Worse) strategy.[7]

The Democratic Party establishment, under the leadership of Debbie Wasserman Schultz, the Chair of the Democratic National Committee from May 4, 2011, to July 28, 2016, was willing to risk serious party damage to halt Bernie Sanders in 2015 and 2016[8]: big-name Democratic economists, former Chairs of the Council of Economic Advisers for Presidents Barack Obama and Bill Clinton, were sent to discredit him during the primary campaign (Alan Krueger, Austan Goolsbee, Christiana Romer, Laura d'Andrea Tyson)[9]; identity politics attacks showcased him as the candidate of young white liberals[10]; and his religious faith, or lack thereof, was used against him.[11] Hillary Clinton finally carried the nomination, to the dismay of Sanders and his supporters who claimed that the primary was rigged[12] and therefore refused to commit to supporting the

---

[6] Gautney, p. x.

[7] Ibid., p. ix. Gautney claims that the Democrats had used the strategy at least since Michael Dukakis in 1988.

[8] Jonathan Martin, Alan Rappeport, "Debbie Wasserman Schultz to Resign D.N.C. Post," *New York Times*, July 24, 2016, https://www.nytimes.com/2016/07/25/us/politics/debbie-wasserman-schultz-dnc-wikileaks-emails.html.

[9] Chris Matthews, "Dem Economists Hit Bernie Sanders with the Ultimate Political Insult," *Fortune*, February 18, 2016, https://fortune.com/2016/02/17/bernie-sanders-open-letter.

[10] Dara Lind, "How Democrats Learned to Love Identity Politics," *Vox*, July 26, 2016, https://www.vox.com/2016/7/26/12280510/democratic-convention-diversity-race-immigrants.

[11] Phil Helsel, "Top DNC Official Apologizes for 'Insensitive' Email After Leak," *NBC News*, July 24, 2016, https://www.cnbc.com/2016/07/24/top-dnc-official-apologizes-for-insensitive-email-after-leak.html.

[12] Sanders's supporters invoked a similar argument in 2020. See: David Siders, "'It Sounds Insane, Actually': Democrats Relive 2016 Primary All Over Again," *Politico*, July 3, 2020, https://www.politico.com/news/2020/03/07/democrats-2016-primary-122951.

winner since, they reckoned, no progressive perspective was ever to be expected should Clinton win the White House come November.

Bernie Sanders's record was astonishing. He was the runner up with 46% of the pledged delegates behind former Secretary of State Hillary Clinton who won the contest with 54%. His call for a political revolution had quickly gained momentum and ignited a "feel the Bern" fever that ultimately drew nearly 1.5 million people to his rallies and to other events across the country.[13] Bernie Sanders started the 2016 primary campaign with a major financial disadvantage to Hillary Clinton. He had raised just $14 million by the end of June 2015 when Clinton's campaign had already raised $47.5 million by that time. Sanders however managed to appeal to even more rank-and-file support than Barack Obama had in 2008, earning donations averaging $27, and finally equaled Clinton with a war chest of $182 million,[14] even slightly surpassing her as of March 31, 2016. That was all the more of an achievement as Bernie Sanders had spoken against *Citizens United*, even asking for a constitutional amendment[15] to overturn the Supreme Court's 2010 decision that opened the floodgates on campaign funding.[16] With the ascension of Bernie Sanders to a national platform and Donald Trump taking over the Republican Party, 2016 was set to be a historic election year, and populism soon became the political catchword.

[13] "Democratic National Convention, 2016," Ballotpedia.org, https://ballotpedia.org/Democratic_National_Convention,_2016.

[14] Robert Yoon, "$182 million: Bernie Sanders Equals Hillary Clinton's Campaign Fundraising," *CNN*, April 21, 2016, https://edition.cnn.com/2016/04/21/politics/2016-bernie-sanders-fundraising-hillary-clinton/index.html.

[15] "Sanders Files Constitutional Amendment to Overturn Supreme Court's Citizens United Decision," Press Release, January 21, 2015, Bernie Sanders, U.S. Senator for Vermont website, https://www.sanders.senate.gov/download/cuamendment?inline=file.

[16] The Supreme Court ruled that laws preventing corporations and unions from using their general treasury funds for independent "electioneering communications" violated the First Amendment's guarantee of freedom of speech. Corporations were allowed to spend unlimited money on campaign ads as long as they did not formally coordinate with candidates or political parties. According to Justice Kennedy, there could not be corruption, because, "[b]y definition, an independent expenditure is political speech presented to the electorate that is not coordinated with a candidate." Citizens United *v. Federal Election Commission*, 558 U.S. 310 (2010).

Much was made of the importance of populism in the 2016 presidential election. Cable news host and former U.S. Representative Joe Scarborough (R-Fla.) penned a significant metaphor in the *Washington Post* during the primary campaign. He claimed that the two parties that had dominated politics in the United States for 150 years had been "commandeered by pirates from outside the establishment" in 2016 and that, too often, "the captains navigating those ships [had] found their passengers cheering for those same pirates." Scarborough argued that "Hamilton, Madison and Washington [had] regained control of their ship of state," but that 2016 leaders seemed "less capable of controlling the mutiny rising in their midst."[17] However, as Charles Postel remarked in August 2016, if Donald Trump and Bernie Sanders were both populists, what, then, did "populist" exactly mean?"[18]

The first known use of the term "populist" in U.S. politics dates back to the Populist movement of the late 1800s, the coalition of Southern and Western farmers, urban workers, as well as utopians and polemicists, who were seen either as forward-looking liberal reformers or as reactionaries trying to recapture an idyllic utopian past. In his 1955 *The Age of Reform*, Richard Hofstadter, the consensus historian,[19] wrote that "somewhere along the way" a large part of the Populist-Progressive tradition "turned sour," became "illiberal and ill-tempered," that the Populists embraced "irrational myths of the past and unreasoned grievances about the present," speculating that the conservative paranoia and witch-hunts of McCarthyism had their roots in the Populist movement of the 1890s.[20]

---

[17] Joe Scarborough, "Alexander Hamilton's Warning to 2016 Voters," *Washington Post*, May 22, 2016, https://www.washingtonpost.com/blogs/post-partisan/wp/2016/05/22/the-modern-populist-mutiny.

[18] Charles Postel, "If Trump and Sanders are Both Populists, What Does Populist Mean?" *The American Historian*, August 2016, https://www.oah.org/tah/issues/2016/february/if-trump-and-sanders-are-both-populists-what-does-populist-mean.

[19] Hofstadter tended to reject that term. He believed that conflict remained an essential aspect of political development. Although he understood the importance of class conflict, his interest was more in the intellectual rather than in the strictly economic roots of that conflict. In the words of one of his biographers: "As the traditional agrarian middle class lost ground to more socially democratic and cosmopolitan interests, the tensions between the two Americas erupted in cultural conflict." See: David S. Brown, *Richard Hofstadter: An Intellectual Biography*, Chicago, IL, The University of Chicago Press, 2006, p. 100.

[20] Richard Hofstadter, *The Age of Reform: From Bryan to F.D.R.*, New York, Vintage, 1955, p. 20.

Yet the very same Populists of the 1890s also shed light on some of the historical roots of Bernie Sanders's own democratic socialism since the Populists were a grassroots movement that fought against many of the economic injustices associated with the Gilded Age. The two perspectives are not mutually exclusive; they help account for the fact that the term "populist" carries several meanings in the contemporary United States, and that Bernie Sanders and Donald Trump each came to be regarded as "the other populist"[21] during the 2016 campaign. From a broader angle, the term "populist" also describes "political phenomena that escape easy labels,"[22] "political appeals that are simply popular,"[23] "easily shifting from left to right,"[24] arguably often quixotic and frustrated, and thereby, to quote Richard Hofstadter again, "sour."[25]

However, populism may not be sufficient in itself to provide a comprehensive explanation of what happened in November 2016. The populist label was also used by the Democratic Party establishment, and by Hillary Clinton herself, to ascribe their electoral defeat to causes that lay outside of the mainstream of American politics.[26] While that type of political spin was not unusual, it certainly obfuscated the fact that many of the causes of the 2016 debacle did indeed lie within the mainstream of American politics, or, as Heather Gautney put it, that 2016 marked "the indictment of party elites on both sides of the aisle, who had more in common with each other than they did with their own respective bases."[27] In other

---

[21] Jonah Goldberg, "Sanders and Trump: Two Populist Peas in a Pod?" *National Review*, August 19, 2015, https://www.nationalreview.com/2015/08/donald-trump-bernie-sanders-populism.

[22] Postel, "If Trump and Sanders are Both Populists," op. cit., p. 6.

[23] Ibid.

[24] Anne Cunningham, ed. *Populism in the Digital Age*, New York, Greenhaven Publishing, 2018, p. 97. See also: Kirk A. Hawkins, Ryan E. Carlin, *et al.*, eds., *The Ideational Approach to Populism: Concept, Theory, and Analysis*, New York, Routledge, 2018.

[25] Hofstadter, op. cit., p. 20.

[26] Multiple causes concur to explain the Democratic defeat. One of them, for example, was that college-educated white women voted for Donald Trump in astonishing proportions although Trump's campaign had been colored by sexist comments.

[27] Gautney, p. 125. Gautney adds that "[d]espite the clear writing on the wall, a surprising number of liberal Democrats persisted in putting forth theories of 'whitelash' to explain Clinton's loss. Most of those hypotheses failed to address regional variations

words, the Democratic Party establishment sold a homegrown extension of the TOGIW—"the other guy is worse"—strategy[28] in 2016. Both "guys," Donald Trump but also Bernie Sanders, were "the other guy." And both guys were "worse." By 2019, three years into the Trump presidency, the Democratic Party still had not changed its course and rumors were aired during the campaign that Barack Obama had privately said that he would eventually speak up to stop Bernie Sanders from becoming the Democratic presidential nominee should Sanders hold a strong lead in the Democratic primary.[29] While the rumor of Obama's private remark was never officially confirmed, one of Obama's close advisors did indeed comment that Sanders was "not a Democrat."[30] Obama himself publicly remarked that "the average American doesn't think we have to completely tear down the system," to which Sanders answered: "Well, it depends on what you mean by tear down the system."[31] This exchange, as we shall see, casts light on a core component of the electoral equation as it spelled out in 2016 and 2020. Did Bernie Sanders only speak like a socialist or did he really speak as one?

The strategies of the Democratic Party and of Barack Obama himself were quite expectedly strategies of political calculations and swing politics. There was certainly reason for the Democratic establishment to compute the electoral data with a view to the upcoming contests. In 1972, Democratic presidential candidate Senator George McGovern[32] (D-S.D.) came to be perceived as a left-wing extremist and was defeated by Richard Nixon in a landslide (Nixon won 60.7% of the popular vote and 49

in political orientation indicated by Obama's electoral popularity in northern industrial states." Ibid, p. 119.

[28] See *supra*, p. 4.

[29] Justine Coleman, "Obama Privately Said He Would Speak Up to Stop Sanders: Report," *The Hill*, November 26, 2019, https://thehill.com/homenews/campaign/472 090-obama-privately-said-he-would-speak-up-to-stop-sanders-report.

[30] Hayley Miller, "Obama Said He Would Speak Up To Stop Bernie Sanders Nomination," *HuffPost* (November 26, 2019), https://www.huffpost.com/entry/obama-bernie-sanders-2020-nomination_n_5ddd31a1e4b00149f724793b.

[31] Barack Obama, Sanders, quoted in Jennifer Medina, Lisa Lerer, "Too Far Left? Some Democratic Candidates Don't Buy Obama's Argument," *New York Times*, November 22, 2019, https://www.nytimes.com/2019/11/16/us/obama-left-democrats-2020.html.

[32] See: George McGovern, *What It Means to Be a Democrat*, New York, Penguin, 2011.

states).[33] Whether McGovern lost because he steered a course too far to the left or because he went too far back to the center in the general election, alienating his primary voters, remains a question up for debate. But the lengthening shadow of George McGovern haunted Democrats in the wake of both the dramatic 2016 Democratic National Convention[34] and of the 2016 presidential election debacle. In November 2019 again, Barack Obama warned Democrats of moving too far left and alienating voters in the presidential race.[35] Whether Obama's argument was valid in 2019, in 2016, neither or both, would be mere speculation here. The drama that surrounded the 2016 Democratic National Convention took place because the sudden surge of Bernie Sanders collided with the political calculations of the Democratic Party establishment, and because the latter arguably failed to recognize an emerging social movement when it saw one. Heather Gautney describes social movements as "organic forms of expression" that are not bound by "the same temporal, political, and institutional horizons as electoral campaigns," that "shape ideas about social change and, if effective, find ways to operationalize those ideas into short—and long—term goals and realize those goals through contestation and organization."[36] Of course, Gautney's analysis may be regarded as an insider's sympathetic view of the 2016 Sanders campaign. But the sociologist Albion Small, as early as 1897, described social movements in a way that somehow prefigured Richard Hofstadter's "sour" appraisal of the Populist-Progressive tradition in 1955[37]:

> The term "Social Movement" is already a cant phrase both in Europe and America. It once had dignity. It is so common now that it is falling into contempt. [...] The social movement is, an unfriendly observer might say, a confusion of fussy, fidgety folk, blocking each other and everybody else by their foolishness. Here it is free soup, and there it is demand for a work-test instead of free soup. It is industrial education here, it is there a trade-union

---

[33] U.S. Presidential Vote, November 7, 1972, Our Campaigns, https://www.ourcampaigns.com/RaceDetail.html?RaceID=1939.

[34] The Democratic National Committee eventually issued an apology to Bernie Sanders and his supporters over leaked emails that showed bias among party officials towards Hillary Clinton.

[35] Obama, Sanders, quoted in Medina, Lerer, op. cit., p. 8.

[36] Gautney, p. 134.

[37] Hofstadter, op. cit., p. 20.

practice to prevent people from learning trades. It is importunity for more law, and it is clamor for no law. It is in one group the prescription of political machinery, and in another the proscription of political machinery. It is in one party outcry for more democracy, and in another it is a wail for revival of aristocracy.[38]

Social movements are often regarded as factions, if not as political tribalism, by those who are in power, and they are almost systematically chastised for steering courses outside of the political mainstream, too far from the center of political gravity. Yet this is arguably a very political judgment, and a rash one to boot. Historian Charles Tilly notably claimed that the American Revolution itself was, as a matter of fact, no other than a social movement.[39] Therein lay much of the substance of the debate between Barack Obama who claimed that "the average American doesn't think we have to completely tear down the system" and Bernie Sanders who answered "[w]ell, it depends on what you mean by tear down the system."[40] Did Bernie Sanders really seek to tear down the system? What did Barack Obama and Bernie Sanders each conceive the system to be? What, then, was exactly Bernie Sanders's democratic socialism?

This volume is not a biography of Bernie Sanders. It was never intended as one. *Bernie Sanders's Democratic Socialism: Holding Utopia Accountable* is not a history of leftism in the United States either. Its structure and organization speak to its overall purpose of providing a framework for understanding and analyzing Sanders's democratic socialism, its origins, its maturation, and its evolution between 1972, when Sanders ran for the Vermont gubernatorial election for the first time, and 2020 when he made his second presidential run. Bernie Sanders is not envisioned here as any sort of historian of the American left either, a figure whose life-story should be told to help make sense of modern-day politics in the United States. If a historian at all, Bernie Sanders, as we shall see, would be a historian of injustice per se, at best a historian of the socialist idea. The

---

[38] Albion W. Small, "The Meaning of Social Movements," *American Journal of Sociology*, vol. 3, n° 3, November 1897, p. 340.

[39] Charles Tilly, *Social Movements, 1768–2004*, Boulder, CO, Paradigm Publishers, 2004, p. 31. Charles Tilly notably refers to an influential lecture series by leading American historian J. Franklin Jameson entitled "*The American Revolution Considered a Social Movement*" (1925).

[40] Obama, Sanders, quoted in Medina, Lerer, op. cit., p. 8.

core argument of this book is that Bernie Sanders's characteristic brand of socialism evolved from the mold of late nineteenth-century utopian radicalism to radical demands for state and corporate accountability in the twenty-first century, turning into a social movement for reparative justice that rose to national prominence in the wake of the Great Recession in 2008 and of the Occupy Wall Street movement in 2011.

* * *

Part I, "Utopianism," examines the dominance of utopian radicalism among early socialists in the United States and the introduction of Marxist ideas in the second half of the nineteenth century, notably by German immigrants, many of whom were exiles of the 1848 Revolution,[41] and of course at the moment of the Russian Revolution in 1917. This is an important backdrop to Bernie Sanders's democratic socialism as Eugene V. Debs, Sanders's political model, came to socialism not directly through Marx but via utopianism. Only later, in the wake of the 1894 demise of the American Railway Union, and under the influence of such socialists as Victor L. Berger,[42] would Eugene Debs lean toward scientific socialism and focus more exclusively on electoral action. Marx and Engels were dismissive of nineteenth-century bourgeois "utopian" socialism, which they contrasted with their own "scientific" socialism, but many of the principles championed by utopian communities and many of the visions reported by American utopians still reflected a milder, distinctively American version of socialism. Bernie Sanders's own thought and political trajectory can be traced back to the intellectual legacy of Debsian

---

[41] See: Heléna Tóth, *An Exiled Generation: German and Hungarian Refugees of Revolution, 1848–1871*, New York, Cambridge University Press, 2014.

[42] Victor L. Berger was born in Austria-Hungary and was a founding member of the Social Democratic Party of America (1898–1901) and its successor, the Socialist Party of America founded in 1901. He was elected as the first socialist to the U.S. House of Representatives in 1910 representing Wisconsin's 5th district (Milwaukee). He was convicted of violating the *Espionage Act* of 1917 for publicizing his anti-interventionist views and therefore denied the seat to which he had been twice elected in the House of Representatives. The verdict was eventually overturned by the Supreme Court in 1921, and Victor L. Berger was elected to three successive terms in the 1920s. In a book entitled *Broadsides* (1913), Berger referred to changing the capitalist system as "drain[ing] the swamp." Victor L. Berger, *Broadsides*, Milwaukee, WI, Social-Democratic Publishing Company, 1913, p. 104, Internet Archive, https://archive.org/details/broadside00berg/page/107/mode/2up.

socialism, and to the subsequent optimistic belief in progressive reform, in a radical but pragmatic, therefore workable, alternative to the capitalist status quo.

Part II, "Realpolitik," deals with the complex relations between Bernie Sanders and the Democratic Party. The term Realpolitik was coined in 1853 by Ludwig von Rochau, a German journalist and politician, in a book entitled *Grundsätze der Realpolitik, angewendet auf die staatlichen Zustände Deutschlands*[43] (*Practical Politics: An Application of Its Principles to the Situation of the German States*) that characterizes the realist tradition in international relations.[44] While the term belongs to the lexicon of foreign policy, qualifying politics based on circumstantial practical and material factors rather than on theoretical or ethical objectives, it may be applied to Bernie Sanders's democratic socialism, not so much because, as we shall see, Burlington, Vermont was a city that had a foreign policy under his mayorship, but essentially because Sanders developed a pragmatic strategy to find his way into the American two-party system. Bernie Sanders put the blame on a Democratic Party that, he believed, had emptied itself of its own doctrine and responsibility to the people of the United States. What we describe as Realpolitik, therefore, was the deliberate endorsement and embrace of the Democratic Party as an empty shell to eventually move into—to "occupy"—that shell with a view to promoting a more radical ideology within a mainstream institutional slot in the two-party system.

Part III, "99 Percent," draws on Gramscian hegemony to reflect on the ways the dominant classes maintain control of society and of the capitalist order. Gramsci's concept of hegemony provides a sophisticated account of the process of class domination and of the roles of intellectuals and also of the "integral state," including the way dominant groups or classes gain power by manufacturing the consent of subordinate groups or classes to prevailing values. The reflection then focuses on what we have labeled the "post-American" promise of Barack Obama as well as on the limitations of the Obama administration in implementing it. The impact of the Great Recession and the confusion in the public eye between the bank bailouts voted by both Democrats and Republicans in the final weeks of the Bush

---

[43] Ludwig von Rochau, *Grundsätze Der Realpolitik, Angewendet Auf Die Staatlichen Zustände Deutschlands*, 1853. Rpt. Sydney, Wentworth Press, 2018.

[44] Jonathan Aslam, *No Virtue Like Necessity: Realist Thought in International Relations Since Machiavelli*, New Haven, CT, Yale University Press, 2002, pp. 183–185.

administration[45] and Barack Obama's own stimulus plan to jumpstart the American economy in early 2009,[46] paved the way for the Occupy Wall Street movement, a popular takeover of lower Manhattan, perceived as the symbolic and geographical location of power in the United States. Occupy Wall Street was the short-lived detonator of social suffering in American society, a protest movement Bernie Sanders aimed to transform into a political movement to demand reparations for economic inequality and to hold Gramsci's "integral state" accountable.

Part IV, "Democratic Socialism as Reparative Justice," tackles the issues of historicism and collective memory to place Bernie Sanders's argument of enduring social and economic inequalities in a diachronic critical perspective. The debate over the different meanings of liberalism in the United States raises corollary issues pertaining to an alleged "failure" of liberalism[47] as well as to state responsibility under the ideological umbrella of liberalism, whether it be political or economic liberalism. In addition to responsibility, the governance-friendly concept of "accountability" (in the sense of answerability, blameworthiness, and ultimately liability) has proved to entail frequent apologies, especially corporate apologies which have become a common feature in recent years. Should apologies be conceived as a way to accept blameworthiness and fend off actual liability? From the perspective of Bernie Sanders's democratic socialism, are corporate apologies and corporate philanthropy to be regarded as strategic vehicles to defuse accusations of corporate "greed" and to pre-emptively discredit potential demands for reparations? As taxation seemed to be the *modus operandi* of Sanders's scheme for reparative justice, could there ever be any overlap between Sanders's vision of society and the reality of the United States? If utopia was being held accountable by Bernie Sanders's democratic socialism, what kind of utopia was that?

[45] "Troubled Asset Relief Program," *Emergency Economic Stabilization Act of 2008*, Pub.L. 110–343, October 3, 2008.

[46] *American Recovery and Reinvestment Act of 2009*, Pub.L. 111–115, February 14, 2009.

[47] See, for example: Patrick J. Deneen, *Why Liberalism Failed*, New Haven, CT, Yale University Press, 2018.

REFERENCES

Aslam, Jonathan. *No Virtue Like Necessity: Realist Thought in International Relations Since Machiavelli*. New Haven, CT: Yale University Press, 2002.

Bellamy, Edward. *Looking Backward, 2000–1887*. Boston, MA: Houghton, Mifflin & Co., 1888. Rpt. Matthew Beaumont, ed. Oxford, New York: Oxford University Press, 2007.

Berger, Victor L. *Broadsides*. Milwaukee, WI: Social-Democratic Publishing Company. 1913. Internet Archive, https://archive.org/details/broadside00berg/page/107/mode/2up.

Brown, David S. *Richard Hofstadter: An Intellectual Biography*. Chicago, IL: The University of Chicago Press, 2006.

Coleman, Justine. "Obama Privately Said He Would Speak Up to Stop Sanders: Report," *The Hill* (November 26, 2019), https://thehill.com/homenews/campaign/472090-obama-privately-said-he-would-speak-up-to-stop-sanders-report.

Cunningham, Anne, ed. *Populism in the Digital Age*. New York: Greenhaven Publishing, 2018.

Deneen, Patrick J., *Why Liberalism Failed*. New Haven, CT: Yale University Press, 2018.

Gautney, Heather, *Crashing the Party: From the Bernie Sanders Campaign to a Progressive Movement*. New York: Verso, 2018.

Goldberg, Jonah. "Sanders and Trump: Two Populist Peas in a Pod?" *National Review* (August 19, 2015), https://www.nationalreview.com/2015/08/donald-trump-bernie-sanders-populism.

Hawkins, Kirk A., Ryan E. Carlin, et al., eds. *The Ideational Approach to Populism: Concept, Theory, and Analysis*. New York: Routledge, 2018.

Helsel, Phil, "Top DNC Official Apologizes for Insensitive Email After Leak." *NBC News* (July 24, 2016), https://www.cnbc.com/2016/07/24/top-dnc-official-apologizes-for-insensitive-email-after-leak.html.

Hofstadter, Richard. *The Age of Reform: From Bryan to F.D.R.* New York: Vintage, 1960.

Lind, Dara. "How Democrats Learned to Love Identity Politics." *Vox* (July 26, 2016), https://www.vox.com/2016/7/26/12280510/democratic-convention-diversity-race-immigrants.

Martin, Jonathan, Alan Rappeport. "Debbie Wasserman Schultz to Resign D.N.C. Post." *New York Times* (July 24, 2016), https://www.nytimes.com/2016/07/25/us/politics/debbie-wasserman-schultz-dnc-wikileaks-emails.html.

Matthews, Chris. "Dem Economists Hit Bernie Sanders with the Ultimate Political Insult." *Fortune* (February 18, 2016), https://fortune.com/2016/02/17/bernie-sanders-open-letter.

McGovern, George. *What It Means to Be a Democrat*. New York: Penguin, 2011.

Medina, Jennifer, Lisa Lerer. "Too Far Left? Some Democratic Candidates Don't Buy Obama's Argument." *New York Times* (November 22, 2019), https://www.nytimes.com/2019/11/16/us/obama-left-democrats-2020.html.

Miller, Hayley. "Obama Said He Would Speak Up to Stop Bernie Sanders Nomination." *HuffPost* (November 26, 2019), https://www.huffpost.com/entry/obama-bernie-sanders-2020-nomination_n_5ddd31a1e4b00149f724793b.

Postel, Charles. "If Trump and Sanders Are Both Populists, What Does Populist Mean?" *The American Historian* (August 2016), https://www.oah.org/tah/issues/2016/february/if-trump-and-sanders-are-both-populists-what-does-populist-mean.

Sanders, Bernard. *Eugene V. Debs: Trade Unionist, Socialist, Revolutionary, 1855–1926.* New York: Folkways Records, 1979.

Scarborough, Joe. "Alexander Hamilton's Warning to 2016 Voters." *Washington Post* (May 22, 2016), https://www.washingtonpost.com/blogs/post-partisan/wp/2016/05/22/the-modern-populist-mutiny.

Siders, David. "'It Sounds Insane, Actually': Democrats Relive 2016 Primary All Over Again." *Politico* (July 3, 2020), https://www.politico.com/news/2020/03/07/democrats-2016-primary-122951.

Small, Albion W., "The Meaning of Social Movements." *American Journal of Sociology*, vol. 3, n° 3 (November 1897), pp. 340–354.

Tilly, Charles. *Social Movements, 1768–2004.* Boulder, CO: Paradigm Publishers, 2004.

Tóth, Heléna. *An Exiled Generation: German and Hungarian Refugees of Revolution, 1848–1871.* New York: Cambridge University Press, 2014.

Von Rochau, Ludwig. *Grundsätze Der Realpolitik, Angewendet Auf Die Staatlichen Zustände Deutschlands, 1853.* Rpt. Sydney: Wentworth Press, 2018.

Yoon, Robert. "$182 Million: Bernie Sanders Equals Hillary Clinton's Campaign Fundraising." *CNN* (April 21, 2016), https://edition.cnn.com/2016/04/21/politics/2016-bernie-sanders-fundraising-hillary-clinton/index.html.

CONTENTS

PART I

Utopianism

CHAPTER 1

Marxism and Socialism in America

There is only one single reference to Karl Marx in *Eugene V. Debs: Trade Unionist, Socialist, Revolutionary, 1855-1926*,[1] the thirty-minute historical documentary Bernie Sanders produced in 1979, shortly after he discovered that most college students in the United States had never even heard of Eugene Victor Debs. Only three weeks after the beginning of the landmark Pullman strike in 1894, the American Railway Union, which represented 35% of Pullman's workforce, and which Eugene Debs had co-founded in 1893, was virtually annihilated and a number of union leaders, Debs himself included, were arrested and sent to jail in Woodstock, Illinois.[2] During his six months in prison, Eugene Debs had time to reflect upon the events of 1894 and upon how the U.S. government had decisively come to the aid of millionaire railroad owners and destroyed a labor union that had fought for the rights of starving workers. "While in prison," Sanders said, Debs began reading "socialist books and literature that friends," including Victor L. Berger, "were sending him, such as

---

[1] Sanders, *Eugene V. Debs*, op. cit., p. 3.

[2] See *infra*, p. 29. On the Pullman strike, see: Richard Schneirov, Shelton Stromquist, Nick Salvatore, eds., *The Pullman Strike and the Crisis of the 1890s*, Urbana and Chicago, University of Illinois Press, 1999.

© The Author(s), under exclusive license to Springer Nature Switzerland AG 2021
N. Gachon, *Bernie Sanders's Democratic Socialism*,
https://doi.org/10.1007/978-3-030-69661-0_1

Marx's 'Das Capital,' and works by Karl Kautsky,[3] the German Marxist."[4] Save a brief mention in *Outsider in the House: A Political Autobiography*[5] (1997), where Sanders refers to his own readings, there are no other references to Karl Marx in any of his later publications, whether it be in *Our Revolution: A Future to Believe In*[6] (2016) or in *Where We Go From Here: Two Years in the Resistance*[7] (2018), or in any of his public speeches. But Bernie Sanders had indeed read Marx. As a student at the University of Chicago in the 1960s, he was taught socialism and felt almost naturally attracted to leftist causes and was fascinated by the Russian Revolution and the Bolsheviks. In *Outsider in the House*, Sanders recalls spending a lot of time burrowed deep in the "stacks," the basement area where most of the books were stored in the university library, and reading mostly about "American and European history, philosophy, socialism, and psychology," and among many other writers, "Jefferson, Lincoln, Fromm,[8] Dewey,[9] Debs, Marx, Engels, Lenin." [10] Sanders developed his own version of Marxism, an American democratic version of Marxism that, maybe, would not make him consistently unelectable in the United States. Sanders adapted his vision of socialism to and for the United States. Years later, on November 19, 2015, as he was giving a speech at Georgetown University in Washington, D.C. to make the case for his own electability at the outset of his first presidential campaign, Sanders confirmed that he was class-conscious but reassured that he was not a Marxist fundamentalist:

[3] Karl Johann Kautsky was a Czech-Austrian theoretician, a prominent promulgator of orthodox Marxism after the death of Friedrich Engels in 1895. See: Karl J. Kautsky, *The Social Revolution and On the Morrow of the Social Revolution*, London, Twentieth Century Press, 1909.

[4] Sanders, band 8, "Internationalizing Socialist Thought."

[5] Id., with Huck Gutman, *Outsider in the House*: A Political Autobiography, New York, Verso, 1997. Rpt. *Outsider in the White House*, 2015.

[6] Id., *Our Revolution: A Future to Believe In*, New York, Thomas Dunne Books, 2016.

[7] Id., *Where We Go from Here: Two Years in the Resistance*, New York, Thomas Dunne Books, 2018.

[8] Erich Fromm, a thinker associated with the Frankfurt School of critical theory, fled the Nazi regime and settled in the United States. See *infra*, p. 137.

[9] About John Dewey (1859–1952), see: John Dewey, *America's Public Philosopher: Essays on Social Justice, Economics, Education, and the Future of Democracy*, ed. Eric Thomas Weber, New York, Columbia University Press, 2020.

[10] Sanders, *Outsider in the House*, p. 15.

I don't believe government should take over the grocery store down the street or own the means of production. But I do believe that the middle class and the working families of this country, who produce the wealth of this country, deserve a decent standard of living and that their incomes should go up, not down.[11]

During that same speech, Sanders made multiple references to Franklin D. Roosevelt and to the New Deal. Douglas Brinkley commented that Sanders was seeking to wrap himself in the mantle of Franklin Roosevelt to remind voters that he was part not only of an important political tradition in American history, but also of a winning one.[12] "Remember," Brinkley pursued, "F.D.R. won four times as essentially a democratic socialist.[13] During his speech at Georgetown University, Bernie Sanders eschewed Marxist symbols and Marxist rhetoric, especially regarding government control of the means of production, not knowing as yet whether that would be sufficient to fend off attacks from his Republican opponents and from the Hillary Clinton campaign alike. At stake was the meaning of socialism in the twenty-first-century United States, and whether that meaning could make political sense in the 2016 presidential campaign.

1.1   MARXIST THOUGHT

Marx spent most of his life in England which he believed to be the historical center of economic industrialism. From 1852 to 1862 he wrote a column in the *New York Tribune*, which the newspaper editor and publisher Horace Greeley had founded in April 1841. With 50,000 copies per issue, the *New York Tribune* was the daily paper with the largest circulation in the United States. At only two cents, the journal was relatively inexpensive and could appeal to the American working class.[14] It

---

[11] Id., *Our Revolution*, p. 166.

[12] Quoted in: Patrick Healey, "Bernie Sanders, Confronting Concerns, Makes Case for Electability," *New York Times*, November 19, 2015, https://www.nytimes.com/politics/first-draft/2015/11/19/bernie-sanders-defends-democratic-socialism-calling-it-route-to-economic-fairness.

[13] Ibid.

[14] On the New York Tribune, see: Adam Tuchinsky, *Horace Greeley's New-York Tribune: Civil War-Era Socialism and the Crisis of Free Labor*, Ithaca, NY, Cornell University Press, 2009.

was progressive and anti-slavery and offered Marx a transatlantic platform to try and undermine the ideas of Henry Charles Carey,[15] the leading economist of the American school of economics and also an advisor to President Abraham Lincoln. And Carey also wrote for the *New York Tribune*. Marx and Carey fundamentally disagreed over the social implications of economic development. Carey believed that economic development could occur without conflict and that different classes, as a universal rule, could find a harmony of interests. As Marx wrote in 1852: "That bourgeois society in the United States has not yet developed far enough to make the class struggle obvious and comprehensible is most strikingly proved by H. C. Carey (of Philadelphia), the only American economist of importance."[16] Henry Charles Carey, who envisioned a new social environment for the United States, if not a classless society at least a society immune to class conflict, somehow prefigured what historians would later describe as the Turner thesis,[17] the belief that "the frontier served to dampen class conflict in the new world."[18]

Marx's appraisal of the American Revolution was not unlike his appraisal of the French Revolution, which he saw as a bourgeois revolution aiming to impose the rule of a capitalist middle class. The United States was a subject of great interest to Marx. Between November 22 and 29, 1864, he co-signed a letter on behalf of the Central Council of the International Workingmen's Association (IWA), often called the First International (1864–1876), to congratulate Abraham Lincoln upon his recent re-election by a large majority. The final paragraph of the letter presented to U.S. Ambassador Charles Francis Adams on January 28, 1865, is very indicative of the way Marx perceived the United States:

[15] See: Henry Charles Carey, *Principles of Political Economy*, Philadelphia, PA, Carey, Lea & Blanchard, 1837.

[16] Karl Marx, Letter to Joseph Weydemeyer, March 5, 1852, quoted in Andrew Dawson, "Reassessing Henry Carey (1793-1879): The Problems of Writing Political Economy in Nineteenth-Century America," *Journal of American Studies*, vol. 34, n° 3, December 2000, p. 465.

[17] See: George Rogers Taylor, *The Turner Thesis: Concerning the Role of the Frontier in American History*, Lexington, MA, D.C. Heath, 1949.

[18] Michael Perelman, *Marx's Crises Theory: Scarcity, Labor, and Finance*, Westport, CT, Praeger, 1987, p. 14.

The workingmen of Europe feel sure that, as the American War of Independence initiated a new era of ascendancy for the middle class, so the American Antislavery War will do for the working classes. They consider it an earnest of the epoch to come that it fell to the lot of Abraham Lincoln, the single-minded son of the working class, to lead his country through the matchless struggle for the rescue of an enchained race and the reconstruction of a social world.[19]

In the American Civil War, in the institution and abolition of slavery, in the advent of freedom in the form of emancipation, Marx read a metaphor of the rise and fall of capitalism, therefore of the rise of the working class.[20] Ambassador Charles Francis Adams penned a cordial, diplomatic answer on the very same day: "Nations do not exist for themselves alone, but to promote the welfare and happiness of mankind by benevolent intercourse and example. It is in this relation that the United States regard their cause in the present conflict with slavery."[21] Marx did regard the United States as a "progressive" country in that he believed that the economic dominance of the middle class would inevitably lead the transition to socialism, hence his 1852 remark about Henry Charles Carey.[22] He had accordingly spoken to justify his support of free trade before the Democratic Association of Brussels, Belgium on January 9, 1848: "In a word the Free Trade system hastens the Social Revolution. It is in this revolutionary sense alone, gentlemen, I am in favour of Free Trade."[23] Marx's nineteenth-century social and economic views opened perspectives on one of the most pressing issues of the twentieth and twenty-first centuries: left to their own devices, free-market economies produce gross inequalities.

Still, Marx remained little known in the United States even though he had some notoriety among the German community, about half a million

---

[19] Robin Blackburn, *An Unfinished Revolution: Karl Marx and Abraham Lincoln*, New York, Verso, 2011, p. 212.

[20] Robert Weiner, "Karl Marx's Vision of America: A Biographical and Bibliographical Sketch," *The Review of Politics*, vol. 42, n° 4, October 1980, p. 470.

[21] Blackburn, p. 213.

[22] Marx, Letter to Joseph Weydemeyer, op. cit., p. 63.

[23] Id., "Speech on the Question of Free Trade," *Karl Marx, Frederick Engels: Collected Works*, vol. 6, London, Lawrence & Wishart, 1976, p. 465. The speech is also available in the Digital Collections of the University of Central Florida: http://ucf.digital.flvc.org/islandora/object/ucf%3A5209.

of whom landed in New York between 1852 and 1854, including German Marxists who arrived after the 1848 revolutions in Europe.[24] It was not until the end of the nineteenth century, toward the end of Marx's life in 1883, that movements to improve the lives of workers really began to gain importance in the United States. Social and economic conflicts and the growth of the labor movement that took shape during the Gilded Age drew considerable attention to socialism and, therefore, to Marxism. *Das Kapital* was largely ignored when the first volume came out in November 1867, and it was not until 1906 that it was published in the United States by the Chicago-based Charles H. Kerr & Company, a leading publisher of socialist, communist, anarchist, and Wobbly (Industrial Workers of the World[25]) works.[26]

Social tensions had increased by then. On May 4, 1886, in Chicago's Haymarket Square, labor protests over the eight-hour workday turned into riots after a bomb was thrown at police, resulting in deaths on both sides. Though the bomber was never identified, eight leading labor activists were convicted, seven were sentenced to death and one was given eight years in prison. Although its involvement could not be proved, the Knights of Labor,[27] the largest and most successful labor union at the time (with nearly 800,000 members in 1886[28]), was blamed for the incident. Three-fourths of its members consequently left the movement in 1886–1887,[29] many joining the American Federation of Labor,

[24] Daniel Bell, *Marxian Socialism in the United States*, Princeton, NJ, Princeton University Press, 1952. Rpt. Ithaca, NY, Cornell University Press, 1996, pp. 18–19.

[25] The Industrial Workers of the World, or "Wobblies," was founded in Chicago, Ill. In 1905. For a story of labor in the United States, see: Philip Dray, *There Is Power in a Union: The Epic Story of Labor in America*, New York, Anchor Books, 2011.

[26] Allen Ruff, *We Called Each Other Comrade: Charles H. Kerr & Company, Radical Publishers*, Oakland, CA, PM Press, 2011, pp. 88–89; Marx, *Capital*, vol. 1, Chicago, IL, Charles H. Kerr, 1906.

[27] The Knights of Labor were initially founded as "the Noble Order of the Knights of Labor" in 1869 by Uriah L. Stephens, James L. Wright, and a number of tailors in Philadelphia, PA.

[28] Its membership had risen after the Great Railroad Strike of 1877.

[29] James Green, Death in the *Haymarket: A Story of Chicago, the First Labor Movement and the Bombing that Divided Gilded Age America*, New York, Anchor Books, 2007.

founded by Samuel Gompers[30] in 1886. The Knights of Labor rejected socialism, and so did the American Federation of Labor. With the demise of the Knights of Labor and the Industrial Workers of the World, business unions—unions opposed to class or to revolutionary unionism, believing that unions and businesses had common interests—eventually prevailed.[31] The Haymarket riot resulted in a major setback for the labor movement, therefore, but it also came to represent a landmark in the struggle for workers' rights. Marx's name also came to be better known and to be associated with working-class revolutions in the context of the Gilded Age. More people now had a sense of his ideas even if they did not really know about *The Communist Manifesto* published with Friedrich Engels in 1848.[32] The first English translation of *Das Kapital* was done in 1887 for William Swan Sonnenschein, a British publisher, a year after the Haymarket incident and four years after Marx's death. The text was translated by Samuel Moore, a friend of Marx's, and Edward Aveling, Marx's son in law, from the third German edition. Frederick Engels then edited the Moore-Aveling translation.[33]

Capital, written over a period of twenty years about the intrinsic instability of the capitalist system, argued that human labor was the source of economic value, and that capitalists paid workers less than the surplus value, the value their labor added to the goods, thus exploiting the laborers. Unemployment, not the pressure of population, *Capital* explained, drove wages down. Unemployment was the direct consequence of capitalism since labor was a mere commodity in the capitalist system. Capitalists could force their workers to work longer hours to earn their subsistence and then reap the surplus value thus created. Marx blamed the capitalist mode of production characterized by private ownership of the means of production which divided the economy into two distinct

[30] Samuel Gompers, a British-born cigar maker, was far from radical. He believed that labor goals could be achieved through collective bargaining without resorting to collective ownership, and in keeping unions out of partisan politics.

[31] See: William M. Dick, *Labor and Socialism in America: The Gompers Era*, Port Washington, NY, Kennikat Press, 1972; Philip Taft, "On the Origins of Business Unionism," *ILR Review*, vol. 17, n° 1, October 1963, pp. 20–38.

[32] Marx, Friedrich Engels, *The Communist Manifesto*, 1848. Rpt. London, Penguin Classics, 2002.

[33] Ruff, op. cit., p. 73.

classes: those who owned the means of production—the capitalist class, or bourgeoisie—and those who did not, the workers—the proletariat.

Workers were alienated, forced to sell their labor as a commodity to the capitalists. The defining moment for Marxism in the United States would come in 1917 after the October Revolution in Russia that brought the downfall of the Romanov monarchy and the creation of a state by the Bolsheviks. Marx's theories had influenced Russian political thought in revolutionary circles and inspired the events leading to the Revolution. Lenin embraced Marx's philosophy, pulling his principles primarily from *Capital* and from *The Communist Manifesto*, notably that the revolution had to be a transition in stages from autocracy to communism, one such stage being a democratic government built on an industrial economic base. In the case of Russia, however, the proletarian revolution took place without going through a period of parliamentary democracy. Because the industrial base on which to build socialism still had to be created, Russia was submitted to Marxism-Leninism, Lenin's adaptation of Marxism in order to establish a socialist state and, later, to develop it further into socialism and eventually communism. In the United States, the Russian Revolution made Karl Marx a household name as his criticism of capitalism gained a wider audience. One decisive factor was that the Socialist Party of America founded in 1901 had now grown and become a significant political force, with Eugene Debs at its head. And Debs, a socialist, had won 900,369 votes (5.99% of the popular vote) in the 1912 presidential election.[34]

1.2   Debsian Socialism

By 1912, over three hundred publications, with a total circulation estimated at more than two million, were spreading the socialist message in the United States. In 1985, the literary and social critic Irving Howe, a prominent figure of the Democratic Socialists of America,[35] described this press as "[e]clectic, vivid, impassioned, erratic," a press that "offered schematic lessons in Marxist economics side by side with essays on popular

[34] "U.S. President National Vote," November 5, 1912, Our Campaigns, https://www.ourcampaigns.com/RaceDetail.html?RaceID=1954.

[35] The Democratic Socialists of America, an organization of democratic socialist, social democratic, and labor-oriented members, was founded in 1982 and has its roots in the Socialist Party of America.

science; fierce calls to direct revolutionary action with bland Christian moralizing."[36] The *Appeal to Reason*, published in Kansas from 1895 to 1922, had an average circulation of 750,000[37] which made it a mainstay of the Socialist Party of America after its creation in 1901. Eugene Debs joined the editorial staff of the *Appeal to Reason* in 1907. The Socialist Party was at the pinnacle of its power in 1912: its membership had grown above 100,000, the Party controlled the administrations of thirty-three cities across the United States,[38] and a socialist leader, Victor L. Berger, had been elected to the U.S. House of Representatives by Wisconsin's 5th district on November 8, 1910.[39] In the words of Bernie Sanders, Eugene Debs was the pivotal figure in the socialist project:

> When American workers needed a radical, independent political party to stand up to the Democratic and Republican parties which represented the interests of the capitalist class—Debs was there. He helped found the Socialist Party—and ran for President on its ticket 5 times.[40]

Not only was 1912 a decisive year because almost a million Americans voted for Eugene Debs in the presidential election, but also because a number of reforms long advocated by socialists had been integrated into the platforms of both the Democratic[41] and Republican[42] parties: trust-busting, maximum-hour and minimum-wage laws, women's suffrage, the abolition of child labor, and the direct election of U.S. senators. Still, Eugene Debs is relatively little known in the contemporary United States. In 1979, with mild Marxist overtones Bernie Sanders explained the

---

[36] Irving Howe, *Socialism and America*, San Diego, CA, Harcourt Brace Jovanovich, 1985, p. 4.

[37] Christine Bold, *The Oxford History of Popular Print Culture*, vol. 6 "U.S. Popular Print Culture 1860-1920," Oxford, Oxford University Press, 2012, p. 245.

[38] Sanders, *Eugene Debs*, band 9, "Debs for President."

[39] Library of Congress, "Topics in Chronicling America - Victor Berger: America's First Socialist Congressman," https://www.loc.gov/rr/news/topics/berger.html.

[40] Sanders, *Eugene V. Debs*, band 2, "An Overview Of Eugene V. Debs."

[41] Democratic Party, "1912 Democratic Party Platform," June 25, 1912, The American Presidency Project, https://www.presidency.ucsb.edu/node/273201.

[42] Republican Party, "Republican Party Platform of 1912," June 18, 1912, The American Presidency Project, https://www.presidency.ucsb.edu/node/273327.

reasons why he believed most younger people had never heard of Eugene Debs:

> Why? Why haven't they told you about Gene Debs and the ideas he fought for? The answer is simple. More than a half century after his death the handful of people who own and control this country—including the mass media and the educational system—still regard Debs and his ideas as dangerous—as a threat to their stability and class rule—and as someone best forgotten about.[43]

However, the fact that American socialism was essentially reformist rather than revolutionary[44] raises the issue of whether American socialism was, or could ever be, Marxist in any way other than rhetorical. The question had repercussions in the perimeter of Bernie Sanders's presidential campaigns and was often deliberately instrumentalized in the political discourse, as when Barack Obama insinuated that Bernie Sanders was a revolutionary to scare voters and to prevent him from gaining the 2020 Democratic nomination. At least Sanders's answer signified that he and the former Democratic president certainly did not view liberalism and the Republic quite in the same way: "Well," Sanders replied, "it depends on what you mean by tear down the system."[45] The word "revolution" does have two meanings, one of them being the return of a body to its initial position after rotating around a fixed axis, and quite a few leftists, Sanders included, estimated that such had been the course of the Obama presidency. The core issue, as we shall see, was not simply what it meant "to tear down the system" but what "the system" itself actually meant. In *A Framework for Political Analysis* (1965), David Easton, arguably of the most influential political scientists in the second half of the last century, provided a definition of the political system: "A political system is a set of interactions abstracted from the totality of social behaviour, through which values are allocated for a society."[46]

[43] Sanders, *Eugene V. Debs*, band 1, "Introduction."

[44] Jack Ross, *The Socialist Party of America: A Complete History*, Lincoln, University of Nebraska Press, 2015, p. 339.

[45] Obama, Sanders, quoted in Medina, Lerer, op. cit., p. 8.

[46] David Easton, *A Framework for Political Analysis*, Englewood Cliffs, NJ, Prentice Hall, 1965, p. 112.

Eugene Victor Debs was born in Terre Haute, Indiana, in 1855, seven years after Marx and Engels published *The Communist Manifesto*. He left school at the age of fourteen and started working in a railroad yard, eventually becoming a fireman on a locomotive. He was initially a member of the Democratic Party, which he later recalled with a measure of disdain: "There was a time in my life, before I became a Socialist," he declared in a 1923 speech, "when I permitted myself as a Democrat to be elected to a state legislature. I have been trying to live it down. I am ashamed of that as I am proud of having gone to jail."[47] Debs was not immediately into socialism either. In 1887, a year after the Haymarket riot, he advocated a distinctly American perspective of social relations, "turning a radical creed into a deeply American one"[48]:

[There] are wrongs which take on some of the forms of slavery, wrongs which work the degradation of men, which sap the foundations of citizenship and imperil the stability of American institutions. The conflict is not between capital and labor, between money and misery, cash and credit, it is between man and man, the man who works and the man who pays, the man who employs and the man employed. It is between the man who holds the office and the man who holds the ballot. It is a conflict between right and wrong, truth and error, justice and injustice, a conflict between citizens who make everything, build everything and the men who simply supervise and manage.[49]

His views evolved during the 1890s. Debs resigned from his position as Secretary of the Brotherhood of Locomotive Firemen, a railroad fraternal benefit society and trade union, and, together with fifty other trade unionists, formed the American Railway Union in Chicago in 1893.[50] He had come to the conclusion that workers could not successfully fight their employers while organized in small craft unions, spending more time and

---

[47] Eugene V. Debs, *Letters of Eugene V. Debs, vol. 1, 1874-1912*, edited by J. Robert Constantine, Urbana and Chicago, University of Illinois Press, 1990, p. liii.

[48] Debs, "Abolitionists," *Locomotive Firemen's Magazine*, vol. 11, n° 2, February 1887, p. 67.

[49] Jill Lepore, "Eugene V. Debs and the Endurance of Socialism," *New Yorker*, February 11, 2019, https://www.newyorker.com/magazine/2019/02/18/eugene-v-debs-and-the-endurance-of-socialism.

[50] For a biography of Eugene Debs, see: Nick Salvatore, *Eugene Debs: Citizen and Socialist*, Urbana and Chicago, University of Illinois Press, 1982.

energy competing against each other than in opposing their employers. The American Railway Union, therefore, was an industrial union, open to all railroad workers in America, regardless of the job performed.[51] Samuel Gompers wanted those workers to join his far less radical trade union, the American Federation of Labor, which he had founded three years earlier. Within a year, however, the American Railway Union became one of the largest unions in America, with 150,000 members.[52] Still, at that time, Debs was not a self-proclaimed radical socialist. He had come to doubt the power of "brotherhood" in the face of ruthless corporations; the strike now seemed to be the weapon of the oppressed. This chain of events was soon to land him in prison.

Debs was directly involved in the Pullman strike that took place from May 11 to July 20, 1894.[53] Pullman, Illinois, was a company town founded in 1880 by George Pullman, the president of the railroad sleeping car company. When nearly 4,000 Pullman Company workers started a strike in response to recent reductions in wages, Debs and the American Railway Union were asked to boycott Pullman cars. The boycott soon evolved into a national rail strike involving 125,000 workers in just four days. President Grover Cleveland sent 14,000 troops into Chicago to break what turned out to be the first national strike in U.S. history. A federal court issued a sweeping injunction against the leaders of the American Railway Union, ordering them to cease the boycott. Debs and the other leaders refused to obey: ending their strike would not only ruin the cause of the Pullman workers, it would also ruin the American Railway Union. But the Union was not strong enough to resist the federal government and the hostility of corporations and of numerous newspapers. The American Railway Union was virtually annihilated in three weeks and Eugene Debs, together with other leaders, was sent to jail in Woodstock, Illinois for defying the injunction. It was a defining moment, as Bernie Sanders explains in his 1979 historical narrative: Debs entered jail in the Spring of 1895 as a militant trade unionist fighting for the rights of workers to earn a decent wage; he left it six months later as a radical

---

[51] And regardless of their race too as of June 1894. See: Debs, "Draws a Race Line: Question of Color Before the American Railway Union," *Chicago Tribune*, vol. 53, n° 170, June 19, 1894, p. 12.

[52] Sanders, *Eugene V. Debs*, band 7, "The Formation and Fall of The American Railway Union."

[53] Schneirov, et al., op. cit., p. 19.

socialist who believed that workers could never receive justice under the capitalist system and that the working class should take over the means of production and the government.[54] While in prison Debs had begun to read socialist books and literature that friends sent him. One such reading was Marx's *Capital*.

In 1900 Eugene Debs stood as the presidential candidate of the short-lived Social Democratic Party which he had co-founded after the demise of the American Railway Union in 1894, convinced as he now was that union action would be insufficient to bring about the liberation of the working class. As of 1904, Debs ran for the newly founded Socialist Party of America. He openly advocated for working-class ownership of the means of production in his opening speech as presidential candidate of the Socialist Party in Indianapolis, Indiana, on September 1, 1904:

> The call of the Socialist party is to the exploited class, the workers in all useful trades and professions, all honest occupations, from the most menial service to the highest skill, to rally beneath their own standard and put an end to the last of the barbarous class struggles by conquering the capitalist government, taking possession of the means of production and making them the common property of all, abolishing wage-slavery and establishing the co-operative commonwealth.[55]

Debs ran again for the Socialist Party of America in 1908, 1912, and 1920. In September 1915, he voiced his opposition to the war, claiming that he was not "a capitalist soldier" but "a proletarian revolutionist."[56] On June 16, 1918, Debs gave a speech in Canton, Ohio, while American troops were fighting in Europe, outlining the socialist opposition to the war and his explicit support to the Russian Revolution.[57] He had also published several articles praising Marx in the previous weeks, notably

---

[54] Sanders, band 8, "Internalizing Socialist Thought."

[55] Debs, "The Socialist Party and the Working Class," September 1, 1904. E.V. Debs Internet Archive, https://www.marxists.org/archive/debs/works/1904/sp_wkingc lss.htm.

[56] Sanders, *Eugene V. Debs*, band 10, "The Speech That Sent Debs To Jail."

[57] Ibid. See also: Debs, "The Canton, Ohio Speech, Anti-War Speech," June 16, 1918. E.V. Debs Internet Archive, https://www.marxists.org/archive/debs/works/1918/can ton.htm.

"Karl Marx the Man: An Appreciation"[58] and "Marx and the Young People."[59] Debs was arrested after the Canton, Ohio speech, charged with violating the 1917 *Espionage Act*,[60] tried, and convicted to ten years in the federal penitentiary of Atlanta, Georgia. He ran a fifth time as the Socialist Party of America's presidential candidate from prison in 1920, receiving close to a million votes.[61] Debs was pardoned by President Warren Harding in 1921, after serving two and a half years of his term, and was returned home to Terre Haute, Indiana at age 66. He died four years later in Elmhurst, Illinois.

Debsian socialism and the persona of Eugene Debs form the starting point to understand how Bernie Sanders's democratic socialism eventually came to appeal to millennials in the twenty-first century, voters who, like Representative Alexandria Ocasio-Cortez (D-N.Y.) who had to face foreclosure with her own family, came of age during the Great Recession of the late 2000s and early 2010s. *Eugene V. Debs: Trade Unionist, Socialist, Revolutionary, 1855-1926*,[62] Sanders's 1979 historical narrative devoted to "Gene Debs," had an important influence on his trajectory, not only because it was his own production but also because Vermont Educational Television (Vermont ETV) refused to broadcast it. The documentary was officially turned down for quality reasons but Sanders saw this as a cover for ideological objections.[63] While Sanders's film would finally run on Vermont ETV, Branko Marcetic explains that "the cycle of setback, persistence, and eventual victory that characterized his battle with ETV would be transplanted to Burlington's City Hall."[64]

---

[58] Debs, "Karl Marx the Man: An Appreciation," *St. Louis Labor*, n° 900 (May 4, 1918), p. 1. E.V. Debs Internet Archive, https://www.marxists.org/history/usa/parties/spusa/1918/0504-debs-marxtheman.pdf.

[59] Id., "Marx and the Young People," *The Young Socialist's Magazine*, vol. 12, n° 5 (May 1918), p. 2. E.V. Debs Internet Archive, https://www.marxists.org/history/usa/parties/spusa/1918/0500-debs-marxandyoung.pdf.

[60] *Espionage Act*, Pub.L. 65–24, June 15, 1917.

[61] "U.S. President National Vote," November 2, 1920, op. cit. p. 3.

[62] Sanders, *Eugene V. Debs*, op. cit., p. 3.

[63] Branko Marcetic, "The Bernie Sanders Origin Story, Part 1," *Jacobin*, November 12, 2019, https://jacobinmag.com/2019/12/bernie-sanders-vermont-mayor-history-elections.

[64] Ibid.

In the late 1970s, Sanders, who had arrived in Vermont from Brooklyn at age 27,[65] had already made four unsuccessful runs as an "unabashed socialist"[66] candidate for the Liberty Union Party of Vermont,[67] twice for governor (in 1972 and 1976) and twice for the Senate (in 1972 and 1974). He was now on the verge of political retirement. By the time Ronald Reagan was elected to the White House in November 1980, Sanders decided to turn away from statewide politics and set his eyes onto the mayor's office in Burlington, Vermont. Located 45 miles south of the border with Canada, 94 miles south of Montreal, Burlington was the most populous city in Vermont with a population of only 37,721 in 1980.[68] Sanders was elected mayor on March 3, 1981.[69] From this point on, his political course was set. After his four terms as mayor, the state of Vermont elected Bernie Sanders to the U.S. House of Representatives in November 1990,[70] then to the Senate in 2006.[71] After all these years, after being reelected in 2012 with 71% of the vote,[72] Sanders told Mark Jacobson that his views were "basically the same" as during his Liberty

[65] Bernie Sanders was born on September 8, 1941. His father Elias Ben Yehuda Sanders (1904–1962) was born to a Jewish family in Słopnice, Austria-Hungary, which, today, is part of Poland. "Eli" Sanders immigrated to the United States in 1921 and later married Dorothy Glassberg (1912–1960), who came from a large Russian Jewish family on New York's Lower East Side. See: Harry Jaffe, *Why Bernie Sanders Matters*, New York, Regan Arts, 2015, pp. 22–25.

[66] Mark Jacobson, "Bernie Sanders for President? Why Not Try a Real Socialist for a Change?" *New York Magazine* (December 28, 2014), http://nymag.com/intelligencer/2014/12/bernie-sanders-for-president-why-not.html.

[67] The Liberty Union Party of Vermont (https://www.libertyunionparty.org) was founded in 1970 as a socialist party by former Representative William H. Meyer (D-Ct.), Peter Diamondstone, and Dennis Morrisseau.

[68] "Population Changes: Summary of Redistricting of the City of Burlington, 1865-Present," op. cit., p. 32.

[69] "Burlington, Vt. Mayor," March 3, 1981, Our Campaigns, https://www.ourcampaigns.com/RaceDetail.html?RaceID=512309.

[70] "Vt. At Large," November 6, 1990, Our Campaigns, https://www.ourcampaigns.com/RaceDetail.html?RaceID=34650.

[71] "Vt. U.S. Senate," November 7, 2006, ibid., https://www.ourcampaigns.com/RaceDetail.html?RaceID=6963.

[72] He was re-elected in 2018 with 67.4% of the vote. "Vt. U.S. Senate," November 6, 2012, Our Campaigns, https://www.ourcampaigns.com/RaceDetail.html?RaceID=507730.

Union days.[73] Sanders's intellectual adhesion to Debsian socialism and his personal admiration for "Gene Debs" himself, "the greatest leader in the history of the American working class,"[74] "a hero of [his],"[75] from whom he derived his own political rhetoric, seem unquestionable, as testified by the plaque honoring Debs in Sanders's Senate office in Washington, D.C.[76] Sanders, however, was less explicit and sometimes much less forthcoming when it came to publicly acknowledging the importance of the socialist canon in his own life and own political course. Individual adhesion is not always tantamount to political cohesion, arguably for reasons of electability in a country like the United States, arguably also due to the multifaceted nature of socialism, to its lack of cohesion. The same question would have been valid about Eugene Debs himself as Debs was not initially a socialist but became one through a process of radicalization while in prison in the wake of the Pullman strike. Eugene Debs eventually blended his initial idealism into Marxist realism at a time when socialism in the United States was by no means an affair of cohesion. Reflecting on Eugene Debs in *Outsider in the White House*, Bernie Sanders wrote: "Unfortunately, his ideas remain sufficiently dangerous not to be widely taught in schools or discussed in the mass media."[77]

1.3   Adhesion Without Cohesion

In *Socialism and America*, Irving Howe referred to Debsian socialism as "an attractive enterprise," "generous in its sentiments, quick to offer solidarity to the oppressed: striking workers, besieged farmers, isolated miners, hungry sharecroppers." It tolerated a wide diversity of opinion within its ranks, "never lusting for the monolithism of later radical movements" and allowed many women to rise to party prominence at a time when women in the United States were still fighting for the suffrage.[78] Yet, even though Bernie Sanders almost idolized the figure of Eugene Debs, he never openly discussed or even explicitly referred to Debsian

---

[73] Jacobson, op. cit., p. 32.

[74] Sanders, *Eugene V. Debs*, band 11, "The Last Days of Eugene Debs."

[75] Id., *Outsider in the White House*, p. 27.

[76] Id., *Outsider in the White House*, p. 27.

[77] Ibid., p. 26.

[78] Howe, pp. 17–18.

socialism during his presidential campaigns. Sanders proclaimed himself to be a "democratic socialist," praised Franklin Roosevelt's New Deal but hardly ever paid tribute to earlier socialist movements. Sanders's popularity in the second decade of the twentieth century partly eclipsed the history of the American socialist movement. In 2019, Jake Altman published a survey entitled *Socialism before Sanders: The 1930s Moment from Romance to Revisionism*[79] to replace the socialist movement of the 1930s within the historical framework of socialism in the United States. There was a discrepancy, a sort of a time warp, between Bernie Sanders's intellectual adhesion to the figure of Eugene Debs and the inchoate reality of socialism as a Marxist doctrine at the turn of the twentieth century.

The main obstacle to ideological cohesion probably was that turn-of-the-twentieth-century socialism was more of a nebula than it was an actual social movement, and that the Socialist Party was not yet capable of mustering majority support the way Eugene Debs could unify a mosaic of social sufferings and demands. The party was fragmented along regional lines, between the descendants of exiles from autocratic Germany in Wisconsin, the cluster of Jewish immigrant socialists in New York, and the socialists that brought farmers together in the South (in 1912, Oklahoma, Texas, Arkansas and Louisiana strikingly gave Eugene Debs 80,000 votes in the presidential election).[80] What most had in common was poverty, affliction, and a feeling of rejection. And the socialism to which they had recently adhered was inseparable from their religious faith. Religion was another factor of complexity, with the Christian socialists on the one side, who were into a non-Marxist social gospel, and the orthodox Marxists, clustered in the cities,[81] on the other side. There were also a few intellectuals, like the muckrakers, or the Chicago literacy renaissance, who, as a group, were smaller in number and therefore also in significance from the perspective of the Socialist Party of America. There were quite a few contradictions and a lack of intellectual cohesion, and sometimes coherence. *The Appeal to Reason*, for example, perpetually sought to blend the socialist faith in progress with "a Marxist," or "vulgar-Marxist," notion of the inevitability of socialism to show that socialism was "a destiny", not

---

[79] Jake Altman, *Socialism before Sanders. The 1930s Movement from Romance to Revisionism*, Cham, Switzerland, Palgrave Macmillan, 2019.

[80] Howe, pp. 9–11.

[81] Ibid., p. 15.

just "a theory." This was "embarrassingly uncomplicated," Irving Howe remarked with a certain irony, but "in 1912 intelligent and serious people held to it firmly."[82]

Socialists lacked cohesion between themselves and, quite significantly also, in their relations with trade unions, in their support of the anarcho-syndicalist Industrial Workers of the World, which Eugene Debs had co-founded, and of the moderate if not conservative American Federation of Labor, whose leadership Bernie Sanders put in the same bag with capitalist politicians in his 1979 documentary on Eugene Debs.[83] The issue was almost inextricable: while some socialists, Eugene Debs included, attacked Samuel Gompers and the American Federation of Labor for class collaboration, literally for treason to the cause of class struggle, they hardly took into account the fact that unionism was also meant to be an instrument of negotiation, and therefore of class collaboration. But other socialists, on the other hand, pushed the cause of class collaboration too far toward business unionism. What was at stake was whether unions should become instruments of the Socialist Party, or whether unions should be regarded as transactional operators of the capitalist society. In addition, like the Socialist Party itself, no trade-union federation could command the majority, or even the large minority,[84] of the American working class that would have given it the political cohesion and authority of a social movement. An unsought form of cohesion came in 1917, the year of the Russian Revolution, when the Socialist Party and unions were both targeted under the *Espionage Act*,[85] and then under its extension through the 1918 *Sedition Act*.[86] In the words of Bernie Sanders, "newspapers opposing the war were barred from the mails, censored and closed down, Socialist Party and trade union offices were wrecked, and large numbers of people were indiscriminately arrested."[87] In fact, as Richard Rorty remarked in *Achieving Our Country: Leftist Thought in Twentieth-Century America* (1997), the closest the left ever came to taking over the government was in 1912, when "a Whitman enthusiast, Eugene Debs,"

---

[82] Ibid., p. 16.

[83] Sanders, *Eugene V. Debs*, band 2, "An Overview of Eugene V. Debs."

[84] Howe, p. 23.

[85] *Espionage Act*, op. cit., p. 31.

[86] *Sedition Act*, Pub.L. 65–150, March 16, 1918.

[87] Sanders, *Eugene V. Debs*, band 8, "Internationalizing Socialist Thought."

ran for president and received almost a million votes,[88] a result which, according to Daniel Bell, was "as unstable a compound as was ever mixed in the modern history of political chemistry."[89]

In a sense Bernie Sanders fulfilled certain of the aspirations Richard Rorty expressed in 1997: "It would be a good thing," Rorty wrote, "if the next generation of American leftists found as little resonance in the names of Karl Marx and Vladimir Ilyich Lenin as in those of Herbert Spencer and Benito Mussolini"; it would be an even better thing, he continued, "if the names of Ely [90] and Croly,[91] Dreiser [92] and Debs, A. Philip Randolph [93] and John L. Lewis [94] were more familiar to these leftists."[95] Such a critique of Marxism echoed a distinctively American approach to the social evils that beset the United States at the turn of the twentieth century. In fact, Rorty continued, "[t]he main thing contemporary academic Marxists inherit from Marx and Engels is the conviction that the quest for the cooperative commonwealth should be scientific rather than utopian, knowing rather than romantic."[96] Marx and Engels were not advocates of utopian socialism due to their own opposition to idealist theories of

---

[88] Richard Rorty, *Achieving Our Country: Leftist Thought in Twentieth-Century America*, Cambridge, MA, Harvard University Press, 1997, p. 52.

[89] Bell, *Marxian Socialism*, p. 45, quoted in Rorty, p. 52. Daniel Bell's quintessential contribution was in the study of post-industrialism. His major works include *The End of Ideology: On the Exhaustion of Political Ideas in the Fifties*, New York, Free Press, 1960 and *The Cultural Contradictions of Capitalism*, New York, Basic Books, 1976.

[90] Richard T. Ely was a progressive political economist and advocate of the Social Gospel. See: Richard T. Ely, his *Introduction to Political Economy*, New York, Chautauqua Press, 1889.

[91] Herbert Croly founded the liberal weekly *The New Republic* in 1914. His most important book was *The Promise of American Life*, London, Macmillan, 1909.

[92] Theodore Dreiser, a novelist and journalist of the naturalist school, is best known for two novels: *Sister Carrie*, New York, Doubleday, Page, 1900 and *An American Tragedy*, New York, Boni & Liveright, 1925.

[93] Asa Philip Randolph was a labor unionist (he was head of the Brotherhood of Sleeping Car Porters in 1941), socialist politician, and civil right activist who organized the 1963 March on Washington.

[94] John L. Lewis was president of the United Mine Workers of America from 1920 to 1960, and founding-president of the Congress of Industrial Organizations (1935), which established the United Steel Workers of America (1942).

[95] Rorty, p. 51.

[96] Ibid., p. 139.

social change, which incidentally reverberated the double meaning of the word utopia as "an ideal place" but also as "no place" at all. But for many Americans, socialism simply meant living by the Golden Rule, a particular brand of socialism that was inseparable from their religious faith, that did not negate the growing class awareness but interpreted that consciousness in a particular, American, cultural context.[97] The cohesion of religious and secular millenarianism provided both a moral right and a moral duty, an inalienable right, to denounce capitalism. America, after all, stood for the promise of a better life.

REFERENCES

Altman, Jake. *Socialism before Sanders. The 1930s Movement from Romance to Revisionism.* Cham, Switzerland: Palgrave Macmillan, 2019.

Bell, Daniel. *Marxian Socialism in the United States.* Princeton, NJ: Princeton University Press, 1952. Rpt. Ithaca, NY: Cornell University Press, 1996.

———. *The End of Ideology: On the Exhaustion of Political Ideas in the Fifties.* New York: Free Press, 1960.

———. *The Cultural Contradictions of Capitalism.* New York: Basic Books, 1976.

Blackburn, Robin. *An Unfinished Revolution: Karl Marx and Abraham Lincoln.* New York: Verso, 2011.

Bold, Christine. *The Oxford History of Popular Print Culture*, vol. 6 "U.S. Popular Print Culture 1860-1920." Oxford: Oxford University Press, 2012.

Carey, Henry Charles. *Principles of Political Economy.* Philadelphia, PA: Carey, Lea & Blanchard, 1837.

Croly, Herbert. *The Promise of American Life.* London: Macmillan, 1909.

Dawson, Andrew. "Reassessing Henry Carey (1793-1879): The Problems of Writing Political Economy in Nineteenth-Century America." *Journal of American Studies*, vol. 34, n° 3, (December 2000), pp. 465–485.

Debs, Eugene V. *Letters of Eugene V. Debs, vol. 1, 1874-1912*, edited by J. Robert Constantine. Urbana and Chicago: University of Illinois Press, 1990.

———. "Abolitionists." *Locomotive Firemen's Magazine*, vol. 11, n° 2 (February 1887), pp. 67–68. E.V. Debs Internet Archive, https://www.marxists.org/archive/debs/works/1887/870200-debs-abolitionists.pdf.

———. "Draws a Race Line: Question of Color Before the American Railway Union." *Chicago Tribune*, vol. 53, n° 170 (June 19, 1894), p. 12.

---

[97] Salvatore, p. 237.

———. "The Socialist Party and the Working Class, Socialist Party Convention Minutes (September 1, 1904). E.V. Debs Internet Archive, https://www.mar xists.org/archive/debs/works/1904/sp_wkingclss.htm.

———. "Karl Marx the Man: An Appreciation," *St. Louis Labor*, n° 900 (May 4, 1918), p. 1. E.V. Debs Internet Archive, https://www.marxists.org/history/ usa/parties/spusa/1918/0504-debs-marxtheman.pdf.

———. "Marx and the Young People," *The Young Socialist's Magazine*, vol. 12, n° 5 (May 1918), p. 2. E.V. Debs Internet Archive, https://www.marxists. org/history/usa/parties/spusa/1918/0500-debs-marxandyoung.pdf.

———. "The Canton, Ohio Speech, Anti-War Speech" (June 16, 1918), E.V. Debs Internet Archive, https://www.marxists.org/archive/debs/works/ 1918/canton.htm.

Dewey, John Dewey. *America's Public Philosopher: Essays on Social Justice, Economics, Education, and the Future of Democracy*, edited by Eric Thomas Weber. New York: Columbia University Press, 2020.

Dick, William M. *Labor and Socialism in America: The Gompers Era*. Port Washington, NY: Kennikat Press, 1972.

Dray, Philip. *There Is Power in a Union: The Epic Story of Labor in America*. New York: Anchor Books, 2011.

Dreiser, Theodore. *Sister Carrie*. New York: Doubleday, Page, 1900.

———. *An American Tragedy*. New York: Boni & Liveright, 1925.

Easton, David. *A Framework for Political Analysis*. Englewood Cliffs, NJ: Prentice Hall, 1965.

Ely, Richard T. *An Introduction to Political Economy*. New York: Chautauqua Press, 1889.

Green, James. *Death in the Haymarket: A Story of Chicago, the First Labor Movement and the Bombing that Divided Gilded Age America*. New York: Anchor Books, 2007.

Healey, Patrick. "Bernie Sanders, Confronting Concerns, Makes Case for Electability." *New York Times* (November 19, 2015), https://www.nytimes. com/politics/first-draft/2015/11/19/bernie-sanders-defends-democratic-socialism-calling-it-route-to-economic-fairness.

Howe, Irving. *Socialism and America*. San Diego, CA: Harcourt Brace Jovanovich, 1985.

Jacobson, Mark. "Bernie Sanders for President? Why Not Try a Real Socialist for a Change?" *New York* (December 28, 2014), http://nymag.com/intell igencer/2014/12/ bernie-sanders-for-president-why-not.html.

Jaffe, Harry. *Why Bernie Sanders Matters*. New York: Regan Arts, 2015.

Kautsky, Karl Johann. *The Social Revolution and On the Morrow of the Social Revolution*. London: Twentieth Century Press, 1909.

Lepore, Jill. "Eugene V. Debs and the Endurance of Socialism." *New Yorker* (February 11, 2019), https://www.newyorker.com/magazine/2019/02/18/eugene-v-debs-and-the-endurance-of-socialism.

Marcetic, Branko. "The Bernie Sanders Origin Story, Part 1." *Jacobin* (November 12, 2019), https://jacobinmag.com/2019/12/bernie-sanders-vermont-mayor-history-elections.

Marx, Karl, Friedrich Engels. *The Communist Manifesto*, 1848. Rpt. London: Penguin Classics, 2002.

———. *Collected Works*, 50 vol. London: Lawrence & Wishart, 1975–2004.

Medina, Jennifer, Lisa Lerer. "Too Far Left? Some Democratic Candidates Don't Buy Obama's Argument." *New York Times* (November 22, 2019), https://www.nytimes.com/2019/11/16/us/obama-left-democrats-2020.html.

Perelman, Michael. *Marx's Crises Theory: Scarcity, Labor, and Finance*. Westport, CT: Praeger, 1987.

Rorty, Richard. *Achieving Our Country: Leftist Thought in Twentieth-Century America*. Cambridge, MA: Harvard University Press, 1997.

Ross, Jack. *The Socialist Party of America: A Complete History*. Lincoln: University of Nebraska Press, 2015.

Ruff, Allen. *We Called Each Other Comrade: Charles H. Kerr & Company, Radical Publishers*. Oakland, CA: PM Press, 2011.

Salvatore, Nick. *Eugene Debs: Citizen and Socialist*. Urbana and Chicago: University of Illinois Press, 1982.

Sanders, Bernard. *Eugene V. Debs: Trade Unionist, Socialist, Revolutionary, 1855-1926*. New York: Folkways Records, 1979.

———, with Huck Gutman. *Outsider in the House: A Political Autobiography*. New York: Verso, 1997. Rpt. *Outsider in the White House*, 2015.

———. *Our Revolution: A Future to Believe In*. New York: Thomas Dunne Books, 2016.

———. *Where We Go from Here: Two Years in the Resistance*. New York: Thomas Dunne Books, 2018.

Schneirov, Richard, Shelton Stromquist, Nick Salvatore, eds. *The Pullman Strike and the Crisis of the 1890s*. Urbana and Chicago: University of Illinois Press, 1999.

Taylor, George Rogers. *The Turner Thesis: Concerning the Role of the Frontier in American History*. Lexington, MA: D.C. Heath, 1949.

Tuchinsky, Adam. *Horace Greeley's New-York Tribune: Civil War-Era Socialism and the Crisis of Free Labor*. Ithaca, NY: Cornell University Press, 2009.

Weiner, Robert. "Karl Marx's Vision of America: A Biographical and Bibliographical Sketch." *The Review of Politics*, vol. 42, n° 4 (October 1980), pp. 465–503.

CHAPTER 2

Utopia and Reform

In his 1987 *Marxism in the United States: A History of the American Left*, Paul Buhle argued that "guilty Calvinism and innocent utopianism" mixed strangely together in virtually every American radical reform movement from the seventeenth century.[1] Brett H. Smith added in *Labor's Millennium: Christianity, Industrial Education, and the Founding of the University of Illinois* (2010) that the utopian millennialism of Calvin's evangelical heirs anticipated the appearance of "a visible American Christian theory of social salvation—the soil from which the Social Gospel movement would grow."[2] One defining challenge for Marxism in the United States lay in a perpetual imperative to reconcile two American idiosyncrasies: Calvinism and utopianism. With such clergymen as Walter Rauschenbusch (1861–1918), who taught at the Rochester Theological Seminary in New York State,[3] and who most notably published *A Theology for the Social Gospel*[4] in 1917, the Social Gospel movement developed at

[1] Paul Buhle, *Marxism in the United States: A History of the American Left*, New York, Verso, 1987. Rpt. 2013, p. 59.

[2] Brett H. Smith, *Labor's Millennium: Christianity, Industrial Education, and the Founding of the University of Illinois*, Eugene, Ore., Picwick Publications, 2010, p. 60.

[3] The Rochester seminary was planted as an offshoot of the Colgate, N.Y. seminary by a group of Baptists. It became a leading progressive theological school. See: Colgate Rochester Crozer Divinity School, https://www.crcds.edu/history.

[4] Walter Rauschenbusch, *A Theology for the Social Gospel*, New York, Macmillan, 1917.

© The Author(s), under exclusive license to Springer Nature Switzerland AG 2021
N. Gachon, *Bernie Sanders's Democratic Socialism*,
https://doi.org/10.1007/978-3-030-69661-0_2

the end of the nineteenth century as a typically American redefinition of Christianity along social lines. The core proposal of the Social Gospel was the application of Christian ethics to social problems, which carried a striking contrast between personal and social salvation. People should live by the Golden Rule as salvation was explicitly tied to good works, to helping other people, especially the needy. Religious liberals progressively stopped preaching a gospel of personal salvation in favor of a social gospel that was eventually more "social" than "gospel." At the very least, social salvation was consistent with the fact that America at large had a special destiny.

2.1   America's Special Destiny

In *American Dreamers: How the Left Changed a Nation* (2011), Nat Kazin posits that radicalism in the United States was always rooted in the promise that individual rights are to be realized in everyday life, and that the nation's founding texts, the Declaration of Independence in particular, bear the very terms of the social contract: "Abolitionists, feminists, savvy Marxists, all quoted the words of the Declaration of Independence, the most popular document in the national canon."[5] While leftists hardly adhere to the notion of self-reliance, to the metaphor of lifting oneself by one's own bootstraps, they embrace the idea that every American is entitled to "the pursuit of Happiness,"[6] independently of class or hierarchical limitations. Drawing on the thinking of his time, Thomas Jefferson justified declaring independence from England in 1776 by referring to the philosophy of natural rights. After John Locke's *Second Treatise of Government*[7] (1690) Jefferson wrote into the Preamble of the Declaration of Independence that "certain unalienable Rights" were God-given, to insist that they could never be taken or even given away, and that among these were "Life, Liberty and the pursuit of Happiness."[8] In fact

---

[5] Nat Kazin, *American Dreamers: How the Left Changed a Nation*, New York, Knopf, 2011, p. xvii.

[6] U.S. Declaration of Independence, Preamble, approved by Congress on July 4, 1776, signed on August 2, 1776, Constitution Center, https://constitutioncenter.org/learn/educational-resources/historical-documents/declaration-of-independence.

[7] John Locke, *The First & Second Treatise of Government* (1690), edited by C. B. Macpherson, Indianapolis, Ind., Hackett, 1980.

[8] Op. cit.

Jefferson simply rephrased, quite elegantly so, John Locke's statement of the fundamental rights of life, liberty, and property, but his own hopes rested primarily on property, as the political elite then also understood it unambiguously. Other contemporaries may have been left to envision an idealized society in which the sole purpose of the government would be to secure these "unalienable rights" for all Americans, but that was arguably not Thomas Jefferson's driving intention. This is typically one of the specifics for which the American utopia would later be held accountable by Bernie Sanders's democratic socialism in the twenty-first-century United States:

"We hold these truths to be self-evident, that all men are created equal; that they are endowed by their Creator with certain unalienable rights; that among these are Life, Liberty, and the pursuit of Happiness; that, to secure these rights, governments are instituted among Men, deriving their just powers from the consent of the governed; that whenever any form of government becomes destructive of these ends, it is the right of the people to alter or to abolish it, and to institute new government, laying its foundation on such principles, and organizing its powers in such form, as to them shall seem most likely to effect their safety and happiness."

Today, while the very rich become richer, the poor become poorer and the middle class disappears, the top 1 percent owns more wealth than the bottom 90 percent, and 95 percent of all new income goes to the top 1 percent.

Today, in terms of life expectancy, poverty has become a death sentence. With better health care, education and nutrition, the top 1 percent has seen an increase in their longevity. They now live 12 years longer than the people at the bottom of the economic ladder, people who are actually seeing a decline in how long they live.

Today, while it is projected that 60 percent of the electorate will not vote in the next national election because they don't see much to vote for, the top 1 percent will be spending hundreds of millions to elect candidates to make them even richer.

Remember the Declaration of Independence: "...governments are instituted among Men (and we would add Women), deriving their just powers from the consent of the governed; that when any form of government becomes destructive of these ends, it is the right of the people to alter or to abolish it..."

> Now is the time to alter our government. Now is the time to stop
> the movement toward oligarchy. Now is the time to create a government
> which represents all Americans, and not just the 1 percent.[9]

The rhetoric of the Declaration of Independence is the rhetoric of
America, of the American "idea," of the American utopia, in all its
complexity and in all its contradictions. Barack Obama, as presidents and
other elected leaders often do, used the exact same metaphor of America
in his Second Inaugural Address in 2013:

> What makes us exceptional—what makes us American—is our allegiance
> to an idea in a declaration made more than two centuries ago: "We hold
> these truths to be self-evident, that all men are created equal; that they
> are endowed by their Creator with certain unalienable rights; that among
> these are life, liberty, and the pursuit of happiness."[10]

The Declaration of Independence appears here as the metaphorical
epicenter of the broader ideological tension between Bernie Sanders and
Barack Obama. At stake is that, as a historical factor, the 2008 Great
Recession initiated a chain of dislocations and conflicts that imposed epis-
temic challenges to what the United States and, for that matter, America,
stand for. One impulse is markedly toward democratic accountability in
the case of Bernie Sanders, the other toward democratic exceptionalism in
the case of former President Obama. Both impulses concur to shed light
on post-crisis utopianism in the U.S. democracy.

Radical reformism and utopianism have always been interwoven
throughout the history of the United States. One fundamental reason
is that nineteenth-century America was much more than a framework
for utopian experiments: nineteenth-century America was arguably a
nationwide utopian experiment itself, one that, from the outset, was
said to be endowed with a special destiny, whatever that may turn out
to be. Socialism appeared in the United States as a utopia on many
accounts, although Marx and Engels insisted on the indispensable distinction between "utopian" and "scientific" socialism. Utopias are extremely

---

[9] Sanders, "The Declaration of Independence: A Revolutionary Document," U.S.
Senator for Vermont Website, July 5, 2014, https://www.sanders.senate.gov/newsroom/
must-read/the-declaration-of-independence-a-revolutionary-document.

[10] Obama, "Inaugural Address," January 21, 2013, The American Presidency Project,
http://www.presidency.ucsb.edu/ws/?pid=102827.

significant in the way they reflect the societies where they are created. Fredric Jameson argues that utopias have always been a political issue,[11] one that still helps to differentiate left and right:

> Thus "utopian" has come to be a code word on the left for socialism or communism; while on the right it has become synonymous with 'totalitarianism' or, in effect, with Stalinism. The two uses do seem somehow to overlap, and imply that a politics which wishes to change the system radically will be designated as utopian—with the right-wing undertone that the system (now grasped as the free market) is part of human nature; that any attempt to change it will be accompanied by violence; and that efforts to maintain the changes (against human nature) will require dictatorship.[12]

Utopias, therefore, help make sense of reality at different moments in time. They help people living at different moments in time cope with modernity. Because economic crises are historical factors that generate dislocations, they are often occasions to debate and to revisit what America is all about, to reconsider the relation between society and the individual, sometimes with momentous consequences when a major political realignment—which Russell J. Dalton defines as "an enduring change in pattern of a social group positions on economic issues"[13]—occurs.

This is most significantly what happened with the New Deal. Economic crises often have dire consequences for parties in power. The economic crises that really become historical moments and are remembered as such are typically those that bring about significant change in their wake. Such was for example not the case of the 1873 panic, Nicolas Barreyre remarks, although it was a crisis which, like any economic event of such magnitude, was "a particularly potent *political* phenomenon."[14] Politics informed the way Americans viewed the crisis and, consequently, how they tried to cope with it. To understand how the long-term effects of the crisis

[11] Fredric Jameson, *Archaeologies of the Future: The Desire Called Utopia and Other Science Fictions*, New York, Verso, 2005, p. x.

[12] Id., "Politics of Utopia," *New Left Review*, vol. 25, January/February 2004, https://newleftreview.org/issues/II25/articles/fredric-jameson-the-politics-of-utopia.

[13] Russell J. Dalton, *Political Realignment: Economics, Culture, and Electoral Change*, Oxford, Oxford University Press, 2018, p. 2.

[14] Nicolas Barreyre, "The Politics of Economic Crises: The Panic of 1873, the End of Reconstruction, and the Realignment of American Politics," *The Journal of the Gilded Age and Progressive Era*, vol. 10, n° 4, October 2011, p. 422.

reshaped society and politics as well as the economy depended on "how the economic event was *embedded* in a political structure and political processes." Barreyre concludes that the reason why the 1873 crisis was "not a *break* in political history" is that "nothing new emerged from it: no political idea, no new political phenomenon,"[15] which serves to explain "why so many historians have passed over the event and rarely choose 1873 as a significant chronological turn in their studies."

After 1886, on the other hand, in the aftermath of the Haymarket riot, there was indeed, to use Nicolas Barreyre's argument, "a *break* in political history."[16] The Haymarket affair was unquestionably "embedded" in political processes, whether it be in the form of labor struggles, of the women's movement, of ethnic and racial clashes,[17] etc. All those utopian and radical ideas and movements "contended for political allegiance,"[18] Francis Shor notes in his introduction to *Utopianism and Radicalism in a Reforming America, 1888-1918*. Economic tension, therefore, did not simply become "a particularly potent *political* phenomenon," economic tension in the form of a class struggle for social justice was "*embedded* in a political structure and political processes."[19] As Francis Shor continues, when economic crises and social conflicts engendered questions about "the legitimacy of the dominant moral and political universe," as in

[15] Ibid. The Great Recession, as we shall see, in that it generated a number of new political phenomena, events, and dislocations—the Occupy movement, the ascension of Bernie Sanders, and the election of Donald Trump—will most likely go down in history as a defining moment that questioned the social compact in the early twenty-first century.

[16] Ibid.

[17] The stories of Lucy Parson and Lizzie Holmes are good examples. Lucy Parsons, who was born a slave in Texas, married Albert Parsons and moved with him to Chicago. A socialist and later an anarchist, the editor of *The Alarm*, an anarchist newspaper, Albert Parsons was of the four Chicago radical leaders convicted of conspiracy and hanged following the Haymarket affair. His wife remained a labor organizer, radical socialist and anarcho-communist after the execution. The assistant editor of *The Alarm* was Lizzie Holmes, an anarchist and organizer of Chicago's working women during the late nineteenth century. After the Haymarket affair, Lizzie Holmes testified in court on behalf of Albert Parsons.

[18] Francis Shor, *Utopianism and Radicalism in a Reforming America, 1888-1918*, Westport, CT, Greenwood Press, 1997, p. xv.

[19] Barreyre, op. cit., p. 45.

the period from 1888 to 1918, "utopianism and radicalism [...] gained prominence."[20]

2.2   EDWARD BELLAMY, LINCOLN STEFFENS

Looking Backward, 2000–1887

Following the dramatic events that surrounded the Haymarket affair in 1886, Edward Bellamy published *Looking Backward, 2000-1887*,[21] a utopian novel about an American future that would transcend the violent tensions of his time. The story is told by Julian West, a Bostonian who goes to sleep by hypnotic means in 1887 and wakes up in the same place 113 years later to discover that the old society and its attendant evils have disappeared, that the city has been transformed into a center of equality, abundance, and harmony, that the United States has become a socialist utopia. Private enterprise has disappeared and has been replaced by a collective organization of the economy that provides opportunity and prosperity for everyone. Through most of the book, Dr. Leete, in whose house Julian West is staying, sits in the drawing room and explains the twentieth century to his guest. *Looking Backward* belongs to the tradition of utopian writing, drawing from classics like Plato's *Republic*,[22] Thomas More's *Utopia*,[23] or from more recent works,[24] but Bellamy's specificity was that it targeted conditions in the United States, notably the growing rift between the rich and poor that had caused the Haymarket affair. *Looking Backward* was the most successful utopian novel ever written.

Edward Bellamy adapted many aspects of pre-Civil War Fourierism into his socialist vision of social organization. Charles Fourier's ideal community consisted of 1,620 persons living on a self-supporting estate of several

---

[20] Shor, op. cit., p. 45.

[21] Edward Bellamy, *Looking Backward, 2000-1887*, Boston, MA, Houghton, Mifflin & Co., 1888. Rpt. Matthew Beaumont, ed., Oxford, New York, Oxford University Press, 2007.

[22] Plato, *The Republic*, c. 375 B.C. Rpt. G. R. F. Ferrari, ed., Cambridge, Cambridge University Press, 2000.

[23] Thomas More, *Utopia: On the Best State of a Republic and on the New Island of Utopia*, 1516. Rpt. Durham, NC, Duke Classics, 2012.

[24] Sylvia E. Bowman, *The Year 2000: A Critical Biography of Edward Bellamy*, London, Octagon Books, 1979, p. 107.

thousand acres called a "phalanx,"[25] in which work was distributed on a rational and rotating basis, according to "the calculus" of "passionate Attraction,"[26] thus ensuring happiness at work. Society, therefore, was scientifically organized into self-sufficient cooperatives. Subsistence was provided out of the common gain and surpluses equitably distributed to reward all members of the Phalanx, proportionally to their contributions in "labor, capital, and talent."[27] Fourier envisioned a society in which people worked together, both rich and poor, to create a social economy that was profitable and also saved time and labor for the citizens. The first American phalanx, the Social Reform Unity, was founded in 1842 in Pennsylvania, and two years later Brook Farm in Massachusetts converted to Fourierism. Before the Civil War, twenty-eight phalanxes were founded in the United States, and there were dozens of Fourierist clubs in cities across the country.[28] At the end of the 1880s, in the wake of the publication of *Looking Backward*, a reform movement took form under the impetus of Bellamyites through the creation of at least 165 Nationalist Clubs across the United States. The movement originated from Boston and was initiated by two journalists, Sylvester Baxter and Cyrus Field Willard,[29] who found in *Looking Backward* an answer to the dislocations of American society and hoped to remake society and the economy through the nationalization of industry. The Nationalist movement was

---

[25] Charles Fourier, *The Utopian Vision of Charles Fourier: Selected Texts on Work, Love, and Passionate Attraction*, edited by Jonathan Beecher, Richard Bienvenu, Boston, MA, Beacon Press, 1971, pp. 99–100.

[26] "I am the inventor of the mathematical calculus of the destinies, a calculus which Newton had within his grasp without realizing it. He determined the laws of material attraction, and I have discovered those of passionate attraction, a theory approached by no one before me." Ibid., p. 84. See also: Jonathan Beecher, *Charles Fourier: The Visionary and His World*, Los Angeles, University of California Press, 1986, p. 66.

[27] Fourier, p. 249.

[28] Edward Bellamy would later call the Fourierists of the 1840s "precursors" of his own movement, and claimed that they were denied their full potential by the coming of the Civil War, or, as Carl J. Guameri puts it, "that antislavery played a key role in diverting utopian socialists from their mission against northern society. Carl J. Guameri, *The Utopian Alternative: Fourierism in Nineteenth-Century America*, Ithaca, NY: Cornell University Press, 1991, p. 368.

[29] Apart from Edward Bellamy himself, Sylvester Baxter and Cyrus Field Willard were arguably the most important leaders in the Nationalist movement, and both were theosophists. Arthur Lipow, *Authoritarian Socialism in America: Edward Bellamy and the Nationalist Movement*, Berkeley, University of California Press, 1982, p. 226.

undercut by the rise of the People's Party, which had gained the support of farmers across the Midwest, South, and West in the 1890s, and had virtually disappeared by 1896.[30]

Edward Bellamy is a very significant figure on several accounts. For one thing, as Carl J. Guameri points out in *The Utopian Alternative: Fourierism in Nineteenth-Century America*, he "deliberately set out to make socialism respectable in America and to separate it from subversive cultural ideas, including foreign theories."[31] Eugene Debs regarded *Looking Backward* and its sequel *Equality*[32] as "valuable and timely contributions to the literature of Socialism [...] which not only aroused the people but started many on the road to the revolutionary movement."[33] There were also important differences with Fourierism. Bellamy did not adhere to the communitarian approach per se. He envisioned socialism as a matter of government ownership with a centralized direction of economic life to be achieved through political action, with a "bureaucratic policy" and the state as "the Great Trust," which, according to Guameri, would have horrified antebellum communitarians but appeared "reasonable" in the late nineteenth century.[34] Edward Bellamy can certainly be regarded as a transitional figure between communitarian and electoral socialism, but his repudiation of the community for the sake of centralization in the hands of the state was also an obstacle for such leaders as Eugene Debs. From their perspective, centralization and state intervention were too often assimilated to the bloody repression of labor movements, from the railroad strikes of 1877 to the Pullman strike of 1894. Many leaders like Eugene Debs were suspicious and even antagonistic to the kind of state sponsorship embraced by the followers of Edward Bellamy.[35]

William Dean Howells once declared that Bellamy "virtually founded the Populist Party," which was an exaggeration although some detractors of the Populists did blame Edward Bellamy for instigating an agrarian

---

[30] The Populists themselves chose to fuse with the Democratic Party in the 1896 election, which caused the movement to collapse after a landslide loss in the electoral college.

[31] Guameri, p. 404.

[32] Bellamy, *Equality*, New York, D. Appleton & Co., 1897. Rpt. Rockville, MD, Wildside Press, 2010.

[33] Quoted in Shor, p. 16.

[34] Guameri, p. 404.

[35] Shor, p. 17.

uprising.[36] A number of Bellamy's proposals, such as the nationalization of the railroad, telegraph, and telephone industries, were also included in Populist politics, which indicates that Bellamy's Nationalism and Populism were certainly close. However, as Charles Postel points out in *The Populist Vision*, there were elements, such as Bellamy's Nationalism, that represented "influential mental constructs" more than a practical system of reform.[37] Postel, who also wrote "If Trump and Sanders Are Both Populists, What Does Populist Mean?" in *The American Historian*,[38] further argues that the Populist movement of the 1890s contained too many diverse and contradictory elements to speak of a single "Populist social blueprint."[39] Populism is an elusive term. In 2016, one striking difference between Donald Trump and Bernie Sanders was that Trump made an extensive use of *ad hominem* attacks while Sanders resorted to blaming the capitalist system itself, the system and its institutions, as the root cause of the symptoms that Trump identified in individuals (some allegedly "crooked"[40]) and groups of individuals. Of course, the personal profile and party affiliation of each respective candidate provides a partial explanation along ideological lines but, as Jan-Werner Müller explains in *What is Populism?*[41] (2016), being critical of elites is a necessary but insufficient condition to account as a populist. Otherwise, if criticism of existing elites was all there was to populism, anyone criticizing the status quo in any country would, almost by definition, be a populist, as would also every presidential candidate in the United States since all presidential candidates run against dysfunctions in the federal capital, against "Washington." In the contemporary sense of the term, Müller proceeds, populists are essentially antipluralist:

[36] Quoted in: Jamie L. Pietruska, *Prediction and Uncertainty in Modern America*, Chicago, IL, University of Chicago Press, 2017, p. 180.

[37] Postel, *The Populist Vision*, Oxford, New York, Oxford University Press, 2007, p. 288.

[38] Id., "If Trump and Sanders Are Both Populists," op. cit., p. 6.

[39] Id., *The Populist Vision*, p. 288.

[40] Donald Trump often referred to Hillary Clinton as "crooked Hillary" during the 2016 campaign, usually in reference to her use of a private email server during her time as Secretary of State in the Obama administration.

[41] Jan-Werner Müller, *What is Populism?* Philadelphia, University of Pennsylvania Press, 2016.

In addition to being antielitists, populists are always *antipluralist*: populists claim that they, and only they, represent the people. [...] When running for office, populists portray their political competitors as just part of the immoral, corrupt elite; when ruling, they refuse to recognize any opposition as legitimate.[42]

Intentionally or not, there is certainly a double standard beneath the "populist" label in contemporary political discourse. The precedent set by people like Edward Bellamy and, as we shall see, Lincoln Steffens helps make an important distinction between utopianism and a form of negativism, if not of nihilism. Utopianism suggests norms while nihilism destroys them.

"I Have Seen the Future, and It Works"

Another expression of a utopian vision was that of Lincoln Steffens, one of the original muckrakers (with such other journalists as Ida Tarbell,[43] Ray Stannard Baker,[44] David Graham Phillips,[45] Charles Edward Russell,[46] or Upton Sinclair[47]) who, at the turn of the twentieth century, wrote extensively to denounce graft and corruption in the United States. Their articles, and the muckraking phenomenon in general, formed what was

---

[42] Ibid., pp. 2–3.

[43] Ida Tarbell is best known for her 1904 book, *The History of the Standard Oil Company*, New York, McClure, Phillips & Co., 1904, published as a series of articles in *McClure's Magazine* between 1902 and 1904.

[44] Ray Stannard Baker also wrote for *McClure's* and later for the muckrakers' own *American Magazine*. He notably explored the situation of black Americans in *Following the Color Line* (*The American Magazine*, LXII, April-August 1907).

[45] David Graham Phillips published a series entitled "The Treason of the Senate" (*Cosmopolitan*, XL-XLII, March–November 1906) that was influential in leading to the passage of Amendment XVII to the U.S. Constitution, which provided for the direct election of U.S. Senators by the people of the states.

[46] Charles Edward Russell, who wrote "At the Throat of the Republic" (*Cosmopolitan*, XLIV, December 1907–March 1908) joined the Socialist Party of America in 1908. He was one of the co-founders of the National Association for the Advancement of Colored People (NAACP) in 1909.

[47] Upton Sinclair wrote the classic muckraking novel *The Jungle*, New York, Doubleday, Page, 1906, about sanitary conditions in meatpacking industry. He was an outspoken socialist.

subsequently referred to as a "literature of exposure" and gave jour-
nalism a new purpose in the progressive nebula, a new voice and a new
perspective beyond mere party politics in American democracy. Lincoln
Steffens was specifically interested in politics, whether it be at the local,
state, or national level. He published *The Shame of the Cities*[48] in 1904,
the book version of a series on municipal corruption he had written
in *McClure's* magazine between 1903 and 1905, and *The Struggle for
Self-Government*[49] in 1906. *The Struggle for Self-Government* regrouped
articles about state corruption also published in *McClure's* between 1903
and 1905. Steffens's methodical, almost scientific analysis of political
corruption, his detailed scrutiny of the workings of the "system," led him
to focus on the underlying corruption of private citizens that, according
to him, was almost mechanically, if not systematically, conducive to a
corrupt government:

> We are pathetically proud of our democratic institutions and our republican
> form of government, of our grand Constitution and our just laws. We are
> a free and sovereign people, we govern ourselves and the government is
> ours. But that is the point. We *let* them divert our loyalty from the United
> States to some "party;" we let them boss the party and turn our municipal
> democracies into autocracies and our republican nation into a plutocracy.
> We cheat our government and we let our leaders loot it, and we let them
> wheedle and bribe our sovereignty from us. True, they pass for us strict
> laws, but we are content to let them pass also bad laws, giving away public
> property in exchange; and our good, and often impossible, laws we allow
> to be used for oppression and blackmail. And what can we say? We break
> our own laws and rob our own government, the lady at the customhouse,
> the lyncher with his rope, and the captain of industry with his bribe and
> his rebate. The spirit of graft and of lawlessness is the American spirit.[50]

Lincoln Steffens would eventually become frustrated with the feeble
achievements of the muckraking movement. Beyond the agitation
surrounding each successive scandal the muckrakers exposed, beyond the
reforms they helped bring about, society was not sufficiently reformed,
and the capitalist system and its excesses still thrived. Steffens and the

---

[48] Lincoln J. Steffens, *The Shame of the Cities*, New York, McClure, Phillips & Co.,
1904. Rpt. Mineola, NY, Dover Publications, 2012.

[49] Id., *The Struggle for Self-Government*, New York, McClure, Phillips & Co., 1906.

[50] Seffens, *Shame of the Cities*, pp. 7–8.

muckrakers believed in divinely directed social evolution in which man retained free will. They believed in science but also in religion, in the law of gravity but also in the Golden Rule.[51] Yet they were disappointed with doctrinal and institutionalized Christianity and, Steffens in particular, pleaded with cities across the United States to awaken their Christian conscience, to feel "shame." Realizing that society would be too slow to reform itself in depth, further disillusioned by the continuing struggle between labor and capital, as well as by the slaughter of World War I, Steffens stepped up a quest to solve all social questions, a quest for certainty, one that would lead him toward Marxist certainty. He was intrigued by strong leaders, like Benito Mussolini, who had the force and energy to rise above the masses, even though that meant setting themselves above the law.

Steffens was captivated by Lenin, whom he interviewed briefly on March 14, 1919, during a three-week visit to Soviet Russia with William C. Bullitt, whose special mission was to negotiate diplomatic relations between the United States and the Bolshevik regime. As a journalist, Steffens did not try to deny the chilling stories of atrocities leaking out of Russia. But at this stage in his trajectory he had come to the conclusion that they were unfortunately necessary. Steffens reported fragments of Lenin's answers to his questions in his autobiography, such as "don't deny the terror. Don't minimize any of the evils of a revolution, we have to pay the price of revolution."[52] Steffens never wavered from his appraisal of the U.S.S.R. Three weeks after meeting Lenin, he wrote to Marie Howe, the wife of renowned progressive reformer Frederic C. Howe[53]: "I have seen the future; and it works."[54] Steffens's projection into a utopian future with a view to actualizing reform, and possibly also revolution although it is highly debatable that Steffens was ever a real revolutionist, is

[51] Nicolas Gachon, *Les Muckrakers et le rêve d'Amérique*, 1900–1912, Lille, ANRT, 1999.

[52] Lenin, quoted in Steffens, *The Autobiography of Lincoln Steffens*, New York, Harcourt, Brace & Co., 1931, p. 797.

[53] Frederic C. Howe fought against corruption and political bosses in Cleveland, Ohio, and was a leader in progressive politics in New York City. Marie Jenney Howe was a prominent feminist and also a Unitarian minister; she was involved with the movement for Women's suffrage in the United States.

[54] Steffens, Letter to Marie Howe, April 3, 1919, *The Letters of Lincoln Steffens*, vol. 1, edited by Ella Winter and Granville Hicks, New York, Harcourt, Brace & Co., 1938, p. 463.

both strikingly similar to and different from Edward Bellamy's outlook in *Looking Backward*. There are obvious similitudes in two comparable references to a utopian future as a model to reform the United States in the present. What is strikingly different, however, is that while Bellamy separated socialism from subversive cultural ideas, notably foreign theories,[55] firmly anchoring the future he envisioned in America, Steffens chose a subversive foreign, un-American model to project a future for the United States. Lincoln Steffens had spent most of his life and career defending American values in the face of industrialization and economic concentration, initially using a distinctively moralizing, even religious rhetoric, as in the title of his series, *The Shame of the Cities*. He later overtly embraced Marxist overtones out of frustration over the inefficiency of reform and the perpetuation of corruption, and even seemed to endorse the Russian Revolution itself to predict a desirable future for his own country.

2.3   UTOPIANISM AS A POLITICAL CHARGE

The charge of utopianism was leveled on numerous occasions against Bernie Sanders who had to fend off the criticism quite often. On September 15, 2015, for example, Bernie Sanders tweeted that it was not "utopian thinking" to say that every man, woman, and child should have access to health care as a right.[56] While he never resorted, unlike like Edward Bellamy or Lincoln Steffens, to a utopian model to retroactively transform the United States accordingly, he did point to a number of policies already in place in other countries so as to counter the characteristic neoliberal argument that nothing else was possible, that no other way of thinking or doing could be deemed practical. Health care was a case in point during the Democratic presidential primary debate on October 14, 2015, notably in this exchange between Bernie Sanders and Hillary Clinton:

> SANDERS: [W]hen you look around the world, you see every other major country providing health care to all people as a right, except the United States. You see every other country saying to moms that, when you have a baby, we're not gonna separate you from your newborn baby, because

---

[55] Guameri, op. cit., p. 47.

[56] Sanders, Twitter post, September 15, 2015, https://twitter.com/berniesanders/status/643764491000369152.

we are going to have—we are gonna have medical and family paid leave, like every other country on Earth. Those are some of the principles that I believe in, and I think we should look to countries like Denmark, like Sweden and Norway, and learn from what they have accomplished for their working people. [...]

CLINTON: [W]ell, let me just follow-up on that [...] because when I think about capitalism, I think about all the small businesses that were started because we have the opportunity and the freedom in our country for people to do that and to make a good living for themselves and their families. And I don't think we should confuse what we have to do every so often in America, which is save capitalism from itself. And I think what Senator Sanders is saying certainly makes sense in the terms of the inequality that we have. But we are not Denmark.[57]

Bernie Sanders was not presenting a foreign subversive model to reform the United States, and Denmark certainly was not Russia. But as Sanders referred to several occurrences of healthcare policies already in place in several Nordic countries, the argument was immediately seized upon by Hillary Clinton to imply that he was positioning himself beside the mainstream of American politics: "But we are not Denmark," Clinton concluded, "[w]e are the United States of America."[58] This was one in numerous moves to paint Bernie Sanders as an unrealistic if not dangerous left-wing extremist before the Democratic nomination. That particular response by Hillary Clinton was rather mild but, on a larger scale, the charge of "un-Americanism" could be politically devastating.

There was a backdrop to Clinton's remark and certain vulnerabilities on the part of Sanders that were expectedly utilized to polarize attitudes about his candidacy. In July 1985, when he was still mayor of Burlington, Bernie Sanders was invited to Nicaragua by President Daniel Ortega to celebrate the sixth anniversary of the Sandinista victory over the Somoza dictatorship. Sanders traveled to Nicaragua. Along with other "foreign dignitaries,"[59] yet the only elected American official to celebrate the

---

[57] "The CNN Democratic Debate Transcript, Annotated," *Washington Post*, October 14, 2015, https://www.washingtonpost.com/news/the-fix/wp/2015/10/13/the-oct-13-democratic-debate-who-said-what-and-what-it-means.

[58] Ibid.

[59] Sanders, *Outsider in the White House*, p. 47.

Sandinista victory in the midst of the Reagan years,[60] Sanders, accompanied by a reporter of the *Burlington Free Press*, declared: "Anyone who believes the Nicaraguan nation is a military threat to the United States is obviously out of their minds."[61] Three years later, after Bernie Sanders married Jane O'Meara on May 28, 1988, the newlyweds flew to Yaroslavl in the Soviet Union in the context of a sister-city relationship on what Sanders himself called "a very strange honeymoon"[62] that lasted ten days. A video taken during the visit[63] resurfaced in 2019 to damage Sanders's reputation. The video showed him bare-chested, sitting at a table lined with vodka bottles, singing "This Land Is Your Land" to his Russian hosts. In 2020, an 89-page Soviet-era file containing letters, telegrams, and internal Soviet documents regarding Sanders's 1988 trip to Yaroslavl, in reality tracking the efforts he had made to find a sister city in Russia for Burlington in the 1980s, also mysteriously emerged from Russian archives.[64] However, the press conference Bernie Sanders gave upon his return to the United States on June 6, 1988, tells a different, unsensational story. Sanders's stay in the U.S.S.R. had taken place while President Ronald Reagan was attending the Moscow Summit from May 29 to June 3, 1988. Sanders explained:

> While we were there the Summit meeting was going on and, without exception, the people there were enthusiastic and delighted by the fact that Ronald Reagan was in Moscow, and in fact they had many kind words to say about Ronald Reagan. The other observation that I would make is that I was surprised by the degree of self-criticism which Soviet officials were

[60] President Reagan accused the Sandinistas of importing Cuban-style socialism and aiding leftist guerillas in El Salvador. He regarded the regime as undemocratic even though foreign observers from democratic nations concluded that the 1984 Nicaraguan general election was generally free and fair.

[61] Russell Banks, "Bernie Sanders, the Socialist Mayor." *The Atlantic*, October 15, 2015, https://www.theatlantic.com/politics/archive/2015/10/bernie-sanders-mayor/407413.

[62] Jaffe, p. 105.

[63] Keiper Bros, "(Drunk and Shirtless) Bernie Sanders sings 'This Land Is Your Land' with Soviets, 1988," January 28, 2019, https://www.youtube.com/watch?v=KgCfJxpqhd0.

[64] Antonio Troianovski, "Excerpts from the Sanders Files in a Russian Archive," *New York Times*, March 5, 2020, https://www.nytimes.com/2020/03/05/world/europe/sanders-russia-excerpts-archive.html.

prepared to make about their own society. Frankly, I thought that they would be there to tell us that everything is wonderful and that certainly was not the case. For example, they are absolutely open in acknowledging that they are not a democratic society, and that those people we spoke to want to become a democratic society, and right now they are in the midst of an extraordinarily important and turbulent point in their history.[65]

That was in 1988, and history would even prove Bernie Sanders right. Perestroika, the political movement for reformation within the Communist Party of the Soviet Union, was active and about to lead to the 1989 Revolutions that resulted in the end of communist rule in Eastern and Central Europe, and to the fall of the Berlin Wall. The specter of foreign subversive roots to Sanders's utopianism was often agitated to combat his political agenda. But in the case of the sister-city program with Yaroslavl, Sanders never changed course. In 2019, he referred to his overseeing this project as mayor of Burlington in order to advocate for his proposal to allocate 1% of the military budget for the funding of exchange programs between foreign and American teenagers: "It was just an incredible experience," he said, "to see these kids getting along as well as they did."[66] Incidentally, an ideological connection between Sanders and communism would have been regarded as strange even by socialists since the Socialist Party of America was strongly anti-communist. A fundamental difference between communism and socialism is that all property and economic resources are owned and controlled by a strong central government under communism while, under socialism, citizens share equally in all economic resources as allocated by a democratically elected government.[67]

Utopianism, and for that matter utopian socialism, is to be understood as unbound from strictly practical considerations. Bernie Sanders

[65] Sanders, "Bernie Sanders on the Soviet Union Press Conference," Channel 17, June 13, 1988, https://www.youtube.com/watch?v=3KCoR6UYs1k.

[66] Id., quoted in Benjamin Wallace-Wells, "Bernie Sanders Imagines a Progressive New Approach to Foreign Policy," *New Yorker*, April 13, 2019, https://www.newyorker.com/news/the-political-scene/bernie-sanders-imagines-a-progressive-new-approach-to-foreign-policy.

[67] Individuals can own property under socialism while there is no such thing as private property under communism. The two doctrines also differ in terms of means: a revolution in which workers rise up against the bourgeoisie is seen as an inevitable part of achieving a pure communist state while socialism seeks change and reform through democratic processes within the existing social and political structure.

regarded practicality, or rather the accusation of impracticality, as the avatar of neoliberal reasoning. On April 15, 2016, in a speech entitled "The Urgency of a Moral Economy" given at the Pontifical Academy of Social Sciences at the Vatican, he spoke of the market economy in terms that the muckrakers of the early twentieth century would have probably endorsed: "There are few places in modern thought that rival the depth and insight of the Church's moral teachings on the market economy."[68] Then, regarding practicality itself, Sanders was more explicit:

> Some might feel that it is hopeless to fight the economic juggernaut, that once the market economy escaped the boundaries of morality it would be impossible to bring the economy back under the dictates of morality and the common good. I am told time and again by the rich and powerful, and the mainstream media that represent them, that we should be "practical;" that we should accept the status quo; that a truly moral economy is beyond our reach.[69]

In fact, the neoliberal accusation of impracticality points to an issue that was already present in the formation of socialism at the end of the nineteenth century and at the beginning of the twentieth century in the United States: the need to find a common ground between utopian aspirations and the need to achieve pragmatic goals. The social dislocations that resulted from the Industrial Revolution, economic concentration, economic crises, the society of the Gilded Age, etc. gave rise to apocalyptic nightmares but also to millenarian visions. The historical context generated conflicting norms and values that, in turn, generated an ideological debate among diverging political interests and visions of society. Accepting "the status quo," to quote from Bernie Sanders's remark, was certainly not an option for those progressives who wanted to inform reality, to *change* the world. Reform was an evolving process, one that was pragmatically optimistic about the future.

---

[68] Sanders, "The Urgency of a Moral Economy," April 15, 2016, *Bernie Speaks: Speeches by Bernie Sanders*, compiled by David Cane, CreateSpace Independent Publishing Platform, Greenbridge Publishing, 2017, p. 48.

[69] Ibid., p. 54.

REFERENCES

Baker, Ray Stannard. "Following the Color Line." *The American Magazine*, LXII (April–August 1907). Rpt. *Following the Color Line: An Account of Negro Citizenship in the Progressive Era.* New York: Doubleday, Page & Co., 1908.

Banks, Russell. "Bernie Sanders, the Socialist Mayor." *The Atlantic* (October 15, 2015), https://www.theatlantic.com/politics/archive/2015/10/bernie-sanders-mayor/407413.

Barreyre, Nicolas. "The Politics of Economic Crises: The Panic of 1873, the End of Reconstruction, and the Realignment of American Politics." *The Journal of the Gilded Age and Progressive Era*, vol. 10, n° 4 (October 2011), pp. 403–423.

Beecher, Jonathan. *Charles Fourier: The Visionary and His World.* Los Angeles: University of California Press, 1986.

Bellamy, Edward. *Looking Backward, 2000-1887.* Boston, MA: Houghton, Mifflin & Co., 1888. Rpt. Matthew Beaumont, ed. Oxford, New York: Oxford University Press, 2007.

———. *Equality.* New York: D. Appleton & Co., 1897. Rpt. Rockville, MD: Wildside Press, 2010.

Bowman, Sylvia E. *The Year 2000: A Critical Biography of Edward Bellamy.* London: Octagon Books, 1979.

Bros, Keiper. "(Drunk and Shirtless) Bernie Sanders sings 'This Land Is Your Land' with Soviets, 1988" (January 28, 2019), https://www.youtube.com/watch?v=KgCfJxpqhd0.

Buhle, Paul. *Marxism in the United States: A History of the American Left.* New York: Verso, 1987. Rpt. 2013.

Dalton, Russell J. *Political Realignment: Economics, Culture, and Electoral Change.* Oxford: Oxford University Press, 2018.

Fourier, Charles. *The Utopian Vision of Charles Fourier: Selected Texts on Work, Love, and Passionate Attraction*, edited by Jonathan Beecher, Richard Bienvenu. Boston, Mass.: Beacon Press, 1971.

Gachon, Nicolas. *Les Muckrakers et le rêve d'Amérique, 1900-1912.* Lille, ANRT, 1999.

Guameri, Carl J. *The Utopian Alternative: Fourierism in Nineteenth-Century America.* Ithaca, NY: Cornell University Press, 1991.

Jaffe, Harry. *Why Bernie Sanders Matters.* New York: Regan Arts, 2015.

Jameson, Fredric. "Politics of Utopia," *New Left Review*, vol. 25 (January–February 2004), https://newleftreview.org/issues/II25/articles/fredric-jameson-the-politics-of-utopia.

———. *Archaeologies of the Future: The Desire Called Utopia and Other Science Fictions.* New York: Verso, 2005.

Kazin, Michael. *American Dreamers: How the Left Changed a Nation.* New York: Knopf, 2011.

Lipow, Arthur. *Authoritarian Socialism in America: Edward Bellamy and the Nationalist Movement*. Berkeley: University of California Press, 1982.

Locke, John. *The First &Second Treatise of Government* (1690), edited by C. B. Macpherson. Indianapolis, IN: Hackett, 1980.

More, Thomas. *Utopia: On the Best State of a Republic and on the New Island of Utopia, 1516*. Rpt. Durham, NC: Duke Classics, 2012.

Müller, Jan-Werner. *What Is Populism?* Philadelphia: University of Pennsylvania Press, 2016.

Obama, Barack H. Inaugural Address (January 21, 2013). The American Presidency Project, http://www.presidency.ucsb.edu/ws/?pid=102827.

Phillips, David Graham. "The Treason of the Senate," *Cosmopolitan*, XL–XLII (March–November 1906).

Pietruska, Jamie L. *Prediction and Uncertainty in Modern America*. Chicago, IL: University of Chicago Press, 2017.

Plato. *The Republic*, c. 375 B.C. Rpt. G. R. F. Ferrari, ed. Cambridge: Cambridge University Press, 2000.

Postel, Charles. *The Populist Vision*. Oxford, New York: Oxford University Press, 2007.

Rauschenbusch, Walter. *A Theology for the Social Gospel*. New York: Macmillan, 1917.

Russell, Charles Edward. "At the Throat of the Republic." *Cosmopolitan*, XLIV (December 1907–March 1908).

Sanders, Bernard. "Bernie Sanders on the Soviet Union Press Conference," Channel 17 (June 13, 1988), https://www.youtube.com/watch?v=3KCoR6UYs1k.

———, with Huck Gutman. *Outsider in the House: A Political Autobiography*. New York: Verso, 1997. Rpt. *Outsider in the White House*, 2015.

———. "The Declaration of Independence: A Revolutionary Document." U.S. Senator for Vermont website (July 5, 2014), https://www.sanders.senate.gov/newsroom/must-read/the-declaration-of-independence-a-revolutionary-document.

———. *Bernie Speaks: Speeches by Bernie Sanders*, compiled by David Cane. CreateSpace Independent Publishing Platform: Greenbridge Publishing, 2017.

Shor, Francis. *Utopianism and Radicalism in a Reforming America, 1888-1918*. Westport, CT: Greenwood Press, 1997.

Sinclair, Upton. *The Jungle*. Doubleday, Page, 1906.

Smith, Brett H. *Labor's Millennium: Christianity, Industrial Education, and the Founding of the University of Illinois*. Eugene, OR: Pickwick Publications, 2010.

Steffens, Lincoln J. *The Shame of the Cities*. New York: McClure, Phillips & Co., 1904. Rpt. Mineola, NY, Dover Publications, 2012.

————. *The Struggle for Self-Government*. New York: McClure, Phillips & Co., 1906.

————. *The Autobiography of Lincoln Steffens*. New York: Harcourt, Brace & Co., 1931.

————. *The Letters of Lincoln Steffens*, vol. 1, edited by Ella Winter and Granville Hicks. New York: Harcourt, Brace & Co., 1938.

Tarbell, Ida. *The History of the Standard Oil Company*. New York: McClure, Phillips & Co., 1904.

Troianovski, Antonio. "Excerpts from the Sanders Files in a Russian Archive." *New York Times* (March 5, 2020), https://www.nytimes.com/2020/03/05/world/europe/sanders-russia-excerpts-archive.html.

Wallace-Wells, Benjamin. "Bernie Sanders Imagines a Progressive New Approach to Foreign Policy." *New Yorker* (April 13, 2019), https://www.newyorker.com/news/the-political-scene/bernie-sanders-imagines-a-progressive-new-approach-to-foreign-policy.

CHAPTER 3

Socialism and Progressivism

In *Where We Go from Here*, two years into the Trump presidency, Bernie Sanders reflected on the ups and downs of the reformist tradition in the United States. He also reflected on his own political trajectory and remarked that, unlike many other presidential candidates who had been defeated in their elections, he did not intend "to fade away into the sunset," that the campaign he had run in 2016 had "brought new progressive ideas into the mainstream and had been enormously successful in engaging millions of people in democracy." Giving up, therefore, was not an option. The struggle had to continue after the election: "We were about more than a political campaign," Sanders wrote, "[w]e were about building a movement."[1] The relentless effort to reform and reconstruct the social environment is a traditional component of utopian social theory in the United States. While utopias are, almost by definition, fictions, one of their most frequent forms being the novel, utopian social theory seeks to expose social evils and suggests alternative—"utopian"—models. Those alternative models are often deemed unrealistic by their critics, hence the political charge conveyed by the term. Utopian social theory,

---

[1] Sanders, *Where We Go from Here*, pp. 21–22.

© The Author(s), under exclusive license to Springer Nature Switzerland AG 2021
N. Gachon, *Bernie Sanders's Democratic Socialism*,
https://doi.org/10.1007/978-3-030-69661-0_3

however, does not only aim to form "a more Perfect Union"[2] but also to experiment America's special destiny and eventually actualize the American utopia. As Robert Fogarty put it in *American Utopianism*, "[t]he belief that citizens could remake their institutions by 'reasoned choice' has been central to American ideology."[3] That continuing commitment to remaking American democracy notably implied a strengthening of the public sphere. Like the Populists of the 1890s, the Progressives of the late nineteenth and early twentieth century invoked the Preamble of the Constitution to assert the purpose of making "We the People"[4] effective in strengthening the federal government's authority to regulate society and the economy.

3.1   Reform as the "Continuing Frontier"

In *Reform in America: The Continuing Frontier*, Robert H. Walker described a "continuing"[5] reform tradition in the history of the United States, arguing, for example, that although the "muckrakers" were named by Theodore Roosevelt in 1906, the "age of the muckrake" had in reality begun at least a generation earlier with such intellectuals as Mark Twain and Charles Dudley Warner (who were the first to call the era "the Gilded Age"[6]), Jacob Riis,[7] and Henry George..[8],[9] The 1890s were a pivotal decade due to the stark clash of two sets of ideas, one focused

[2] U.S. Constitution, Preamble, signed in convention September 17, 1787, ratified June 21, 1788, Constitution Center, https://constitutioncenter.org/interactive-constitution/preamble.

[3] Robert Fogarty, ed., *American Utopianism*, Itasca, Ill., E. F. Peacock, 1972, p. ix. Quoted in Shor, p. xiv.

[4] U.S. Constitution, op. cit., p. 61.

[5] Robert H. Walker, *Reform in America: The Continuing Frontier*, Lexington, University of Kentucky Press, 1985.

[6] Mark Twain, Charles Dudley Warner, *The Gilded Age: A Tale of Today*, Hartford, CT, American Publishing Company, 1874.

[7] Jacob A. Riis, a Danish-American social reformer and social documentary photographer, notably published *How the Other Half Lives: Studies Among the Tenements of New York*, New York, Charles Scribner's Sons, 1890.

[8] Henry George (1839–1897) published *Progress and Poverty An Inquiry into the Cause of Industrial Depressions and of Increase of Want with Increase of Wealth: The Remedy*, New York, Appleton and Co., 1879, in which he advocated for the single tax.

[9] Walker, p. 167.

on individualism and laissez-faire, the other on collective welfare and social controls.[10] Perhaps, as Eric Foner, reflected in 1984, "because mass politics, mass culture, and mass consumption came to America before it did to Europe," American socialists were the first to face "the dilemma of how to define socialist politics in capitalist society."[11] Robert Walker added that the last years of the nineteenth century were not without positive advances: the interests of farm and labor had been marshaled, railroads had been successfully prosecuted for rate discrimination, a civil service and antitrust bill had been passed.[12] The consequence was that the ability to realize utopian or radical ideals were somehow obstructed by the developing role of the state which, by incorporating certain reforms, managed to implement its own agenda while displacing radicals to the margins of the mainstream of American politics. In a sense, therefore, progressivism[13] undercut socialism, or rather "contained" socialism, as Alan Dawley remarked:

> [T]he social-justice planks in the Progressive platform incorporated watered-down socialist demands on wages, hours, and working conditions, and Roosevelt himself was convinced beyond a doubt that if conservatives did not come forward with reform, the masses would turn to socialism.[14]

The continuity motif, reform as "the continuing frontier,"[15] the idea that progressivism succeeded in containing socialism through legislation in

---

[10] Ibid., p. 168.

[11] Eric Foner, "Why Is There No Socialism in the United States?" *History Workshop*, n° 17, Spring 1984, p. 76.

[12] Walker, p. 167.

[13] Shelton Stromquist argues that "a Progressive movement constituted itself in response to the mounting social crisis of the late nineteenth century that was most clearly revealed in the battles between labor and capital and in the campaigns to save the wasted lives produced by industrial growth. Through diverse and overlapping networks intellectuals, social gospel reformers, young educated women, labor activists, and insurgent politicians developed over time a sense of participating in what they came to call a 'movement.'" Stromquist, *Reinventing 'The People': The Progressive Movement, the Class Problem, and the Origins of Modern Liberalism*, Chicago, University of Illinois Press, 2006, p. 3.

[14] Alan Dawley, *Struggles for Justice. Social Responsibility and the Liberal State*, Cambridge, MA, Belknap Press of Harvard University Press, 1991, p. 136. Quoted in Shor, p. 187.

[15] Walker, op. cit., p. 62.

the early twentieth century had repercussions in Bernie Sanders's later political posture.

Bernie Sanders's ideological positioning relative to Elizabeth Warren's was extremely telling in that while both agreed on most issues (a single-payer health insurance system, stronger labor unions, a Green New Deal, a $15 per hour minimum wage, free public college tuition, extended childcare and family leave policies, etc.) and were the two most left-wing candidates in the 2020 Democratic Party nomination, the ideological markers they embraced were different from one another. While Sanders identified as a "democratic socialist," Senator Warren (D-Mass.) famously called herself "a capitalist to [her] bones"[16] in 2018, adding that markets need rules. Elizabeth Warren belonged to a populist-progressive tradition that emerged in the Gilded Age. Like the Populists in the People's Party of the 1890s, she attacked monopoly power: "In many ways," she said, "tech monopolies are similar to the oil and sugar and railroad trusts of the nineteenth century."[17] While Warren identified the source of political corruption that undermined U.S. democracy in the influence of big business, her solutions to the structural inequalities entailed by corporate capitalism typically relied on government regulation, the favorite tool of the middle-class progressives who followed the Populists:

> The big fight now is to make the Justice Department and the [Federal Trade Commission] and other agencies use the tools they already have to protect competition. I'll give you three steps that the federal government can take to revive competition: Block anticompetitive mergers; stop anticompetitive conduct; and prioritize protecting competition.[18]

Elizabeth Warren's proposal was not one that would seek to reverse the deregulation that had been the rule since the 1980s, and it was also reminiscent of Theodore Roosevelt's "New Nationalism" speech at Osawatomie, Kansas, on August 31, 1910:

[16] Ted Rall, "The The Left Is Lukewarm on Elizabeth Warren," *Wall Street Journal*, November 6, 2018. https://www.wsj.com/articles/the-left-is-lukewarm-on-elizabeth-warren-1541548548.

[17] George Zornick, "Elizabeth Warren's 'Big Fight' Against Monopolies," *Nation*, February 15, 2018, https://www.thenation.com/article/elizabeth-warrens-big-fight-against-monopolies.

[18] Ibid.

It has become entirely clear that we must have government supervision of the capitalization, not only of public service corporations, including, particularly, railways, but of all corporations doing an interstate business. I do not wish to see the nation forced into the ownership of the railways if it can possibly be avoided, and the only alternative is thoroughgoing and effective legislation, which shall be based on a full knowledge of all the facts, including a physical valuation of property. This physical valuation is not needed, or, at least, is very rarely needed, for fixing rates; but it is needed as the basis of honest capitalization.[19]

About Theodore Roosevelt, Elizabeth Warren declared:

No one had done it when Teddy Roosevelt stepped up. And yet the American people supported him. And then antitrust law fell largely by the wayside, until Franklin Roosevelt, during the Great Depression, revived the use of antitrust law. And once again, giant corporations complained loudly. But the people supported the president.[20]

Although ideologically close, Elizabeth Warren can hardly be said to belong to the same tradition of American radicalism as Bernie Sanders.

Bernie Sanders's democratic socialism evolved from a tradition that, at its origin, was intellectually rooted in the great democratic uprisings that had swept Europe in 1848, and in the socialist revolutionary thought of Karl Marx and Friedrich Engels that gradually ran across the European working class and gave rise to the Social Democratic Party of Germany in the 1890s. The social critique was always systemic, putting the blame on class injustice rather on the corruption of corrupt individuals. In its American version, socialism never meant violent seizure of power except for limited occurrences, as with the Industrial Workers of the World[21] but, as we saw with Eugene Debs, who rapidly distanced himself from the positions of the IWW, which he had co-founded, socialism and even revolution meant winning democratic elections before aiming to reorganize society. Except for his personal admiration for the persona of Eugene

---

[19] Theodore Roosevelt, "The New Nationalism," August 31, 1910, Theodore Roosevelt Association, https://theodoreroosevelt.org/content.aspx?page_id=22&club_id=991271&module_id=33836.

[20] Quoted in Zornick, op. cit., p. 64.

[21] Joseph R. Corlin, "The IWW and the Question of Violence," *The Wisconsin Magazine of History*, vol. 51, n° 4, Summer 1968, pp. 316–326.

Debs, Bernie Sanders hardly ever referred to the early twentieth-century origins of his democratic socialism, preferring, as he did in June 2019 at the George Washington University, to relate it to Franklin D. Roosevelt's New Deal, which made political sense for a candidate running for the nomination of the Democratic Party:

> Over eighty years ago Franklin Delano Roosevelt helped create a government that made transformative progress in protecting the needs of working families. Today, in the second decade of the 21st century, we must take up the unfinished business of the New Deal and carry it to completion. This is the unfinished business of the Democratic Party and the vision we must accomplish. In order to accomplish that goal, it means committing ourselves to protecting political rights, to protecting civil rights—and to protect economic rights of all people in this country. As FDR stated in his 1944 State of the Union address: "We have come to a clear realization of the fact that true individual freedom cannot exist without economic security and independence."[22]

But Bernie Sanders referred to himself as a "democratic socialist" while Mimi Soltysik, the leader and presidential candidate of the Socialist Party USA, would not even recognize him as a socialist:

> From what I see of Bernie Sanders, he appears to be delivering a social-democratic message. That's not where I am coming from. I do not see solutions existing within the capitalist system. Capitalism cannot be reformed. Capitalism is inherently classist, racist and sexist. Do we want kinder and gentler classism, racism and sexism? Kinder oppression? I know that I don't. I may have seen Sanders define himself as a democratic socialist. I suppose he can define himself however he chooses. What I see is something of a reformist, and as I mentioned, a social democrat. I think what's important at the moment is developing some sort of dialogue with those who are supporting Sanders.[23]

---

[22] Sanders, "Sanders Calls For 21st Century Bill of Rights," Speech at the George Washington University, June 10, 2019, Not me. *Us* (2020 campaign website), https://berniesanders.com/en/sanders-calls-21st-century-bill-rights/.

[23] Devon Douglas-Bowers, Colin Jenkins, "Socialism and Electoral Politics in the US: An Interview with Mimi Soltysik," June 30, 2015, The Hampton Institute, http://www.hamptoninstitution.org/mimi-soltysik-interview.html#.XhM4xi17Siv.

Mimi Soltysik's argument arguably had a European prism. Social democracy is traditionally associated with the Nordic model and with Keynesianism due to the longstanding governance by social democratic parties during the post-war consensus, and to their influence on socioeconomic policy in the Nordic countries. The "social-democratic message," or New Deal-style welfarism from a more strictly American perspective, Soltysik accused Sanders of embodying was indeed compatible, and remained compatible, with capitalism. Sanders never envisioned state-centered technocratic planning for the United States. The difficulty in pinning down Bernie Sanders's political identity often resulted in misleading assumptions, some of them benign, as when Bernie Sanders and Elizabeth Warren were often regarded as perfectly interchangeable, and sometimes less benign, as when Barack Obama deliberately argued that Sanders's political strategy aimed "to tear down the system."[24] The present volume argues that Bernie Sanders evolved from promoting social reform to promoting social reparations in the wake of the Great Recession and the Occupy Wall Street movement, with the ingrained conviction that the future of the United States could indeed be changed, therefore with an incurable optimism, although Bernie Sanders did often appear, as Harry Jaffe put it in *Why Bernie Sanders Matters*, as "a rumpled old man ranting about rich people."[25]

3.2 Progressive Reform and Optimism

Alan Dawley's argument that progressivism "contained"[26] socialism through legislation could be regarded as an early instance of political triangulation. Another major reason why progressivism was successful in containing socialism was that it was successful in mobilizing utopian hopes. Francis Shor referred to "an incurable optimism,"[27] to a sense of inevitable progress that comforted the socialists, as this 1913 extract from the *Western Comrade*, a Los Angeles-based socialist magazine published from 1913 to 1918, seems to confirm: "[Socialism] is an irresistible spirit and there is not likely to come out of capitalism any immovable object

[24] Obama, Sanders, quoted in Medina, Lerer, op. cit.

[25] Jaffe, p. xi.

[26] Dawley, op. cit., p. 63.

[27] Shor, p. 188.

to halt its progress."[28] While the argument is certainly illuminating, one might add that the optimism of the socialists was seriously tempered after the Russian Revolution, in the aftermath of the passage of the *Espionage Act*,[29] and during the wartime crusade against radicals that culminated in the postwar red scare. As Francis Shor himself explained: "For many radicals the Russian Revolution transformed what had been a utopian longing for a good place outside of history into a historical site for that good place."[30] Edward Bellamy and Lincoln Steffens[31] are perfect representatives of each of these utopian motives or aspirations. Steffens's remark, however, was embedded with another cause for optimism, an explicitly pragmatic outlook voiced in strikingly Jamesian fashion: Steffens had seen the future—*and it worked.*[32]

Optimism—"the doctrine that thinks the world's salvation inevitable"[33]—was inherent to William James's pragmatism, to a philosophical project to change the world. In *Pragmatism: A New Name for Some Old Ways of Thinking*, James explained what it meant to follow the pragmatic method:

> You must bring out of each word its practical cash-value, set it at work within the stream of your experience. It appears less as a solution, then, than as a program for more work, and more particularly as an indication of the ways existing realities may be *changed*.
> *Theories thus become instruments, not answers to enigmas, in which we can rest.* We don't lie back upon them, we move forward, and, on occasion, make nature over again by their aid.[34]

James's pragmatism, or radical empiricism, was an efficient platform for reform, one that denounced the nihilism of determinism:

---

[28] Ibid.

[29] *The Espionage Act of 1917*, op. cit., p. 31.

[30] Shor, p. 188.

[31] See *supra*, pp. 46, 50.

[32] Steffens, Letter to Marie Howe, op. cit., p. 52.

[33] William James, *Pragmatism: A New Name for Some Old Ways of Thinking*, New York, Longmans, Green & Co., 1907. Rpt. 1922, p. 285.

[34] Ibid., p. 53.

Calling a thing bad means, if it means anything at all, that the thing ought not to be, that something else ought to be in its stead. Determinism, in denying that anything else can be in its stead, virtually defines the universe as a place in which what ought to be is impossible, in other words, as an organism whose constitution is afflicted with an incurable taint, an irremediable flaw.[35]

In other words, much of the progressive optimism lay in William James's pragmatic conception of truth, therefore of reality:

"Grant an idea or belief to be true," [pragmatism] says, "what concrete difference will its being true make in one's actual life? How will the truth be realized? What experiences will be different from those which would obtain if the belief were false? What, in short, is the truth's cash-value in experiential terms?"[36]

Hence, the importance of Lincoln Steffens's remark that the future he had seen in Russia actually "work[ed]."[37] Had it not worked, socialism would have had no value "in experiential terms."[38] Richard Rorty, a neo-pragmatist, wrote in 1997 that "disgust with American hypocrisy was pointless" for William James, "unless accompanied by an effort to give America reason to be proud of itself in the future,"[39] quoting from James himself: "Democracy is a kind of religion, and we are bound not to admit its failure. Faith and utopias are the noblest exercise of human reason, and no one with a spark of reason in him will sit down fatalistically before the croaker's picture."[40] In its resistance to determinism, therefore, James's pragmatism holds that the present can indeed be changed:

Hence arises the idea that our minds are not here to copy a Reality that is already complete. [...] In point of fact the *use* of most of our thinking is to help us to change the world. We must for this know definitely *what*

[35] Id., "September 1884," in *The Will to Believe an Other Essays in Popular Philosophy*, New York, Longmans, Green & Co., 1897. Rpt. *The Will to Believe, Human Immortality, and Other Essays*, New York, Dover Publications, 1956, pp. 161–162.

[36] Id., *Pragmatism*, p. 200.

[37] Steffens, Letter to Marie Howe, op. cit., p. 52.

[38] James, *Pragmatism*, op. cit., p. 67.

[39] Rorty, p. 9.

[40] James, "The Social Value of the College-Bred," quoted in ibid.

we have to change; and thus theoretic truth must at all times come before practical application.[41]

A distinctively American philosophy, pragmatism lies at the core of the progressives' optimism and also forms the matrix that made it possible for an activist like Bernie Sanders to blend the intellectual roots of his own thinking, some of them European and Marxist-related, into the American reform movement in a very idiosyncratic way. Pragmatism took Sanders a step further than Debs. While the final argument of this volume will be that Bernie Sanders eventually sought to change the world by exacting reparations for the 99%, the integration of pragmatism in his thinking does not simply mean, as Harry Jaffe put it, that "Sanders is a pragmatist," that "[l]ike William Jennings Bryan in 1896, he knows that the best chance of actually getting president is through one of the two main parties."[42] Of course political and electoral calculations are part and parcel of political campaigns, but politics and ideologies cannot simply be erased by the apparent superficiality of political discourse. When Barack Obama claimed in 2019 that "the average American doesn't think we have to completely tear down the system,"[43] he was aiming to discredit Bernie Sanders in the perspective of the Democratic primary by linking him to ideologies regarded as typically un-American, Marxist and utterly revolutionary. Sanders replicated that, "[w]ell, it depends on what you mean by tear down the system,"[44] a very pragmatic answer indeed from someone who had argued tirelessly that capitalism was deeply flawed. Obama meant destruction, Sanders meant that, in almost Jamesian rhetoric, "[c]alling a thing bad means, if it means anything at all, that the thing ought not to be, that something else ought to be in its stead."[45] At bottom the issue was not whether Barack Obama or Bernie Sanders was more or less American or un-American. Both endorsed American values. The issue pertained to a tension between an optimist-reformist vision for America,

---

[41] James, *Manuscript Essays and Notes*, Cambridge, MA, Harvard University Press, 1988, pp. 228–229.

[42] Jaffe, p. 180.

[43] Obama, quoted in Medina, Lerer, op. cit., p. 8.

[44] Ibid.

[45] James, *Pragmatism*, op. cit., p. 67.

possibly a utopian one, and a determined conservative-centrist conception of U.S. politics. Barack Obama's first presidential campaign slogan, "Change We Can Believe In," was no longer a matter of real choice, but one of acceptance, if not of resignation.

3.3   KARL POLANYI'S SOCIALISM

In terms of changing the world, Karl Polanyi's *The Great Transformation*,[46] published in 1944, the exact same year Franklin D. Roosevelt promised a "Second Bill of Rights,"[47] also provides some insights into Bernie Sanders's democratic socialism. Polanyi considered that free-market capitalism itself was also a utopian vision, the utopia of a self-regulating market. And he defined socialism as "the tendency inherent in an industrial civilization to transcend the self-regulating market by consciously subordinating it to a democratic society."[48] In a significant reversal, the aim was explicitly to make the economy serve the needs of the people, not the opposite. The intention was not to "tear down the system"[49] but to legislate to make sure the system could better serve social needs. From that angle, Sanders's brand of democratic socialism appears much less likely to "tear down the system" and more in keeping with what Polanyi advocated:

> I don't believe government should take over the grocery store down the street or own the means of production. But I do believe that the middle class and the working families of this country, who produce the wealth of this country, deserve a decent standard of living and that their incomes should go up, not down.[50]

Karl Polanyi took issue with traditional economic thought and claimed that laissez-faire was not a universal law, that free trade classical

---

[46] Karl Polanyi, *The Great Transformation: The Political and Economic Origins of Our Time*, Boston, MA, 1944. Rpt. 2001.

[47] Franklin D. Roosevelt, State of the Union Address, January 11, 1944, Franklin D. Roosevelt Presidential Library and Museum, http://www.fdrlibrary.marist.edu/archives/address_text.html.

[48] Polanyi, p. 176.

[49] Obama, quoted in Medina, Lerer, op. cit., p. 10.

[50] Sanders, *Our Revolution*, op. cit., p. 20

economists aimed to bring all nations into one giant market under the auspices of the gold standard. "Laissez-faire was planned," Polanyi wrote, "planning was not."[51] It took state intervention, therefore, and repression, to impose the logic of the market and its consequences on society and the people. Polanyi was opposed to the market liberals who denounced the erection of protective barriers against the working of the global market as conspiracies. "While laissez-faire economy was the product of deliberate state action," Polanyi wrote, "subsequent restrictions on laissez-faire started in a spontaneous way."[52]

Polanyi described this as a "double movement" by which "the market expanded continuously" but was met by "a countermovement checking the expansion in definite directions."[53] Welfare and other forms of social protections for labor were examples of this resistance:

> To allow the market mechanism to be sole director of the fate of human beings and their natural environment [...] would result in the demolition of society. For the alleged commodity "labor power" cannot be shoved about, used indiscriminately, or even left unused, without affecting also the human individual who happens to be the bearer of this peculiar commodity. In disposing of a man's labor power the system would, incidentally, dispose of the physical, psychological, and moral entity "man" attached to that tag. Robbed of the protective covering of cultural institutions, human beings would perish from the effects of social exposure; they would die as the victims of acute social dislocation [...]. Nature would be reduced to its elements, neighborhoods and landscapes defiled, [...] the power to produce food and raw materials destroyed. Finally, the market administration of purchasing power would periodically liquidate business enterprise, for shortages and surfeits of money would prove as disastrous to business as floods and droughts in primitive society.[54]

In "Karl Polanyi for President," an article published in *Dissent*[55] in 2016, Patrick Iber and Mike Konczal advance that Bernie Sanders and his

[51] Polanyi, p. 147.
[52] Ibid.
[53] Ibid., p. 136.
[54] Ibid., pp. 76–77.
[55] Patrick Iber, Mark Konczal, "Karl Polanyi for President," *Dissent*, May 23, 2016, https://www.dissentmagazine.org/online_articles/karl-polanyi-explainer-great-transformation-bernie-sanders.

supporters were not Marxists but Polanyians even though Bernie Sanders and his supporters were unfamiliar with the Hungarian social theorist. This is certainly true in part. Sanders's democratic socialism was indeed Polanyian in its belief that a political revolution would use democracy to change the rules governing the national political economy. But Sanders's democratic socialism was also, as we saw, Debsian, populist, progressive, and pragmatic. And it bore many similitudes with Franklin Roosevelt's "Second Bill of Rights," which included:

> The right to a useful and remunerative job in the industries or shops or farms or mines of the Nation;
> The right to earn enough to provide adequate food and clothing and recreation;
> The right of every farmer to raise and sell his products at a return which will give him and his family a decent living;
> The right of every businessman, large and small, to trade in an atmosphere of freedom from unfair competition and domination by monopolies at home or abroad;
> The right of every family to a decent home;
> The right to adequate medical care and the opportunity to achieve and enjoy good health;
> The right to adequate protection from the economic fears of old age, sickness, accident, and unemployment;
> The right to a good education.[56]

What best characterizes Bernie Sanders's call for "Revolution,"[57] at this stage, resides in what it was not: an actual revolution in the Marxist sense of the term. Yet the concept carried many different connotations, positive or negative, and possible interpretations which will be dealt with in subsequent chapters.

In the wake of the Great Recession and of the Occupy Wall Street movement, Bernie Sanders's democratic socialism gained a wider audience in mainstream politics. A Gallup Poll published in October 2018 revealed that when asked to explain their understanding of the term "socialism," only 17% of Americans now defined it as government ownership of the means of production, against 34%—i.e., half the number—who defined it this way in 1949. As of 2018, Americans were more likely to

---

[56] Franklin D. Roosevelt, op. cit., p. 70.

[57] Sanders, *Our Revolution*, op. cit., p. 19.

define socialism as connoting equality for everyone (23% in 2018 against 10% in 1949).[58] That was a significant though limited departure from Louis Hartz's argument in *The Liberal Tradition in America* (1955) that because the United States was created as a "nonfeudal society,"[59] "the American community is a liberal community,"[60] a society "indifferent to the challenge of socialism."[61]

References

Corlin, Joseph F. "The IWW and the Question of Violence." *The Wisconsin Magazine of History*, vol. 51, n° 4 (Summer 1968), pp. 316–326.

Dawley, Alan. *Struggles for Justice. Social Responsibility and the Liberal State.* Cambridge, MA: Belknap Press of Harvard University Press, 1991.

Douglas-Bowers, Devon, Colin Jenkins. "Socialism and Electoral Politics in the US: An Interview with Mimi Soltysik" (June 30, 2015), The Hampton Institute, http://www.hamptoninstitution.org/mimi-soltysik-interv iew.html#.XhM4xi17Siv.

Fogarty, Robert, ed. *American Utopianism.* Itasca, IL: E. F. Peacock, 1972.

Foner, Eric. "Why Is There No Socialism in the United States?" *History Workshop*, n° 17 (Spring 1984), pp. 57–80.

George, Henry. *Progress and Poverty an Inquiry into the Cause of Industrial Depressions and of Increase of Want with Increase of Wealth: The Remedy.* New York: Appleton and Co., 1879.

Hartz, Louis. *The Liberal Tradition in America: An Interpretation of American Political Thought Since the Revolution.* New York: Harcourt, Brace, 1955.

Iber, Patrick, Mark Konzcal. "Karl Polanyi for President." *Dissent* (May 23, 2016), https://www.dissentmagazine.org/online_articles/karl-polanyi-explai ner-great-transformation-bernie-sanders.

Jaffe, Harry. *Why Bernie Sanders Matters.* New York: Regan Arts, 2015.

James, William. *The Will to Believe an Other Essays in Popular Philosophy.* New York: Longmans: Green & Co., 1897. Rpt. *The Will to Believe, Human Immortality, and Other Essays.* New York: Dover Publications, 1956.

---

[58] "The Meaning of 'Socialism' to Americans Today," Gallup, October 4, 2018, https://news.gallup.com/opinion/polling-matters/243362/meaning-socialism-americ ans-today.aspx.

[59] Louis Hartz, *The Liberal Tradition in America: An Interpretation of American Political Thought Since the Revolution*, New York, Harcourt, Brace, 1955, p. 5.

[60] Ibid., p. 3.

[61] Ibid., p. 6.

————. *Pragmatism: A New Name for Some Old Ways of Thinking*. New York: Longmans, Green & Co., 1907. Rpt. 1922.

————. *Manuscript Essays and Notes*. Cambridge, MA: Harvard University Press, 1988.

Medina, Jennifer, Lisa Lerer. "Too Far Left? Some Democratic Candidates Don't Buy Obama's Argument." *New York Times* (November 22, 2019), https://www.nytimes.com/2019/11/16/us/obama-left-democrats-2020.html.

Polanyi, Karl. *The Great Transformation: The Political and Economic Origins of Our Time*. Boston, MA: Beacon Press, 1944. Rpt. 2001.

Rall, Ted. "The Left Is Lukewarm on Elizabeth Warren?" *Wall Street Journal* (November 6, 2018), https://www.wsj.com/articles/the-left-is-lukewarm-on-elizabeth-warren-1541548548.

Riis, Jacob. *How the Other Half Lives: Studies among the Tenements of New York*. New York: Charles Scribner's Sons, 1890.

Roosevelt, Franklin D. State of the Union Message (January 11, 1944). Franklin D. Roosevelt Presidential Library and Museum, http://www.fdrlibrary.marist.edu/archives/address_text.html.

Roosevelt, Theodore. "The New Nationalism" (August 31, 1910). Theodore Roosevelt Association, https://theodoreroosevelt.org/content.aspx?page_id=22&club_id=991271&module_id=338365.

Rorty, Richard. *Achieving Our Country: Leftist Thought in Twentieth-Century America*. Cambridge, MA: Harvard University Press, 1997.

Sanders, Bernard. *Our Revolution: A Future to Believe In*. New York: Thomas Dunne Books, 2016.

————. *Where We Go from Here: Two Years in the Resistance*. New York: Thomas Dunne Books, 2018.

————. "Sanders Calls For 21st Century Bill of Rights." Speech at the George Washington University (June 10, 2019), Not me. Us. (2020 campaign website), https://berniesanders.com/en/sanders-calls-21st-century-bill-rights.

Shor, Francis. *Utopianism and Radicalism in a Reforming America, 1888-1918*. Westport, CT: Greenwood Press, 1997.

Steffens, Lincoln J. *The Letters of Lincoln Steffens*, vol. 1, edited by Ella Winter and Granville Hicks. New York: Harcourt, Brace & Co., 1938.

Stromquist, Shelton. *Reinventing 'The People': The Progressive Movement, the Class Problem, and the Origins of Modern Liberalism*. Chicago: University of Illinois Press, 2006.

Twain, Mark, Charles Dudley Warner. *The Gilded Age: A Tale of Today*. Hartford, CT: American Publishing Company, 1874.

Walker, Robert H. *Reform in America: The Continuing Frontier*. Lexington: University of Kentucky Press, 1985.

Zornick, George. "Elizabeth Warren's 'Big Fight' Against Monopolies." *Nation* (February 15, 2018), https://www.thenation.com/article/elizabeth-warrens-big-fight-against-monopolies.

PART II

Realpolitik

CHAPTER 4

An Experiment in Municipal Socialism

In his 1979 historical narrative devoted to Eugene Debs, Bernie Sanders recounts how "as a young labor leader Debs not only believed in capitalism, but was an active member of the Democratic Party," and that although he had "an excellent future as a Democratic politician, he stopped running for office as a Democrat" after one term in the Indiana House of Representatives, "when his bill in support of railroad workers got whittled down to nothing by politicians in the state capitol."[1] Sanders would run an opposite course, first as a candidate of the Liberty Union Party and then, later in his political life, under the banner of the Democratic Party. As of 1979, Sanders told a scathing story of class interest and political treason:

> The workers know that under Republican rule and Democratic rule, conditions for them have remained unchanged. [...] They know, too, that under both Democrat and Republican rule the President is on the side of the capitalists, that the governors are all on the side of the capitalists, that Congress and the state legislators respond to the demands of the capitalists, that the courts are uniformly for the capitalists, while soldiers and injunctions and jails are for the exclusive benefit of the workers.[2]

---

[1] Sanders, *Eugene V. Debs*, band 6, "The Early Background of Eugene Debs."

[2] Ibid., band 5, "Democrats, Republicans, and Capitalists."

© The Author(s), under exclusive license to Springer Nature Switzerland AG 2021
N. Gachon, *Bernie Sanders's Democratic Socialism*,
https://doi.org/10.1007/978-3-030-69661-0_4

Political treason, Sanders argued, came in the garb of democracy: "Every four years the Democratic and Republican parties come forward and tell the working people of this country all that they are going to do for them."[3] In political lies by the two major parties lay the fundamental justification for socialism for Sanders. What was needed, he said as he recorded Debs's story, was "an economic system in which the working people owns the means of production—and in which we produce goods and services for the use of all—and not profits for the few."[4] Sanders's November 19, 2015, argument at Georgetown University that he did not believe government should "take over the grocery store down the street or own the means of production"[5] sheds light on how his political positioning evolved, from an all-out ideological approach, arguably from a nineteenth-century definition of class, to a more corrective-reparative approach for all those who do not belong to the ruling class: "I do believe that the middle class and the working families of this country, who produce the wealth of this country, deserve a decent standard of living and that their incomes should go up, not down."[6]

4.1   Mayor Sanders of Burlington

Arguably because of a recurrent debate over the limitations of democracy under capitalism and over the State as the instrument of the ruling class, leftists in the United States tend to not participate very actively in electoral politics. In *The Progressive City: Planning and Participation, 1969-1984* (1986), Pierre Clavel describes as "educational campaigns"[7] the campaigns Bernie Sanders ran as a candidate of the Liberty Union Party in the 1970s, twice for governor of Vermont in 1972 and 1976 and twice for the U.S. Senate in 1972 and 1974, never receiving more than 6.1% of the vote. Educational campaigns use the legitimacy of elections and media attention to channel public attention into specific issues or perspectives, with the inherent risk of leaning too heavily on proposals and

---

[3] Ibid.

[4] Ibid.

[5] Id., Our Revolution, op. cit., p. 20.

[6] Ibid.

[7] Pierre Clavel, *The Progressive City: Planning and Participation, 1969-1984*, New Brunswick, NJ, Rutgers University Press, 1986, p. 164.

not enough on mobilizing voters, and of letting their arguments vanish as quickly as they were publicized. Bernie Sanders's candidacy in the 1981 mayoral election in Burlington was intended as a very different scenario:

> This was not to be an "educational" campaign. The goal of this contest was to win. For this reason, the campaign was issue-oriented, focused on the most serious problems facing Vermont's largest city, problems ignored by city government. While I often placed these issues within the context of what was going on nationally, and made it clear that a fundamental change of priorities was needed at the national level, virtually all of my energy was spent addressing the concerns that faced the people of Burlington. I was running for mayor, not U.S. senator. The people of the city wanted to know how I would improve the quality of life at the local level if I became mayor. Those were the issues I addressed.[8]

Sanders, who was "happily retired from politics"[9] after his electoral losses in state politics, and who had left the Liberty Union Party in 1977, ran as an independent against the five-time incumbent Democrat Gordon Paquette, who had served as mayor of Burlington since 1971. The decision came after his friend Richard Sugarman,[10] a political consultant and a professor of religion at the University of Vermont, showed Sanders that even though he had received only 6.1% of the vote statewide in the

---

[8] Sanders, *Outsider in the White House*, p. 35.

[9] Ibid., p. 34. Bernie Sanders was still politically active between 1976 and 1981, although not as a politician. He founded and directed the American People's Historical Society, a small independent production company. His biggest project was the documentary he produced on Eugene Debs in 1979 (op. cit, p. 3). Hillary Clinton attacked Sanders during his campaign for the 2020 Democratic nomination for being a career politician who never actually worked until he was 40. Sanders holds a Bachelor of Arts in political science from the University of Chicago (1964) and claims that he worked from 1964 to 1976 as a freelance writer, carpenter, youth counselor, and state employee. See: Jade Scipioni, "Hillary Clinton Says Bernie Sanders Didn't Get a Real Job Until He Was 41—Here's a Copy of His Actual Resume from the '80s," CNBC, March 2, 2020, https://www.cnbc.com/2020/03/03/photos-bernie-sanders-resume-as-mayor-of-burlington-vermont.html. On the American People's Historical Society, see: "Before Bernie Sanders Made History, He Sold It," Special Collections, University of Vermont Libraries, June 16, 2015, https://blog.uvm.edu/uvmsc-specialcollections/?p=152.

[10] Richard Sugarman was an advisor to Bernie Sanders on his 2016 presidential campaign.

1976 gubernatorial election,[11] he had carried 12% in Burlington, and over 16% in the two working-class wards of the city. The 1980-1981 campaign for the mayorship of Burlington marked Sanders's return to electoral politics: "The campaign itself functioned as a crash course in Burlington's problems and politics. In truth, I knew very little about Burlington city government,"[12] Sanders later wrote. His campaign built a coalition of "leaders of the low-income community, college professors, the Burlington Patrolmen's Association, environmentalists, and conservative homeowners worried about rising property taxes."[13] Former members of the Liberty Union Party, a party which Russell Banks described as "an umbrella under which a diverse crowd could gather, from doctrinaire Marxists to liberal Democrats, from 'outside agitators' to home-grown environmentalists, from micro-chipping libertarians to marijuana growers,"[14] also played active roles in the campaign.[15]

Sanders's close victory over Gordon Paquette (43.83–43.72%)[16] came as a major defeat for the Democratic Party after three decades of winning elections. Gordon Paquette, who had never lost a race, had hardly bothered to campaign against Bernie Sanders, who had never won one. In the debate, however, Sanders had surprised Burlington constituents by turning out to be a lot more knowledgeable about local issues than anyone expected. The conservative structure of the Democratic Party had been caught asleep. It had failed to recognize the agitation within the population, as well as the changes in demographics: young workers moving to high-technology and service jobs, University of Vermont students moving from dormitories into city neighborhoods, the lowering of the voting age to 18 and the soaring rental and medical costs affecting

---

[11] Bernie Sanders Lost by Only Ten Votes: 4,330 to 4,320. "Vt. Governor," November 2, 1976, Our Campaigns, https://www.ourcampaigns.com/RaceDetail.html?RaceID=93728.

[12] Sanders, *Outsider in the White House*, p. 37.

[13] Ibid.

[14] Banks, op. cit., p. 54.

[15] Sanders, *Outsider in the White House*, p. 37.

[16] The other defeated candidate was Richard Bove (I), 11.04%. Burlington, Vt. Mayor, March 3, 1981, Our Campaigns, https://www.ourcampaigns.com/RaceDetail.html?RaceID=512309.

the aging and the poor.[17] The Democratic organization pledged that it would not be caught asleep again in the next election and that Bernie Sanders would be a one-term mayor. Sanders had run on "equity" themes, advocating tax reform, higher pay for municipal workers, and programs redirecting services to city youth and redirecting housing and medical care to the less affluent.[18] Yet his first year in office was characterized by stalemate due to the obstructionism of the Democratic majority on the Board of Aldermen and of a number of commissions. As he explained in *Outsider in the White House*, Sanders "knew that a progressive agenda could never be implemented without the efforts of a strong and successful political movement,"[19] which led him to work with other progressives and activists in Burlington in order to create the Burlington Progressive Coalition.[20] The strategy of the Democratic Party eventually backfired. *The Burlington Free Press* published an editorial stating that "the Democrats were more preoccupied with tarnishing [Sanders's] credibility than with the interests of the people."[21] Sanders and his supporters finally fought the opposition to a standstill and the mayor was reelected in 1983, 1985, and 1987.

Even more striking than Bernie Sanders's 1981 victory, therefore, was his reelection in the Burlington mayoral races by larger margins in 1983 (52.1%)[22] and 1985 (56.1%),[23] and once more in 1987 with 55.9%.[24]

[17] Dudley Clendinen, "It's New Politics vs. Old in Vermont as Mayor Strives to Oust Alderman," *New York Times*, February 28, 1982, https://www.nytimes.com/1982/02/28/us/it-s-new-politics-vs-old-in-vermont-as-mayor-strives-to-oust-alderman.html.

[18] Clavel, p. 169.

[19] Sanders, *Outsider in the White House*, p. 134.

[20] About the Burlington Progressive Coalition, see: David Reynolds, *Democracy Unbound: Progressive Challenges to the Two-Party System*, Boston, MA, South End Press, 1997, pp. 165–170.

[21] *Burlington Free Press*, April 8, 1882, p. 12.

[22] Sanders (I) ran against Judy Stephany (D), 30.68%, and James Gibson (R), 17.21%. "Burlington, Vt. Mayor," March 1, 1983, Our Campaigns, https://www.ourcampaigns.com/RaceDetail.html?RaceID=512316.

[23] Sanders (I) ran against Brian D. Burns (D), 31.9%, and Diane Gallagher (I), 12%. Burlington, Vt. Mayor, March 5, 1985, Our Campaigns, https://www.ourcampaigns.com/RaceDetail.html?RaceID=512321.

[24] Sanders (I) ran against Paul Lafayette (D), 30.7%. Burlington, Vt. Mayor, March 3, 1987, Our Campaigns, https://www.ourcampaigns.com/RaceDetail.html?RaceID=512323.

Sanders's terms as mayor of Burlington turned out to be an experiment in municipal socialism, a successful one by most accounts, and a mostly uncontroversial one had it not been for the "socialist" label hovering over his administration. While he was a controversial figure in national politics, his record in municipal politics tells a different story. Sanders did not conquer Burlington on a distinctively socialist agenda: he made no promise to municipalize the banks, to expropriate the wealthy, or to disarm the police.[25] For one thing, he promised to raise property taxes less than incumbent Mayor Gordon Paquette (to 25 instead of 65 cents per $100 of assessed value) and to tax tourism-oriented businesses more instead of taxing property owners,[26] which turned out to be a successful policy. Sanders improved city government and introduced procedural and financial reforms that were often supported by the Republican members of the Board of Aldermen. As Russell Banks explained in a piece for *The Atlantic*:

> Allen Gear, a Republican member of the Board of Aldermen since 1979, looking back over Sanders's tenure as mayor, says, "He's done things I don't think we Republicans could have done, because the two traditional parties in a town like this are very close. We interact with each other on business over coffee, over tea, crumpets and marmalade, if you will, and it would have been very hard for us, us being Republicans, if we had the Chief Executive's spot, to have done some of the things Bernie has done. [...] He's taken a lot of very Republican ideas and put them in place. Such as combining all of the garages of the various city departments and putting them into a single public-works department, initially a Republican proposal, to gain efficiency in handling city rolling stock. [...] He's put a lot of modern accounting practices and money-management practices into place that are good Republican business practices. [...] And he has surrounded himself with some very talented, vigorous people."[27]

Sanders, therefore, was successful as a third-party politician with a socialist profile in the context of a national conservative trend and a hostile state government in a city that had voted for conservative Democrats since 1965. In 1983, Jon Margolis, writing for the *New Republic*, suspected

---

[25] Jon Margolis, "Bernie of Burlington," *New Republic*, March 14, 1983, https://newrepublic.com/article/122285/bernie-burlington.

[26] Ibid.

[27] Banks, op. cit., p. 54.

that Sanders's supporters would want him to run for the U.S. Senate should he be reelected but estimated that it was "extraordinarily unlikely" that Sanders could get elected statewide, that he probably would have little impact outside of Burlington and that he would most likely "prefer to make the revolution in one city, fill the potholes, and keep the taxes down." "All this may not be what Debs and Thomas[28] had in mind," Margolis concluded, "[b]ut then, they never got elected."[29] While he was largely successful and uncontroversial as mayor of Burlington, however, Bernie Sanders often veered outside municipal politics during the Reagan era.

4.2   ALL THAT SOCIALIST "PORNOGRAPHY"

In 1980, the Socialist Workers Party ran three candidates for the presidency: Clifton DeBerry, Andrew Pulley, and Richard Congress (who was on the ballot only in Ohio). While he was running for mayor of Burlington as an independent, Bernie Sanders built ties with the Socialist Workers Party and supported DeBerry and Pulley. He even was an elector for the presidential slate of the Socialist Workers Party in 1980. The Socialist Workers Party, which was Trotskyist, was distinct from the Socialist Party.[30] As would be the case with his alleged connections with communists in Yaroslavl in 1988, Sanders's political connections were perceived as murky by many.[31] Even though the tensions between socialists, communists, and Trotskyists can be difficult to ponder for anyone outside of the radical left, what was certain was that the three groups tended to combat one another, which made it at least extremely atypical, and certainly highly eclectic, for Sanders to be really involved with all three. In 1988, on the occasion of his first appearance as mayor of Burlington on C-SPAN, which consistently labeled him as a "socialist" on screen, Sanders was asked by the audience about his 1980 support for the Socialist Workers Party and briefly confirmed it: "In 1980 I was an elector for the Socialist Workers Party. I am not a member. And I am not a

---

[28] Altman, op. cit., p. 34. Norman Thomas was a socialist candidate for governor of New York in 1924 and ran six times for president beginning in 1928.

[29] Margolis, op. cit.

[30] The Socialist Workers Party was formed in 1937 after a split from the Socialist Party of America.

[31] See *supra*, p. 54.

member of any party, and was not a member at that point. I was asked to put my name on the ballot and I did, that's true."[32] He then declared his support for Mel Mason, the Socialist Workers Party's 1984 presidential candidate, in a letter to *The Militant*, a socialist newsweekly connected to the Socialist Workers Party: "At a time when the Democratic and Republican parties are intellectually and spiritually bankrupt, it is imperative for radical voices to be heard which offer fundamental alternatives to capitalist ideology. I wish Mel Mason good luck on his campaign."[33] Sanders was then repeatedly attacked by his political opponents for having supported the Socialist Workers Party when most Americans were voting for Ronald Reagan, Jimmy Carter, or John Anderson,[34] for campaigning for the Socialist Workers Party in the 1980 and 1984 presidential campaigns, and for being investigated by the FBI over his ties to the Marxist group.[35] Sanders's support, however, was arguably less a matter of coherent ideological adhesion than a support for alternative radical voices in the heyday of neoliberalism during the Reagan era, even if they advocated more radical positions than his own, which Mel Mason himself seemed to confirm in a 2019 exchange with the *Washington Examiner*: "We had a long-distance relationship [with Bernie Sanders], but that kind of changed after he ran for Congress. I didn't have as much contact anymore. I have a lot of respect for him, but I just don't think the programs he put forward are what workers need in this country."[36]

On May 21, 1981, Andrew Pulley, the Socialist Workers Party's 1980 presidential nominee, visited Burlington while on tour to publicize an ongoing Socialist Workers Party suit against political victimization by the federal government. As mayor, Bernie Sanders gave remarks to introduce

[32] Sanders, "Urban Issues of Concern," C-SPAN, January 20, 1988, https://www.c-span.org/video/?240-1/urban-issues-concern.

[33] Id., "It Is Imperative for Radical Voices to Be Heard," *The Militant*, January 20, 1984, p. 13, https://themilitant.com/1984/4801/MIL4801.pdf.

[34] John Anderson was a Republican representative fom Illinois (1961–1981) who ran an independent campaign for president in 1980. See: Doug Bandow, "Is Bernie Sanders Still a Communist at Heart?" *American Spectator*, November 23, 2019, https://spectator.org/is-bernie-sanders-still-a-communist-at-heart.

[35] Joseph Simonson, "Bernie Sanders Campaigned for Marxist Party in Reagan Era," *Washington Examiner*, May 30, 2019, https://www.washingtonexaminer.com/news/campaigns/bernie-sanders-campaigned-for-marxist-party-in-reagan-era.

[36] Ibid.

Pulley and made the following statement on what he described as the instrumentalization of the socialist epithet:

> In the '50s, with McCarthyism, they created a system of bugaboos, with the bugaboo of communism. Any person who stood up for working people, or for low-income people, or for peace, was associated with the "communist front." Now the word is "terrorist." [...] I think there's a way to deal with that terrible word—that pornographic word which they hate so much in this country—called socialism. I think the best way is to be up front about that word, not to run away from that word. To deal with it in a straightforward way, and explain exactly what we mean by that word. Along with Andrew, we are antitotalitarian. We believe in democracy. Then there's nothing they can do. I can't be called a socialist anymore. I admit it. What are they going to do with us?[37]

To assess Bernie Sanders's radicalism, and to draw contemporary implications from his 1981 argument, one should take into account the existing political space to his left, those people for whom Sanders is in fact "a moderate,"[38] if not the advocate of "a kinder, gentler system of exploitation."[39] Jeff Mackler, for example, the national secretary of Socialist Action, a Trotskyist party founded in 1983, supports the abolition of capitalism in the United States, a 100% tax rate on all incomes above $150,000, the elimination of the military budget, the nationalization of the energy and banking industries, open borders, and the creation of a state-run healthcare system. He was a presidential candidate in 2016 and 2020. In June 2016, a month before the Democratic National Convention in Philadelphia, Jeff Mackler gave an interview in which he scoffed at Bernie Sanders and delivered a scathing critique of his political relevance as a "democratic socialist":

---

[37] Sanders, "Andrew, We're Delighted to Have You," *The Militant*, June 12, 1981, p. 10, https://themilitant.com/1981/4522/MIL4522.pdf.

[38] Annie Lowrey, "The People Who Think Bernie Is Moderate," *The Atlantic*, August 29, 2019, https://www.theatlantic.com/ideas/archive/2019/08/real-socialists-left-bernie/596890.

[39] Nick Baker, "Interview with Socialist Action's Presidential Candidate, Jeff Mackler," Socialist Action, June 26, 2016, https://socialistaction.org/2016/06/26/interview-with-socialist-presidential-candidate-jeff-mackler.

> Bernie has been traveling the country for the past year campaigning for a "kinder and gentler" capitalism, for a "kinder, gentler" system of exploitation and minority rule, dressed, of course, in the garb of "democratic socialism." And now Sanders is preparing his long-anticipated shift to supporting the kind of cold-blooded racist, warmongering Hillary Clinton-style capitalism that his soon-to-be-bewildered supporters had hoped to flee from with his candidacy. As we anticipated, Sanders, along with Clinton, will now deploy the lesser evil "Trump" card to once again frighten the unwary back into the Democratic Party, as the graveyard of social movements.[40]

While the term "socialism" seemed demonetized by people like Bernie Sanders according to Jeff Mackler, it was also consistently over-monetized, given an ideological overcharge for political reasons, in the mainstream political arena. During the Trump administration, in the context of a shrinking percentage of Democrats who preferred capitalism over socialism as a more humane system,[41] the president tweeted the socialist epithet as the avatar of un-Americanism: "We will never be a Socialist or Communist Country. IF YOU ARE NOT HAPPY HERE, YOU CAN LEAVE! It is your choice, and your choice alone. This is about love for America. Certain people HATE our Country...."[42] Annie Lowrey described this as "an old rhetorical move, not a serious piece of contemporary politics," consistent with the fact that "Republicans have termed whatever the Democrats have wanted as 'socialism' and whomever they choose to run as a 'socialist' regularly since the New Deal."[43] From the outset, therefore, Bernie Sanders's campaign for "democratic socialism" was also a campaign of disambiguation. He needed to break the binary opposition between freedom and capitalism on the one side, and, on the other, to combat the use of the socialist label as a ploy to discredit any attempt for leftist reform. Sanders opted for a bottom-up approach from the shores of Lake Champlain in Burlington, Vermont, to try to achieve that:

[40] Ibid.

[41] "Democrats More Positive About Socialism Than Capitalism," August 13, 2018, Gallup, https://news.gallup.com/poll/240725/democrats-positive-socialism-capitalism.aspx.

[42] Donald Trump, Twitter post, July 15, 2019, https://twitter.com/realdonaldtrump/status/1150874781744607232.

[43] Lowrey, op. cit., p. 84.

As the mayor of Burlington, and someone committed to grassroots democracy, I saw no magic line separating local, state, national, and international issues. How could federal cuts in education not be a local issue? They affect our public schools. How could environmental degradation not be a local issue? It affects the water we drink and our health. How could issues of war and peace not be a local issue? It is local youngsters who fight and die in wars. Ultimately, if we're going to revitalize democracy in this country, local government will have to assume a much stronger and more expansive role.[44]

Democratic centralism, therefore, certainly did not seem to be the matrix of Bernie Sanders's democratic socialism.

4.3   Foreign Policy as a Local Issue

"As you may recall," Sanders wrote in *Outsider in the White House*, "I was not the only elected official in America during the 1980s. There was that other fellow, Ronald Reagan."[45] And that was a pivotal moment in national politics. President Reagan pursued a policy of relentless opposition to the Soviet Union and its ideological allies. Reagan's foreign policy initiatives meant building up military spending at home and providing resources for anti-Communist forces overseas. As soon as he took office in January 1981, Reagan increased military aid and sent Special Forces instructors to El Salvador, whose army was fighting the leftist guerrillas of the Farabundo Martí National Liberation Front. "Many Burlingtonians," Sanders continued, "including myself, supported the Sandinista government in Nicaragua. President Reagan did not. We disagreed with him. We expressed our displeasure."[46] Burlington, therefore, became a city that now had a foreign policy:

If children in Nicaragua were suffering because of U.S. policy, it was our responsibility to try to change that policy. If children in the United States were going hungry because the federal government was spending more

[44] Sanders, *Outsider in the White House*, p. 85.
[45] Ibid., p. 81.
[46] Ibid.

than was necessary on the military, we also had a responsibility to work on changing that.[47]

A city with a foreign policy, Sanders argued, meant that "as progressives," people "understood we all live in one world."[48] Burlington forged a sister-city relationship with Yaroslavl[49] in the Soviet Union, which Sanders recalled as "just an incredible experience to see these kids getting along as well as they did,"[50] and forged another one with Puerto Cabezas, a remote town on the Nicaraguan coast. Assuredly, his connections, and destination choice—Yaroslavl—for his honeymoon were extremely political. This was a significant moment in Sanders's and political trajectory. He would later seem less involved in foreign policy issues when running for president of the United States, sometimes even dodging a number of distinctively global issues such as terrorism. And he would accordingly be attacked on his thin foreign policy experience.[51]

On October 17, 1983, Sanders sent a letter to President Reagan, as mayor of Burlington, on the issue of the human, political, ethical, and economic implications of war in Nicaragua:

> Dear President Reagan,
> In the strongest possible terms, I urge you to stop the CIA war against the people of Nicaragua and allow them to develop their independent nation as best they can after the horrors imposed upon them by the forty years Samosa dictatorship.

[47] Ibid., p. 85.

[48] Ibid.

[49] See *supra*, p. 54.

[50] Sanders, quoted in Wallace-Wells, op. cit., p. 56.

[51] As senator, Bernie Sanders consistently voted to limit American military interventions abroad, and opposed bills that took Israel's side in the Middle East peace process. He focused on domestic issues during the 2016 and 2020 presidential campaigns, in part because the foreign policy establishment accused him of championing a foreign policy aligned with socialist regimes around the world. Another reason, arguably, was that Democrats usually do not fare well when competing on the national stage with Republicans on international affairs and national security. Foreign policy issues helped Ronald Reagan win his first term and George W. Bush win his second. On Bernie Sanders's positions pertaining to Israel, see: Jewish Telegraphic Agency, "Where Bernie Sanders Stands on Issues That Matter to Jewish Voters in 2020," *The Times of Israel*, November 20, 2019, https://www.timesofisrael.com/where-bernie-sanders-stands-on-issues-that-matter-to-jewish-voters-in-2020.

There are many ways in which American taxpayers' money can be better spent than in attempts to destabilize the Sandinista government by CIA bombings of oil storage depots and industrial targets in the poverty-stricken nation of Nicaragua. At a time when your administration has imposed horrendous cutbacks to the American people in such areas as housing, aid to education, environmental protection and health care, I am appalled that you are using taxpayers' money to destroy the government of a small nation.

The people of the United States are looking to our Federal Government for help in providing meaningful jobs for our youth, adequate Social Security benefits for our elderly and programs which will improve the quality of life for all the people in our nation. We are not looking forward to the continuation of the century old American policy toward Latin America which suggests that the United States has the right to overthrow any government there which disagrees with us.

I urge you to immediately call a halt to the CIA attacks against Nicaragua.

Respectfully Yours,
Bernard Sanders
Mayor[52]

"Not only was the war against Nicaragua illegal and immoral, it was an outrageous waste of taxpayer money. As a mayor, I wanted more federal funds for affordable housing and economic development," Sanders wrote in *Outsider in the White House*. His opposition to Reagan's Latin American policies, including in Guatemala and El Salvador, was rooted in his own socialist anti-corporate perspectives:

What is really going on in terms of the United States' relationship with Nicaragua of course has nothing to do with Nicaragua. The nature of the conflict that now exists is based on the fact that, for the last hundred and fifty years or so, the United States government, in its wisdom, has decided that Latin America should be a colony of the United States government,

[52] Sanders, Letter to President Ronald Reagan, October 17, 1984, quoted in David Matthews, "Bernie Sanders' 1980s Nicaragua Letters Show His Early Interest in Foreign Policy," Splinter News, February 12, 2016, https://splinternews.com/bernie-sanders-1980s-nicaragua-letters-show-his-early-i-1793854724.

and that countries which attempt to stand up and do thing for their own people rather than for American corporations are not to be tolerated.[53]

That speech was given in July 1985 in Puerto Cabezas, Nicaragua, on the Atlantic coastline, where the details of the sister-city program with Burlington had just been discussed with local officials. Sanders had traveled to Managua, Nicaragua at the invitation of the Nicaraguan government for the anniversary of the Sandinista Revolution. During the trip Sanders met with Daniel Ortega, the president of Nicaragua, as well as other government officials, including Father Miguel D'Escoto, then the Nicaraguan foreign minister, in a small church in Managua where D'Escoto was lying in bed, fasting in protest against American support for the contras. He also met with some of the opposition, including Jaime Chamorro, the editor of the opposition newspaper, *La Prensa*.[54] It was certainly a bold step, with strong political and ideological implications in the context of the Reagan era, especially considering Sanders's strong skepticism of American power, but what he actually said in an interview upon his return was somewhat more nuanced than what many of critics have often blamed him for:

> I mean, no one should think that the Sandinista government has the support of a 100% of the people, they certainly do not, they had an election where all they got was 62 or 63% of the vote, then 35% of the people voted for somebody else. [...] [W]e talked to people, and among poor and working people there was a very strong feeling that the revolution that they had made was their revolution, that they had fought against the very horrible Samoza dictatorship [...], and most of the poor people and the working people that I talked to felt that the situation was much better now than it had been before. There was, and make no mistake about this, serious concerns about economic conditions in Nicaragua. People would tell you "it just cost us a fortune to get this item and that item." And some of those people are blaming the government.[55]

---

[53] Id., Address at Puerto Cabezas Sister City Public Meeting, July 10, 1985, CCTV, https://www.cctv.org/search/node/Puerto%20Cabezas%20Sister%20City%20Program.

[54] Id., *Outsider in the White House*, p. 82.

[55] Id., "Interview with Mayor Sanders After His Trip to Nicaragua," August 8, 1985, CCTV, https://www.cctv.org/watch-tv/programs/interview-mayor-sanders-after-his-trip-nicaragua.

Sanders also pointed out to what he claimed was a confusion on the part of quite a few Americans: the fact that 35% of people voted against the Sandinistas did not mean that they wanted to support an invasion of their own country. "I voted against Ronald Reagan," Sanders added, "does that mean to say that I want an invasion of the United States to get rid of Ronald Reagan? We will deal with our own problems in our own way. I hope we will vote Reagan out and reactionary Republicans out."[56] That was visibly foreign policy, from local Burlington, but with a national agenda. Michael Crowley and Michael Cruse, writing for Politico, added that, in fact, Sanders's visit to Nicaragua "wasn't exactly subversive," that other members of the U.S. Congress traveled to the country in the mid-1980s, "including a freshman senator named John Kerry," and that the Reagan State Department did not oppose the visits.[57]

Sanders's comments on Cuba that same year were arguably more subversive than those made over the Nicaragua affair. He recalled how, in 1961, "everybody was totally convinced that Castro was the worst guy in the world and that all the Cuban people was going to rise up in rebellion against Fidel Castro," and that it did not happen because "he educated the kids, gave them health care, totally transformed the society." Sanders denied that Fidel Castro or Cuba were "perfect" but remarked that "just because Ronald Reagan dislike[d] those people" did not mean that the Cuban people felt the same way. So, the United States "expected this tremendous uprising in Cuba and it never came."[58] Sanders's foreign policy positions as mayor of Burlington were certainly fodder to his opponents, Republicans and Democrats alike, more than they were actually subversive. His two sister-city programs, in Yaroslavl and Puerto Cabezas, were no revolutions. Sanders himself acknowledged that he and his wife Jane later visited Cuba in 1989, that he had hoped to meet with Fidel Castro, that it "didn't work out" but that he "did meet with the mayor of Havana and other officials."[59] Sanders had no revolutionary credentials that could have caught Castro's eye. Yet he was building his political persona while pointing to an alternative path for the United States in

[56] Ibid.

[57] Michael Crowley, Michael Kruse, "The Foreign Minister of Burlington, Vt," Politico, July 31, 2015, https://www.politico.com/story/2015/07/the-foreign-minister-of-burlington-vt-120839.

[58] Sanders, "Interview with Mayor Sanders After His Trip to Nicaragua," op. cit., p. 88.

[59] Id., *Outsider in the White House*, p. 85.

the midst of the Reagan era. Sanders needed to be perceived as a radically different kind of political figure more than he was a radical himself. His homegrown socialism from among the green hills of Burlington, Vermont, would hopefully do just that. Having castigated and sometimes vilified both the Republican Party and the Democratic Party, Sanders would now have to come to terms with the two-party system.

REFERENCES

Altman, Jake. *Socialism before Sanders. The 1930s Movement from Romance to Revisionism*. Cham, Switzerland: Palgrave Macmillan, 2019.

Baker, Nick. "Interview with Socialist Action's Presidential Candidate, Jeff Mackler." *Socialist Action* (June 26, 2016), https://socialistaction.org/2016/06/26/interview-with-socialist-presidential-candidate-jeff-mackler.

Bandow, Doug. "Is Bernie Sanders Still a Communist at Heart?" *American Spectator* (November 23, 2019), https://spectator.org/is-bernie-sanders-still-a-communist-at-heart.

Banks, Russell. "Bernie Sanders, the Socialist Mayor." *The Atlantic* (October 15, 2015), https://www.theatlantic.com/politics/archive/2015/10/bernie-sanders-mayor/407413.

Clavel, Pierre. *The Progressive City: Planning and Participation, 1969-1984*. New Brunswick, NJ: Rutgers University Press, 1986.

Clendinen, Dudley. "It's New Politics vs. Old in Vermont as Mayor Strives to Oust Alderman." *New York Times* (February 28, 1982), https://www.nytimes.com/1982/02/28/us/it-s-new-politics-vs-old-in-vermont-as-mayor-strives-to-oust-alderman.html.

Crowley, Michael, Michael Kruse. "The Foreign Minister of Burlington, Vt." Politico (July 31, 2015), https://www.politico.com/story/2015/07/the-foreign-minister-of-burlington-vt-120839.

Jewish Telegraphic Agency. "Where Bernie Sanders Stands on Issues That Matter to Jewish Voters in 2020." *The Times of Israel* (November 20, 2019), https://www.timesoMATTHEWSfisrael.com/where-bernie-sanders-stands-on-issues-that-matter-to-jewish-voters-in-2020.

Lowrey, Annie. "The People Who Think Bernie Is Moderate." *The Atlantic* (August 29, 2019), https://www.theatlantic.com/ideas/archive/2019/08/real-socialists-left-bernie/596890.

Margolis, Jon. "Bernie of Burlington." *New Republic* (March 14, 1983), https://newrepublic.com/article/122285/bernie-burlington.

Matthews, David. "Bernie Sanders' 1980s Nicaragua Letters Show His Early Interest in Foreign Policy." Splinter News (February 12, 2016), https://splinternews.com/bernie-sanders-1980s-nicaragua-letters-show-his-early-i-179 3854724.

Reynolds, David. *Democracy Unbound: Progressive Challenges to the Two-Party System*. Boston, MA: South End Press, 1997.

Sanders, Bernard. *Eugene V. Debs: Trade Unionist, Socialist, Revolutionary, 1855-1926*. New York: Folkways Records, 1979.

———. "Andrew, We're Delighted to Have You." *The Militant* (June 12, 1981), p. 10, https://themilitant.com/1981/4522/MIL4522.pdf.

———. "It Is Imperative for Radical Voices to Be Heard." *The Militant* (January 20, 1984), p. 13, https://themilitant.com/1984/4801/MIL4801.pdf.

———. "Interview with Mayor Sanders After His Trip to Nicaragua." CCTV (August 8, 1985), https://www.cctv.org/watch-tv/programs/interview-mayor-sanders-after-his-trip-nicaragua.

———. "Urban Issues of Concern." C-SPAN (January 20, 1988), https://www.c-span.org/video/?240-1/urban-issues-concern.

———, with Huck Gutman. *Outsider in the House: A Political Autobiography*. New York: Verso, 1997. Rpt. *Outsider in the White House*, 2015.

———. *Our Revolution: A Future to Believe In*. New York: Thomas Dunne Books, 2016.

Scipioni, Jade. "Hillary Clinton Says Bernie Sanders Didn't Get a Real Job Until He Was 41—Here's A Copy of His Actual Resume from the '80s." CNBC (March 2, 2020), https://www.cnbc.com.

Simonson, Joseph. "Bernie Sanders Campaigned for Marxist Party in Reagan Era." *Washington Examiner* (May 30, 2019), https://www.washingtonexaminer.com/news/campaigns/bernie-sanders-campaigned-for-marxist-party-in-reagan-era.

Wallace-Wells, Benjamin. "Bernie Sanders Imagines a Progressive New Approach to Foreign Policy." *New Yorker* (April 13, 2019), https://www.newyorker.com/news/the-political-scene/bernie-sanders-imagines-a-progressive-new-approach-to-foreign-policy.

CHAPTER 5

Embracing the Democratic Party

On March 5, 2019, in the early stages of his second presidential run, Bernie Sanders was required by new Democratic National Committee rules to formally declare himself a member of the Democratic Party before seeking the nomination in 2020. The document signed and notarized by Sanders read as follows:

> I hereby affirm that, upon publicly announcing my candidacy for the Democratic nomination for President of the United States in the 2020 election, I am a member of the Democratic Party. I will run as a Democrat, accept the nomination of my Party, and will serve as a Democrat if elected. […]
>
> Further, I acknowledge that the National Chairperson of the Democratic National Committee is authorized to determine whether a presidential candidate has established substantial support for their nomination as the Democratic candidate for the Office of the President of the United States is a bona fide Democrat […].[1]

---

[1] Sanders, Presidential Candidate Written Affirmation, March 5, 2019, NBC News, https://www.documentcloud.org/documents/5759487-Bernie-Sanders-signs-DNC-loyalty-pledge.html.

N. Gachon, *Bernie Sanders's Democratic Socialism*, https://doi.org/10.1007/978-3-030-69661-0_5

The day before, on March 4, 2019, Sanders had also filed to be a candidate for the U.S. Senate in 2024, but as an independent.[2] A similar odd scenario had already been played out in 2016 when Sanders filed as a Democrat to run for the Democratic nomination and then filed as an independent for his 2018 Senate campaign. On August 2, 2019, the Democratic National Committee consequently adopted a new rule forcing the party's presidential candidates to identify as Democrats in an effort to try and keep outsider candidates like Bernie Sanders from winning the nomination in 2020.[3] The Democratic National Committee was determined to avert the drama that had surrounded the 2016 convention in Philadelphia and arguably paved the way for the debacle in the presidential election that year.

The drama was still luring however, even after the Democratic National Committee decided on August 25, 2018, to drastically scale back the controversial superdelegate system that gave Democratic Party dignitaries tremendous power to cast decisive votes on the first ballot[4] of presidential nominating conventions. The superdelegates had become even more controversial in the context of the 2016 Democratic National Convention, especially after Sanders's supporters criticized the Democratic Party establishment for purportedly supporting Hillary Clinton. Eliminating superdelegates had subsequently been a top priority for Sanders, a necessary step toward rebuilding trust and healing the wounds of the 2016 primary. The 2018 measure that limited the role of superdelegates was welcome, therefore, as a step in the right direction. However, the Democratic National Committee's new rule that visibly asked for more loyalty from candidates in return, requiring them to affirm that they were indeed Democrats and that they would run and serve as Democrats angered Sanders's supporters. Mark Longabaugh, a senior adviser to Sanders's 2016 presidential campaign, bristled:

[2] Id., Statement of Candidacy, March 4, 2019, Federal Election Commission, https://docquery.fec.gov/pdf/416/201903049145600416/201903049145600416.pdf.

[3] Democratic National Committee, Regulations of the Rules and Bylaws Committee for the 2020 Democratic National Convention, December 1, 2018, Democratic Party, https://democrats.org/wp-content/uploads/sites/2/2019/07/Regulations-of-the-RBC-for-the-2020-Convention-12.17.18-FINAL.pdf.

[4] The new procedure allowed superdelegates to vote for any candidate in the (unlikely) event a presidential candidate was not nominated on the first ballot.

I really don't get the motivation for the resolution at all. You know, Bernie Sanders got 13 million votes in 2016. Thousands, if not millions, of those votes were young people and independents he brought into the Democratic Party. And I'm just stunned that the Democratic Party's rules committee would want to try to make the Democratic Party an exclusive club, for which we want to exclude voters and large segments of the American electorate.[5]

At stake behind the Democratic National Committee's new rule was Bernie Sanders's long-standing complex, murky relationship with the Democratic Party, a party he had called "spiritually bankrupt"[6] in 1984, a party whose nomination he sought in presidential elections while running as an independent in congressional elections and claiming to be a "democratic socialist."

5.1   FROM LOCAL TO STATE AND NATIONAL POLITICS

Bernie Sanders was at times ironical about his complex relationship with the Democratic Party, or with the "Democratic" label which he probably found as disturbing as registered Democrats found the "socialist" label. Sanders lamented that the Democratic and Republican parties were little more than empty labels for middle-of-the-road politics that had proven inefficient. In 1988, as he was still mayor of Burlington, Sanders ran for the U.S. House of Representatives as an independent against Republican candidate Peter Smith. That was "an interesting political year," Sanders wrote in his memoir: "I became a Democrat—for all of one night."[7] The reason was that Reverend Jesse Jackson was running for the Democratic nomination for president of the United States. The progressives in Vermont were divided: some refused to get involved because Jackson was the candidate of the Democratic Party, others launched a Vermont chapter of the "Rainbow Coalition"[8] to support Jesse Jackson. The

---

[5] Quoted in David Siders, "DNC Rule Change Angers Sanders Supporters," August 6, 2018, *Politico*, https://www.politico.com/story/2018/06/08/dnc-rule-change-sanders-supporters-634998.

[6] Sanders, "It Is Imperative for Radical Voices to Be Heard," *op. cit.*, p. 83.

[7] Id., *Outsider in the White House*, p. 100.

[8] The original "Rainbow Coalition" (Rainbow Coalition of Revolutionary Solidarity) was a multicultural political organization active in the late 1960s and early 1970s, founded

Burlington Progressive Coalition finally decided to endorse Jackson and Bernie Sanders campaigned for Jackson when the latter visited Burlington. Sanders explained how, on the evening of the "nonbinding"[9] Vermont Democratic Party caucus, he participated "in a formal Democratic party function for the first and last part of [his] life."[10] Democratic Governor of Vermont Madeleine Kunin gave the nominating speech for Michael Dukakis and Sanders gave the nominating speech for Jesse Jackson. Sanders recalled how his presence was sometimes no longer welcome after the progressives had defeated the Democrats as the local governing party: "a number of old-line Dems staged a silent protest by standing up and turning around as I delivered my speech. And when I returned to my seat, a woman in the audience slapped me across the face. It was an exciting evening."[11] Another reason was that Sanders had run for governor of Vermont as an independent two years earlier, because the state legislature refused to let Burlington and other cities reform their property tax system. And he had run against Madeleine Kunin who had been elected the first woman governor of Vermont in 1984 and was seeking reelection in 1986. Still, Sanders was proud to endorse Jackson who eventually won the Burlington caucus overwhelmingly and carried the state. Sanders, however, later expressed his disappointment that Jackson's progressive positions were not incorporated into the Democratic Party platform later that year.[12]

At the end of his term as mayor of Burlington in May 1989, Sanders was unemployed. He lectured in political science for a while at Harvard Kennedy's School of Government, at Hamilton College[13] (Clinton, New York), and at the State University of New York in Binghampton, and he was faced with three possible options: dropping out of politics; running for governor again in 1990 (Democratic Governor Kunin was not seeking

---

in Chicago by Fred Hampton of the Black Panther Party The name "Rainbow Coalition" was appropriated by Jesse Jackson in forming his own, more moderate coalition, Rainbow/PUSH.

[9] In Vermont, at the time, the primary process was totally open, allowing anyone to identify with any party.

[10] Sanders, *Outsider in the White House*, p. 101.

[11] Ibid.

[12] Sanders, *Where We Go from Here*, p. 13.

[13] At Hamilton College, Sanders took courses on cities and democratic socialism. See Dennis Gilbert, "Adventures with Bernie Sanders in 1990," *HuffPost*, January 12, 2017, https://www.huffpost.com/entry/adventures-with-bernie-sa_b_8963690?guccounter=1.

a fourth term); or running for Congress once more against Peter Smith, whom he had already fought in the 1988 election for the U.S. House of Representatives. His decision was finally to run against Peter Smith again. That was a challenging task. Defeating an incumbent is generally an uphill battle. Yet Sanders (37.50%) had lost to Smith (41.21%) by only 3.71%, and since the Democratic candidate, Paul Poirier, had only obtained 18.88%,[14] chances were that the Democrats would not run a strong candidate. The calculus was right: Dolores Sandoval, a professor at the University of Vermont, ran a weak campaign for the Democratic Party and Sanders reaped the lion's share of the Democratic vote. Another factor was that the social and political landscape had changed considerably in the aftermath of the Reagan era: "The rich were getting richer, the middle class was shrinking, the new jobs being created were low-wage jobs, and the people of Vermont were increasingly dissatisfied with status quo politics,"[15] Sanders wrote. With a weak Democratic candidate in the race, Sanders hoped to put his two opponents back to back, convinced as he was that a candidate outside of the two-party system could be appealing to voters, using his typical line to approach virtually everyone on the campaign trail: "Hi, I'm Bernie Sanders, running for Congress. If you like what's going on in Congress, then vote for Peter Smith. If not, you might want to consider voting for me."[16] Peter Smith, who was initially leading slightly, made two strategic mistakes during the campaign:[17] he voted for the 1990 budget reconciliation[18]

[14]Vermont Secretary of State, "1988 U.S. House General Election," Vermont State Archives and Records Administration, https://vtelectionarchive.sec.state.vt.us/elections/view/75810.

[15]Sanders, *Outsider in the White House*, p. 107.

[16]Id., quoted in Jaffe, p. 110.

[17]In addition, the National Rifle Association (NRA) turned against Peter Smith. A few months after taking office in 1988, an office to which he had been elected with the support of the NRA, Smith had announced his intention to vote in favor of background checks on firearm purchasers and of a five-day waiting period on purchases (*Brady Handgun Violence Prevention Act*, Pub.L. 103–159, February 28, 1994). The NRA and Vermont's sportsmen community were angered by his about-face and worked hard to defeat him. That context benefited Sanders although the NRA never endorsed him or financed any of his campaigns.

[18]A budget reconciliation bill makes legislation easier to pass in the Senate. The budget cannot be stalled in the Senate by filibuster, and it does not need the president's signature. Instead of 60 votes, a reconciliation bill only needs a simple majority in the Senate.

bill which proposed major cuts in Medicare, which gave Sanders a slight edge; and he "produced the most negative television ads that anyone in Vermont had ever seen,"[19] describing Sanders as becoming "nauseous" upon hearing John F. Kennedy's inaugural speech, or posting Sanders on a split screen with Fidel Castro. The Sanders campaign eventually carried thirteen of Vermont's fourteen counties on November 6, 1990. Sanders was elected as an independent to the U.S. House of Representatives with 56% of the vote, before Peter Smith (39.52%) and Democratic candidate Dolores Sandoval (3.01%).[20] Sanders's election to the U.S. House of Representatives in 1990 was a major landmark in his political trajectory, eighteen years after running for statewide office and receiving only 1.15% of the vote.[21] The unwavering rhetoric of the "Socialist Ex-Mayor" was in the *New York Times* the next morning, November 7, 1990:

> What we need is a mass movement of tens of millions of people prepared to say that we want national health care, that we want the millionaires and multinational corporations who are not paying their fair share to pay their fair share. [...] We want money going to environmental and educational programs. We want no more Star Wars or Stealth bombers.[22]

Sanders's election to the U.S. House of Representatives in 1990[23] was also a significant turning point in his relationship with the Democratic Party, in his strategy to embrace the Democratic Party. During the campaign, Bernie Sanders had made it clear that he would "seek entry into the Democratic Caucus, while remaining an Independent."[24] While quite a few Democratic legislators shared Sanders's views, for example on

---

[19] Sanders, *Outsider in the White House*, p. 107.

[20] Vermont Secretary of State, "1990 U.S. House General Election," Vermont State Archives and Records Administration, https://vtelectionarchive.sec.state.vt.us/elections/search/year_from:1990/year_to:1990/office_id:5/show_details:1. Peter Diamondstone of the Liberty Union Party earned 0.9% of the votes.

[21] "Vt. Governor," November 7, 1972, Our Campaigns, https://www.ourcampaigns.com/RaceDetail.html?RaceID=144194.

[22] Sanders, quoted in "The 1990 Elections: The Message—Vermont; Socialist Ex-Mayor Elected to House," *New York Times*, November 7, 1990, p. 6, https://www.nytimes.com/1990/11/07/us/the-1990-elections-the-message-vermont-socialist-ex-mayor-ele cted-to-house.html.

[23] "Vt. At Large," November 6, 1990, Our Campaigns, *op. cit.*, p. 32.

[24] Sanders, *Outsider in the White House*, p. 115.

the need for a national healthcare system, or on environmental protection measures, those same legislators were proud Democrats as much as
Sanders was a proud independent. Some of them, like Charlie Stenholm
(D-Texas), a leader of the conservative Blue Dog Democrats,[25] considered that having a socialist in the caucus may meet with fierce opposition
from their constituents. Unsurprisingly, all Representative Stenholm had
to do to bar Sanders was to circulate a document containing less than
flattering observations Sanders had made on the Democratic Party. With
a share of humor, Sanders declared himself "surprised by the quality of
[Stenholm's] research" and admitted that the quotes were "accurate,"
that he had been "extremely critical" of the Democratic Party over the
years, of "its tepidness about fighting for the working families of this
country."[26] Sanders had to work out a compromise with Speaker Tom
Foley (D-Wash.) and Majority Leader Dick Gephardt (D-Mo.) by which
he was *not* to become a member of the Democratic Caucus but would be
treated as a Democrat in terms of committee assignments and seniority.
Despite claims that Sanders had always caucused with Democrats, his first
election to the U.S. House of Representatives revealed that such was
not exactly the case as his initial overtures were rebuffed by the Democratic Caucus. Sanders's remark in *Where We go from Here* is therefore
technically inaccurate, at least for what regards the U.S. House of Representatives: "in Washington, I have been a member of the Democratic
Caucus in the House for the sixteen years I served there and a member
of the Democratic Caucus in the Senate for the last twelve years."[27] Most
members elected as independents or under the banner of a minor party
usually caucus either with the Democrats or the Republicans. Sanders's
campaign announcement that he would caucus with the Democrats,
therefore, was not unheard of. In 1990, however, the problem was that
Bernie Sanders was requesting membership in the House Democratic
Caucus but, resisting caucus rules, refused to call himself a Democrat.

---

[25] The Blue Dog Coalition is a caucus of U.S. Democratic representatives who identify
as fiscally conservative, centrist Democrats.

[26] Sanders, *Outsider in the White House*, p. 116.

[27] Id., *Where We Go from Here*, p. 214.

5.2   THE ROAD TO THE U.S. SENATE

Jim Jeffords, the Republican Senator of Vermont who had defected to become an independent in 2001, tipping control of the Senate in favor of the Democrats, [28] announced in 2005 that he would not seek reelection due to concerns about his health and that of his wife. Jeffords was a moderate Republican, a champion for the environment and for education who had grown disenchanted over the years with the conservative stance of the Republican Party. Immediately, Democrats and Republicans sought to frame the 2006 race in Vermont. Bernie Sanders, who was the U.S. Representative for Vermont, immediately issued a public statement that he intended to run for Jim Jeffords's seat. Since Howard Dean, the former governor of Vermont and now the chairperson of the Democratic National Committee, indicated that he was not interested, Bernie Sanders, against all odds, emerged as the likely Democratic contender. As of 2005, however, the likelihood of a Senate run by an independent and "democratic socialist" for the state of Vermont shortly after the reelection of George W. Bush was almost infinitesimal. The seat Sanders wanted to run for as a radical independent was probably the most permanently Republican Senate seat in the country, with a Republican winning streak that had extended from before the Civil War through the 2000 election.[29] The likely candidate was certainly a moderate Republican, or perhaps a moderate Democrat. Bernie Sanders was neither. But he was endorsed by Senate Democratic Leader Harry Reid (Nevada), whom he had never met, and by Senator Charles (Chuck) Schumer (D-N.Y.). Sanders was grateful as their endorsements might help ease down possible Democratic opposition in Vermont. Barack Obama, then still senator of Illinois, also came to Vermont to campaign for Sanders.

The Republican candidate turned out to be Richard Tarrant, "the wealthiest person in the state," according to Sanders, a near-billionaire Vermont software entrepreneur and major Republican Party donor. During the debate organized before the election, Tarrant touted the good works of his family's charitable foundation, which donated money to

---

[28] "The text of Sen. Jim Jeffords' announcement Thursday in Burlington, Vt," CBS News, May 24, 2001, https://www.cbsnews.com/news/text-of-jeffords-speech.

[29] John Nichols, "Afterword: Outsider in the Presidential Race," in Sanders, *Outsider in the White House*, p. 310.

Vermont schools and hospitals,[30] only to see it cited in the independent press as another sign of privilege, not to speak of his taste for luxurious Florida real estate. Sanders highlighted his excessive campaign spending, "with ad after ad portraying me as an enemy of humanity," and claimed that "Tarrant spent more money per vote in 2006 than any Senate candidate had in American history up to that point."[31] On November 7, 2006, Sanders was elected to succeed incumbent Senator Jim Jeffords with 65.4% of the vote against 32.3% for Richard Tarrant.[32] Bernie Sanders was now on his way to the U.S. Senate, set to become the first socialist senator in American history. Sanders's election was certainly an achievement in that "democratic socialism" had so far never been a vote-winning label in a country where even the word "liberal" is often regarded as an epithet, and in a state that had elected Republicans to that seat since the Civil War. After representing Vermont's at-large House district as an independent for sixteen years (1991–2007), Bernie Sanders had first won the Democratic primary in Vermont, then declined the nomination in order to run as an independent, thus making sure that no Democrat would be on the ballot in the general election to split the vote. Yet there was a contradiction in declining the Democratic nomination while feeling "grateful"[33] for the support of national Democrats like Chuck Schumer, Harry Reid, or Barack Obama. Whether or not Bernie Sanders had cut a deal with the Democratic devil, or had sympathy for the devil, neither or both, was up for debate. As of 2007, it was a double-entry question about a double-edged sword as the Democratic Party establishment was also trying to cut a deal with Sanders, a political devil they had a measure of sympathy for, or maybe trying to give the devil the kiss of death.

On May 22, 2005, Howard Dean, the chair of the Democratic National Committee, appeared on NBC's "Meet the Press" and was interviewed by Tim Russert who asked him if there was room in the Democratic Party for a socialist. The answer was as calculated as the question was simple:

[30] Richard Tarrant, Vermont Senate Debate, October 23, 2006, C-SPAN, https://www.c-span.org/video/?195068-1/vermont-senate-debate.

[31] Sanders, *Our Revolution*, p. 44.

[32] "Vt. U.S. Senate," November 7, 2006, Our Campaigns, https://www.ourcampaigns.com/RaceDetail.html?RaceID=6963.

[33] Sanders, *Our Revolution*, p. 43.

DEAN: Well, a Democratic socialist—all right, we're talking about words here. And Bernie can call himself anything he wants. He is basically a liberal Democrat, and he is a Democrat that—he runs as an Independent because he doesn't like the structure and the money that gets involved. And he actually has, I think, some good points about campaign finance reform. The bottom line is that Bernie Sanders votes with the Democrats 98 percent of the time. And that is a candidate that we think...

RUSSERT: So you'd support him?

DEAN: We may very well end up supporting him. We need to work some things out because it's very important for us not to split the votes in some of the other offices as well.[34]

Accordingly, the way Bernie Sanders was welcome and integrated into the Senate Democratic Caucus was strikingly different from what had happened in the House of Representatives in 1990, even though Sanders's own strategy had not changed:

> When I was elected in 2006, the Democrats, by two votes, took control of the U.S. Senate. Senator Harry Reid, the new majority leader, was extremely kind to me and appointed me to most of the committees I wanted.
>
> I had requested of Senator Ted Kennedy, the longtime leader of the Senate Health, Education, Labor and Pensions Committee, the opportunity to serve with him on that very important committee. I was very appreciative that he consented. My interest in environmental issues was long-standing, and I was fortunate to be appointed to the two major environmental committees, the Committee on Energy and Natural Resources and the Committee on Environment and Public Works. The Environment Committee was led by an old friend of mine from California, Barbara Boxer. As a strong advocate for veterans, I also was delighted to be appointed to the U.S. Senate Committee on Veterans' Affairs, as well as to the Budget Committee, which gave me an important say in the development of national priorities.[35]

For many observers, for Sanders's opponents as well as for a number of socialists, Sanders was not—but was—a Democrat.

---

[34] Howard Dean, Meet the Press, May 22, 2005, NBC News,http://www.nbcnews.com/id/7924139/ns/meet_the_press/t/transcript-may/#.XiBLzy17Sis.

[35] Sanders, *Our Revolution*, p. 44.

Ashley Smith, a member of the International Socialist Organization, in a piece published for *Socialist Worker* on November 17, 2006, painted an alternative portrait of Bernie Sanders and of his recent election to the U.S. Senate:

> While it was fantastic to see Tarrant humiliated, Sanders' election to the Senate doesn't represent a radical departure from politics as usual. He may have a portrait of Eugene Debs hanging in his office, but his politics have little in common with that great American socialist.[36]

"To put an exclamation point on his all-but-declared membership in the Democratic Party," Smith added, "Sanders celebrated his election victory, contrary to his tradition of hosting a separate party, with the Democrats."[37] Especially damning was her reminder that Sanders had made the following statement on Vermont Public Television during the 2004 presidential election, calling it "capitulation" to the Democrats: "I am going to vote for John Kerry, I am going to run around this country and do everything I can to dissuade people from voting for Ralph Nader. I am going to do everything I can, while I have differences with John Kerry, to make sure that he is elected."[38] Bernie Sanders's presidential strategy will be discussed in the final part of this volume but, as testified by Ashley Smith's argument about Ralph Nader, Sanders's election to the Senate in 2006 was understood by many as a possible path toward presidential politics. Could a socialist really run for president in the United States? But was Bernie Sanders a real socialist? In the context of the 2006 senatorial election, Ashley Smith's point was that Bernie Sanders could or should have run like Ralph Nader ran for president, as an independent opposing both capitalist parties, the Republicans and the Democrats. However, Sanders apparently refused to risk the spoiler effect of vote splitting, i.e., drawing votes from a major candidate with similar views and possibly causing an opponent to win. This is the reason why Bernie Sanders, and Ashley Smith blamed him for it, "supported Bill Clinton as a lesser evil"[39] in 1992, and John Kerry in 2004. Ralph Nader had run

---

[36] Ashley Smith, "A Socialist in the Senate?" *Socialist Worker*, November 17, 2006, p. 11, https://socialistworker.org/2006-2/610/610_11_BernieSanders.php.

[37] Ibid.

[38] Ibid.

[39] Ibid.

as the Green Party[40] nominee in 2000 and cost Al Gore, Bill Clinton's vice president, two states, Florida and New Hampshire, which had been crucial to George W. Bush's election.[41] A similar scenario took place in 2004, with a more limited impact since Bush was a much more polarizing figure in 2004 than he had been in 2000. Ashley Smith's arguments were very significant in that they already prefigured the next—presidential—step in Bernie Sanders's political trajectory. For socialist purists, Sanders's strategy of caucusing with the Senate Democrats was a typical liberal strategy to transform the Democratic Party from within which had not only failed but been counterproductive for generations: it had not shifted the Democrats to the left and instead had dragged the leftists who joined the Democrats to the right. Sanders, they thought, would be no exception. Sanders was not a radical from such a perspective, and Ashley Smith claimed that he had betrayed his own political model:

> Anything we want from Sanders or the Democrats we will have to fight for. And if we want a genuine socialist alternative, we should follow the lead of Sanders' hero, Eugene Debs, who said, "The differences between the Republican and Democratic Parties involve no issue, no principle in which the working class have any interest."[42]

Were American leftists to sacrifice electoral success for ideological purity? Bernie Sanders believed both could one day be achieved in the United States and he adopted a more pragmatic course upon entering the U.S. Senate.

5.3   Bernie Sanders's Congressional Record

Bernie Sanders's pragmatic course in the U.S. Congress cannot be regarded as one of actual leadership in terms of legislative achievements. As of January 2020, he had co-sponsored 4781 bills (3070 in

---

[40] The Green Party USA was founded in 1991 and dissolved in 2019. It was succeeded by the Green Party of the United States, founded in 2001 when the Association of State Green split from the Green Party USA.

[41] Charlie Cook, "The Next Nader Effect," *New York Times*, March 9, 2004, https://www.nytimes.com/2004/03/09/opinion/the-next-nader-effect.html.

[42] Ashley Smith, "A Socialist in the Senate?" *Socialist Worker*, November 17, 2006, p. 11, https://socialistworker.org/2006-2/610/610_11_BernieSanders.php.

the House and 1711 in the Senate) but sponsored only 379 (236 in the House and 143 in the Senate).[43] Of the bills he sponsored, only three became law: two to rename post offices in Vermont,[44] and one to increase the disability compensation rate for American veterans and their families.[45] All bills combined, his six main policy areas (out of thirty-one) throughout his presence in the U.S. Congress were health (1010 bills), armed forces and national security (555 bills), taxation (426 bills), government operations and politics (322 bills), education (290 bills), and labor and employment (277 bills).[46] GovTrack.us stated that Bernie Sanders ranked "most liberal" during the 2019 legislative year (January 3, 2019–December 31, 2019) compared to other senators serving ten or more years,[47] and also, statistically, "most absent" due to his two campaigns for the 2016 and 2020 presidential elections.[48] While Sanders was arguably the most liberal member of Congress, his importance, therefore, was not one of actual legislative leadership. He was an "outsider" in the House of Representatives from the outset, as the title and contents of his memoir first published in 1997 suggested:

> The way the debate on the House floor shaped up was nothing new. Same old lies. Same old bullshit. Same old empty sound-and-fury. Suddenly Dick Armey, Newt Gingrich, and others who had received millions in contributions from corporate America and the rich were deeply concerned about

[43] Congress.gov,   https://www.congress.gov/member/bernard-sanders/S000033. Bernie Sanders also introduced 884 amendments, 550 resolutions 294 concurrent resolutions, and 274 joint resolutions (House and Senate combined).

[44] H.R.5245—To designate the facility of the United States Postal Service located at 1 Marble Street in Fair Haven, Vermont, as the "Matthew Lyon Post Office Building," Pub.L. 109–263, August 2, 2006; S.885 - A bill to designate the facility of the United States Postal Service located at 35 Park Street in Danville, Vermont, as the "Thaddeus Stevens Post Office," Pub.L. 113–189, November 26, 2914.

[45] Veterans' Compensation Cost-of-Living Adjustment Act, Pub.L. 113–152, May 8, 2013.

[46] Congress.gov, *op. cit.*, p. 103.

[47] Of "all" senators, those serving less than ten years included, Kamala Harris (D-Calif.) ranked "most liberal" in 2019.

[48] Sen. Bernard "Bernie" Sanders's 2019 Report Card, GovTrack.us, https://www.gov track.us/congress/members/bernard_sanders/400357/report-card/2019. Among "all" senators the "most absent" in 2019 were presidential candidates: Sen. Cory Booker (D-N.J.), Sen. Bernie Sanders (I-Vt.), Sen. Kamala Harris (D-Calif.), Sen. Elizabeth Warren (D-Mass.), Sen. Amy Klobuchar (D-Minn.).

the well-being of low-income workers. Raising the minimum wage, they declaimed with melodramatic handwringing, would hurt the poor, not help them. [...] The theatrics bordered on the comic.[49]

Sanders's legislative accomplishments, however, were far from inexistent. In August 2005, Matt Taibbi of *Rolling Stone* argued that the legislative efficacy of the amendment process should also be taken into account:

Amendments occupy a great deal of most legislators' time, particularly those lawmakers in the minority. Members of Congress do author major bills, but more commonly they make minor adjustments to the bigger bill. Rather than write their own anti-terrorism bill, for instance, lawmakers will try to amend the Patriot Act, either by creating a new clause in the law or expanding or limiting some existing provisions. The bill that ultimately becomes law is an aggregate of the original legislation and all the different congresspersons along the way.

Sanders is the amendment king of the current House of Representative. Since the Republicans took over Congress in 1995, no other lawmaker – not Tom DeLay, not Nancy Pelosi – has passed more roll-call amendments (amendments that actually went to a vote on the floor) than Bernie Sanders. He accomplishes this on the one hand by being relentlessly active, and on the other by using his status as an Independent to form left-right coalitions.[50]

As John Nichols put it in his afterword to the 2015 edition of *Outsider in the White House*, one of the reasons that Sanders said he wanted to go to the Senate was because he believed that, as an independent, he could build unlikely alliances "[i]n the sense," Sanders explained, "that we are trying to develop left-right coalitions, we are also trying to redefine American politics."[51] Sanders, however, did not really succeed in redefining U.S. politics from within the walls of the U.S. Congress even though his congressional legitimacy gave considerable resonance to his radical voice. In strictly legislative terms, his Senate record is hardly revolutionary and even leans toward the Democratic mainstream:

---

[49] Sanders, *Outsider in the White House*, p. 121.

[50] Matt Taibbi, "Inside the Horror Show That is Congress," *Rolling Stone*, August 25, 2005, https://www.rollingstone.com/feature/inside-the-horror-show-that-is-congress-177955. See also: William F. Grover, "In the Belly of the Beast: Bernie Sanders, Congress and Political Change" *New Political Science*, vol. 28/29, Winter-Spring 1994, pp. 31-52.

[51] Nichols, "Afterword: Outsider in the Presidential Race," *op. cit.*, p. 320.

As a member of the Senate, I am proud to have passed some major legislation. Majority Leader Harry Reid, Congressman Jim Clyburn of South Carolina, and I succeeded in putting $11 billion into community health centers throughout the country, as part of the Affordable Care Act. This enabled some 6 million more Americans, regardless of their income, to access primary health care, dental care, low-cost prescription drugs, and mental health counseling. We also substantially increased funding for the National Health Service Corps, which brought thousands of doctors, dentists, and nurses into medically underserved areas throughout the country.[52]

Sanders took a number of bold steps, as when he took the floor of the Senate for eight and a half hours on December 10, 2010, to filibuster the extension of the Bush-era tax cuts by the Obama administration, tax cuts that the Democratic Party had been denouncing for years. From an ideological standpoint, outside of Congress, it was certainly comforting for progressives to see that someone in the country could still take a stand for the view that upper-income households did not need a tax cut, but there was no doubt that the bill, supported by most Republicans and enough Democrats, would eventually pass. Sanders's trajectory in Congress, by many accounts, was one of a solo radical who managed to grab the spotlight, to boost his national reputation, and to become a sort of hero for the left.

Sanders was an activist in Congress, and he used the media accordingly: "There are some great people out there who can say, and are saying, exactly what I'm saying. They're not United States Senators."[53] Sanders often appeared on progressive talk-radio shows like those hosted by Thom Hartmann and Ed Schultz, and on MSNBC. He was a guest on public television's "Bill Moyers Journal," and also on programs unlikely to host a democratic socialist, like NBC's "Meet the Press" and ABC's "This Week."[54] Sanders used the same tools that had built the so-called Republican Revolution of 1994, when the airwaves were literally turned into a political weapon and conservative talk-radio hosts became the ideological mouthpieces of the Republican Party. In January 1995, the Congressional Progressive Caucus was the first group inside the U.S.

[52] Sanders, *Our Revolution*, pp. 44–45.

[53] *Id., Outsider in the White House*, pp. 308–309.

[54] Ibid.

Congress to propose a detailed, comprehensive legislative alternative to Speaker Newt Gingrich (R-Ga.) and to the "Contract with America" signed by over 300 Republican candidates and presented at a press conference just six weeks before the 1994 midterm elections. Sanders remarked that "[w]hile most Democrats responded with confusion and paralysis to the Republican victory, the members of the Progressive Caucus immediately mobilized to fight back—both in Congress and back home at the grassroots level."[55] Back in 1994, "[w]e were not confused or hesitant," Sanders wrote, "[w]e knew exactly what we had to do. Intellectually, we had to expose the Contract with America for exactly what it was: a vicious assault on working people and the poor."[56] Sanders was not only a member but a founder, arguably the initiator, and the first chairperson of the Congressional Progressive Caucus.

The Congressional Progressive Caucus was established in 1991 by six U.S. Representatives: Ron Dellums (D-Calif.), Lane Evans (D-Ill.), Thomas Andrews (D-Maine), Peter DeFazio (D-Ore.), Maxine Waters (D-Calif.) and Bernie Sanders (I-Vt). Sanders's inspiration came from the "alternative budget" that was introduced by the Black Caucus every year and which "[i]n a very simple and effective manner [...] exposed the moral bankruptcy of congressional priorities."[57] For years, Sanders realized, the Black Caucus had been the progressive caucus in Congress, but not every progressive was black. So Sanders started promoting the idea of a caucus that would bring all progressives together—white, black, Hispanic, Asian, male, and female—in order to stand together in fighting for progressive priorities. That meant pushing for activism on an "ideological" and "class" basis to represent all Americans who were struggling for a better standard of living while the Black Caucus would keep fighting for the particular needs of the black community, the Hispanic Caucus for the particular needs of Hispanics, and the Women's Caucus on the particular needs of women.[58] Sanders initially approached Ron Dellums, then Peter DeFazio, Lane Evans, and finally Maxine Waters.

The Congressional Progressive Caucus has grown steadily since it was founded in 1991 and is now, with 98 members, the second-largest caucus

[55] Sanders, *Outsider in the White House*, p. 329.

[56] Sanders, *Outsider in the House*, p. 200

[57] Ibid., p. 153.

[58] Ibid.

within the Democratic Party and the third largest caucus in the U.S. Congress. It is often referred to as the progressive faction of the Democratic Party and, with its large numbers, its range of progressive ideas, and the left-wing political figures in its ranks, is ideally positioned to be extremely influential on Capitol Hill. As such, it can and should be regarded as a significant initiative on the part of Bernie Sanders, and others, to alter the legislative course of the Democratic Party. Yet it was not really radical and was, to a large extent, absorbed into the mainstream of the Democratic Party. On March 19, 2019, Representative Ro Khanna (D-Calif.), the Congressional Progressive Caucus's first Vice Chair, reposted an article by Paul Blest for Splinter News, a left-leaning news and opinion website, about the political limits of the Caucus:

> While Republican groupings like the House Freedom Caucus operate as a unified army, the CPC tends to let its members go their own way. And despite its name, it doesn't even have an ideologically unified makeup; in fact, over a dozen members of the CPC also have membership in the New Democratic Coalition, which has historically represented the more pro-business wing of the party.[…] The CPC was launched during the final year of the Soviet Union and a year before Bill Clinton won the presidency. The Democratic Party's priorities of the time reflected that rightward drift.[59]

For one thing, Sanders and his colleagues never succeeded in turning the Congressional Progressive Caucus into a political movement ("a unified army"). It is indeed a fact that any significant swerve to the left of the Democratic mainstream had to be taken individually, as when Bernie Sanders decided to filibuster Barack Obama's extension of the Bush-era tax cuts in 2010. In the same article, Paul Blest argues that "if Obama's tenure marginalized progressive priorities, that [was] in part because of choices that the left made," that, as a consequence, "the Democrats were always more interested in cutting a deal with the right of the caucus or even the GOP than they were with the left."[60] Too often, political compromise had led to ideological step back and Bernie Sanders had

---

[59] Paul Blest, "What will it take for the Congressional Progressive Caucus to win?", Splinter News, March 19, 2019. Reposted by Rep. Ro Khanna, https://khanna.house. gov/media/in-the-news/what-will-it-take-congressional-progressive-caucus-win.

[60] Ibid.

not been able to make any "radical" difference from within the Congressional Progressive Caucus he had helped create. Of course, the fuel of social suffering and discontent was everywhere but there was detonator to start off a radical movement, and that detonator was not likely to be found within the walls of the U.S. Congress. Another reason had to do with Bernie Sanders's ideological matrix as he sold it to the American people. That matrix was not Marxism, not Debsian socialism, not even democratic socialism per se. Quite confusingly sometimes, Bernie Sanders proclaimed himself to be "a democratic socialist" while equating his own ideological matrix with New Deal liberalism—a doctrine already co-opted by each and every Democratic member of Congress, and a project Franklin D. Roosevelt himself intentionally never called socialism.

References

Blest, Paul. "What Will It Take for the Congressional Progressive Caucus to Win?" Splinter News (March 19, 2019), https://splinternews.com/what-will-it-take-for-the-congressional-progressive-cau-1833071375.
Cook, Charlie. "The Next Nader Effect," New York Times, March 9, 2004, https://www.nytimes.com/2004/03/09/opinion/the-next-nader-eff ect.html.
Gilbert, Dennis. "Adventures with Bernie Sanders in 1990." HuffPost (January 12, 2017), https://www.huffpost.com/entry/adventures-with-bernie-sa_b_8 963690?guccounter=1.
Grover, William F. "In the Belly of the Beast: Bernie Sanders, Congress and Political Change." New Political Science, vols. 28/29 (Winter–Spring 1994), pp. 31–52.
———. "Stranger in the House? Bernie Sanders in Congress." Voices of Dissent: Critical Readings in American Politics, 2nd ed., edited by William F. Grover and Joseph G. Peschek. New York: HarperCollins, 1996, ch. 5.
———. "Congress and Movement-Building: Bernie Sanders and the Congressional Progressive Caucus." Voices of Dissent: Critical Readings in American Politics, 5th ed., edited by William F. Grover and Joseph G. Peschek, New York: Pearson, 2004, ch. 7.
———, Joseph G. Peschek. "The Wild Ride of President-Elect Bernie Sanders." CommonDreams, (June 17, 2015), https://www.commondreams.org/views/ 2015/06/17/wild-ride-president-elect-bernie-sanders.
———. "It Is Clear the Establishment and Corporate Media Would Prefer Trump Reelection to President Bernie Sanders." CommonDreams (January 15, 2020), https://www.commondreams.org/views/2020/01/15/it-clear-establishment-and-corporate-media-would-prefer-trump-reelection-president.

Jaffe, Harry. *Why Bernie Sanders Matters*. New York: Regan Arts, 2015.
———. "It Is Imperative for Radical Voices to Be Heard." *The Militant* (January 20, 1984), p. 13. https://themilitant.com/1984/4801/MIL4801.pdf.
———, with Huck Gutman. *Outsider in the House: A Political Autobiography*. New York: Verso, 1997. Rpt. *Outsider in the White House*, 2015.
———. *Our Revolution: A Future to Believe In*. New York: Thomas Dunne Books, 2016.
———. *Where We Go from Here: Two Years in the Resistance*. New York: Thomas Dunne Books, 2018.
———. Statement of Candidacy (March 4, 2019). Federal Election Commission, https://docquery.fec.gov/pdf/416/201903049145600416/201903049145600416.pdf.
———. Presidential Candidate Written Affirmation (March 5, 2019). NBC News, https://www.documentcloud.org/documents/5759487-Bernie-Sanders-signs-DNC-loyalty-pledge.html.
SIDERS, David. "'It Sounds Insane, Actually': Democrats Relive 2016 Primary All Over Again." Politico (July 3, 2020), https://www.politico.com/news/2020/03/07/democrats-2016-primary-122951.
Smith, Ashley. "A Socialist in the Senate?" *Socialist Worker* (November 17, 2006), p. 11, https://socialistworker.org/2006-2/610/610_11_BernieSanders.php.
Taibbl, Matt. "Inside the Horror Show That Is Congress." *Rolling Stone* (August 25, 2005), https://www.rollingstone.com/feature/inside-the-horror-show-that-is-congress-17795.

CHAPTER 6

Bernie Sanders's Liberal Matrix

In 1928, for the first of his six consecutive campaigns as the presidential nominee of the Socialist Party, Norman Thomas campaigned on a platform that, among other planks, called for the nationalization of natural resources and basic industries, promising to achieve something Marx had envisioned.[1] It has often been argued that the social vision of the Socialist Party was fulfilled by the New Deal, that Franklin D. Roosevelt put into practice virtually every social program that Norman Thomas had been espousing.[2] Norman Thomas, however, rejected the claim that Roosevelt had carried out the Socialist Party platform, and even claimed that, for lack of more profound or radical changes to the system, the New Deal was even an implicit concession to state capitalism:

> What Roosevelt did was temporarily to stabilize capitalism with a few concessions to workers that are poor copies of Socialist immediate demands. In no true sense is the New Deal socialism. It is state capitalism [...].[3] That both [the Democratic and Republican] parties are

---

[1] Socialist Labor Party of America, "National Platform," May 14, 1928, http://www.slp.org/pdf/platforms/plat1928.pdf.

[2] Altman, p. 196.

[3] Norman Thomas, *The New Deal: A Socialist Analysis*, Chicago, IL., Socialist Party of America, Committee on Education and Research, 1934, p. 3, https://digital.library.pitt.edu/islandora/object/pitt%3A31735061544668.

© The Author(s), under exclusive license to Springer Nature Switzerland AG 2021
N. Gachon, *Bernie Sanders's Democratic Socialism*, https://doi.org/10.1007/978-3-030-69661-0_6

alike and both quite confused, is to be expected in a country in which the major parties are paid by and serve the same owning class. [...] Those who expected Socialism from a Democratic President deserve to be disappointed.[4]

This issue was a defining one for Bernie Sanders's own brand of socialism. On November 19, 2015, as he was speaking at Georgetown University to define what he exactly meant by "democratic socialism," Sanders asserted "simply and straightforwardly" that democratic socialism "builds on what Franklin Delano Roosevelt said when he fought for guaranteed economic rights for all Americans." "That was Roosevelt's vision 70 years ago," Sanders added—"[i]t is my vision today."[5]

6.1   The Lexicon of New Deal Liberalism

In a February 2016 interview with the Daily Beast, Larry Sanders described his brother Bernie, then a candidate to be the presidential nominee of the Democratic Party, as "a genuine socialist in his sense of class warfare," in his belief that "there is not a national interest so much as there is an interests with sectors of the population."[6] While this argument was an explicit throwback to the Marxist conception of socialism, Bernie Sanders took a significantly diverging approach when he said, and wrote, for example in *Our Revolution*, that he did not believe "government should take over the grocery store down the street or own the means of production."[7] Since the very definition of socialism is based on public ownership and control of the means of production and natural resources, one is bound to wonder why, in consistently proclaiming himself to be a "democratic socialist," Bernie Sanders came to define "democratic social-ism" as something that, as a matter of fact, was not socialism. Sanders's democratic socialism had come a long way since 1979, a time when he

[4] Ibid., p. 19.

[5] Sanders, "Democratic Socialism in the U.S.A.," November 19, 2015, *Bernie Speaks*, pp. 81–82.

[6] Larry Sanders, quoted in Nico Hines, "Bernie Sanders's Brother: He Backs 'Class Warfare,' Bill Clinton Was Worse Than Bush," The Daily Beast, February 19, 2016, https://www.thedailybeast.com/bernie-sanderss-brother-he-backs-class-warfare-bill-clinton-was-worse-than-bush.

[7] Id., *Our Revolution, op. cit.*, p. 20.

eulogized his socialist model Eugene Debs as someone who understood how "necessary" it was "for the working class, itself, to take over the means of production and the government."[8]

Bernie Sanders made relatively few references to Roosevelt's New Deal until he was pressed, as a presidential hopeful, to define what he exactly meant by "democratic socialism." In *Outsider in the House* (1997) and its 2015 reedition as *Outsider in the White House*, Sanders simply claimed that the United States needed "to pass labor legislation that ensure[d] equity in contract negotiations between workers and management" and that the task was certainly achievable since "legislation to achieve the same purpose was passed during the New Deal."[9] Roosevelt's New Deal could not really be regarded as a core component of Sanders's ideological matrix at that point. To most people, his ideological matrix was and remained socialism. Sanders's references to the New Deal sought, almost pragmatically, to project what was largely perceived and often debunked as a mere socialist utopia into the realm of political praxis, not unlike what Lincoln Steffens wrote about his trip to Russia in 1919: "I have seen the future, and it works."[10] Sanders's point was to counter the neoliberal argument that no alternative legislative course was ever possible. There were to be more frequent references to Roosevelt and to the New Deal in *Our Revolution* in 2016 and in *Where We Go from Here* in 2018. Sanders opened the umbrella of New Deal liberalism wider before the 2016 presidential election, during his first presidential campaign. The speech he gave in Gaston Hall at Georgetown University on November 19, 2015 was both a pivotal moment and a conventional exercise in political communication as Bernie Sanders was speaking of Franklin D. Roosevelt's inaugural remarks of January 1937 to speak about himself:

> President Franklin Delano Roosevelt looked out at the nation and this is what he saw. He saw tens of millions of its citizens denied the basic necessities of life. He saw millions of families trying to live on incomes so meager that the pall of family disaster hung over them day by day. He saw millions denied education, recreation, and the opportunity to better their lot and the lot of their children. He saw millions lacking the means to buy products they needed and by their poverty and lack of disposable income

---

[8] Id., *Eugene V. Debs*, band 8, "Internalizing Socialist Thought," *op. cit.*, p. 3.

[9] Id., *Outsider in the House*, p. 236; *Outsider in the White House*, p. 293.

[10] Steffens, Letter to Marie Howe, *op. cit.*, p. 52

denying employment to many other millions. He saw one-third of a nation ill-housed, ill-clad, ill-nourished. And he acted.[11]

Those remarks concerned the United States in the wake of the Great Recession. What Roosevelt had seen was what Sanders was seeing now. He was seeking to make himself presidential, to embody a future that could be functional because it had worked earlier in similar circumstances. In the same speech, Sanders made a pointed reference to another landmark speech by Franklin D. Roosevelt, his 1944 State of the Union address in which he proposed a "Second Bill of Rights." Again, Sanders's strategy could be read through the prism of political communication:

> In that speech, Roosevelt described the economic rights that he believed every American was entitled to: The right to a decent job at decent pay, the right to adequate food, clothing, and time off from work, the right for every business, large and small, to function in an atmosphere free from unfair competition and domination by monopolies. The right of all Americans to have a decent home and decent health care.[12]

This campaign speech by Bernie Sanders a year before the 2016 presidential election used the lexicon of New Deal liberalism rather than its substance, keywords applicable to the post-Great Recession period— "economic rights," "decent job," "decent pay," "adequate food," "adequate [...] clothing," "time off from work," "unfair competition," "domination by monopolies," "decent home," "decent health care"— rather than a comprehensive account of Roosevelt's legacy in implementing the New Deal. Perhaps even more significant was that Sanders's 2015 speech contained no mention of his model, Eugene Debs, or of Norman Thomas, the Socialist Party's candidate for president in each of Roosevelt's four elections, who wrote that Roosevelt, in fact, had temporarily stabilized capitalism, and that the New Deal was not socialism.[13]

Sanders's references to the New Deal also eschewed the transition between the first and the second New Deal. Roosevelt's first hundred days (March–June 1933) saw him win passage of numerous bills designed to

---

[11] Sanders, "Democratic Socialism in the U.S.A.," *Bernie Speaks*, p. 75.

[12] Ibid., p. 81.

[13] Thomas, *op. cit.*, p. 111.

end the nation's economic troubles. The first New Deal (1933–1934), therefore, looked to stabilize the financial system of the United States, to provide relief and jobs, and to reenergize the capitalist economy. From that angle, Norman Thomas's 1934 argument that "[w]hat Roosevelt did was temporarily to stabilize capitalism"[14] was factual. However, faced with growing criticism, especially from the left, Roosevelt took a left turn as the 1936 presidential election came into view. In 1935, during the second hundred days (June–August 1935), Roosevelt won passage of progressive legislation that provided a minimum level of social and economic protection for all Americans. Three initiatives represented the administration's turn to the left: the Works Progress Administration, the Wagner Act,[15] and the Social Security Act.[16] In 1937–1938, however, industrial production declined by 33%, wages by 35%, national income by 13%, while unemployment rose by 5% with an estimated 4 million workers losing their jobs.[17] The so-called Roosevelt recession was due to the decline in federal spending, which led a reluctant Roosevelt to finally endorse Keynesian economics and to ask Congress for a substantial increase in federal spending in April of 1938. Then, Sanders's reference to the Second Bill of Rights (1944) was, again, essentially rhetorical as the 1944 State of the Union was delivered during World War II, only fifteen months prior to Roosevelt's death. It was therefore never really implemented. The legacy and importance of the New Deal is a question open for debate. World War II, however, more than the New Deal, arguably ended the Great Depression by sparking massive job creation as well as enough public and private spending to lift the United States out of the slump.

Bernie Sanders's recurrent references to New Deal liberalism raise a number of issues and were often regarded as inconsistent, or at least as puzzling. Why would Sanders seek to be associated with the New Deal when even Democrats tended to distance themselves from such a symbol of big government? Again, it is important to distinguish political substance from political communication. While Sanders's attempt to

---

[14] Ibid.

[15] *National Labor Relations Act*, Pub.L. 74–198, July 6, 1935.

[16] *Social Security Act*, Pub.L. 74–271, August 14, 1935.

[17] Patrick J. Maney, *The Roosevelt Presence: The Life and Legacy of FDR*, Berkeley, University of California Press, 1998, p. 103.

define democratic socialism in his 2015 address at Georgetown University was expectedly one of disambiguation, it was also, intentionally, one of strategic ambiguation: by linking democratic socialism to New Deal liberalism, Sanders was bringing democratic socialism into the lexicon of mainstream American politics. The attempt was all the easier as the New Deal was perceived as an expression of socialist values by many observers in the 1930s. President Roosevelt was often labeled as a socialist for supporting such programs as Social Security, the minimum wage, unemployment compensation, jobs programs, agricultural assistance, or the end of child labor. Of course Roosevelt was not as socialist, nor did he adopt the substance of the Socialist Party platform, but Bernie Sanders visibly understood that, by proclaiming liberal democratic goals that resonated with the ideas of many socialists, Norman Thomas included, Roosevelt had succeeded in attracting the swing voters who had defeated the Republicans in 1932[18] into a New Deal coalition that won the congressional elections of 1934 and reelected the president with 61% of the popular vote and 523 of 531 electoral votes in 1936.[19] By using the lexicon of New Deal liberalism when he launched his first presidential campaign, Bernie Sanders sought to address subliminal messages to liberals across the board with a view to building a potentially electable coalition, broader than the radical ranks of democratic socialism—a coalition assimilable to the mainstream of American politics.

6.2   MARTIN LUTHER KING JR., LYNDON B. JOHNSON

Mainstream Class Warfare

A similar sequence can be observed regarding Martin Luther King Jr. There are no references to Dr. King in *Outsider in the House* (1997) or in *Outsider in the White House* (2015). There are several references in *Our Revolution* (2016), and a whole chapter in *Where We Go from Here* (2018).[20] As in the case of Franklin Roosevelt, the rhetoric of the November 19, 2015, speech at Georgetown University aimed not only to

---

[18] "U.S. President National Vote," November 8, 1932, Our Campaigns, https://www.ourcampaigns.com/RaceDetail.html?RaceID=1949.

[19] "U.S. President National Vote," November 3, 1936, ibid., https://www.ourcampaigns.com/RaceDetail.html?RaceID=1948.

[20] Sanders, "Remembering Dr. King," *Where We Go from Here*, pp. 172–177.

place Sanders in the footsteps but also to literally wrap him in the mantle of Martin Luther King Jr.: "What Roosevelt was stating in 1944, what Martin Luther King Jr. stated in similar terms 20 years later and what I believe today, is that true freedom does not occur without economic security."[21] Democratic socialism, Sanders added, built on what Martin Luther King Jr. had said in 1968: "This country has socialism for the rich, and rugged individualism for the poor."[22] Although it became more open and explicit when Sanders started running for president, his admiration for Martin Luther King Jr. seemed coherent and sincere. In *My Song: A Memoir of Art, Race, and Defiance*, Harry Belafonte, an early supporter of the civil rights movement and a confidant of Martin Luther King Jr., described King as "a socialist and a revolutionary thinker" who "spoke not just in anger, but in anguish," and recalled and exchange with him about the 1968 Poor People's Campaign he was organizing during the last months of his life:

> "The trouble," Martin went on, "is that we live in a failed system. Capitalism does not permit an even flow of economic resources. With this system, a small privileged few are rich beyond conscience and almost all others are doomed to be poor at some level." Taking a sip from his glass, he continued, "That's the way the system works. And since we know that the system will not change the rules, we're going to have to change the system."[23]

Sanders described Dr. King's Poor People's Campaign as "an effort to bring low-income blacks, whites, Latinos, and Native Americans together to change our national priorities and to create a society where all people

[21] Id., "Democratic Socialism in the U.S.A.," *Bernie Speaks*, p. 81.

[22] Ibid., p. 82. Martin Luther King's argument described cynically inverted ideological prisms. The implicit reference was to Herbert Hoover October 22, 1928 address in which he expressed his belief that the American system was based on "rugged individualism" and "self-reliance," phrases that were associated with the policies of the Republican Party and were meant to laud economically successful people and to discredit socialism: "We were challenged with a choice between the American system of rugged individualism and a European philosophy of diametrically opposed doctrines—doctrines of paternalism and state socialism." See Herbert Hoover, "Rugged Individualism," Campaign Speech, October 22, 1928, Digital History, http://www.digitalhistory.uh.edu/disp_textbook_p rint.cfm?smtid=3&psid=1334.

[23] Harry Belafonte, Michael Shnayerson, *My Song: A Memoir of Art, Race, and Defiance*, New York, Vintage, 2012, p. 328.

could live with dignity and security."[24] And again, Sanders projected King's activism into the realm of political praxis, into a project that, maybe, he himself would be able to make real for the twenty-first-century United States:

> It is my strong view that Dr. King's vision and organizing tactics should continue to guide those of us who want to transform our economic and political systems. Dr. King understood that the only time we bring about real change in this country is when we mobilize people at the grassroots level.[25]

Martin Luther King Jr., after all, Sanders also wrote, was "a nonviolent revolutionary who wanted to see our nation undergo 'a radical revolution of values,' against not just the evils of Jim Crow and segregation but also the triple evils of poverty, racism, and militarism."[26] Dr. King's figure, therefore, was brandished by Bernie Sanders as the symbol of a nonviolent, almost mainstream revolution. Sanders's implication was that America had drifted away from its own mainstream, and that the peaceful revolution he was advocating would restore America's own fundamental set of values. Hence, for example, the tension between Barack Obama and Bernie Sanders over what it means to "tear down the system."[27] As if he was speaking about himself, Sanders argued that King's "bold leadership also made mainstream America uncomfortable," and that "[a] 1966 Gallup poll found that almost two-thirds of Americans had an unfavorable opinion of Dr. King."[28] The seamy side of Sanders's political communication strategy was there for all to see, especially in that linking up with Martin Luther King Jr.'s legacy was certainly a most valuable argument to try and draw African Americans into a "democratic socialist" coalition. The ideological filiation, however, was legitimate although it came to fruition only after the 2008-2009 Great Recession. Sanders, who never met Martin Luther King in person but indicated many times that he was present at the 1963 March on Washington, reminded his readers in *Where We Go from Here* that "the Great March on Washington that

---

[24] Sanders, "Remembering Dr. King," *Where We Go from Here*, p. 175.

[25] Ibid.

[26] Ibid., p. 174.

[27] Medina, Lerer, *op. cit.*, p. 8.

[28] Sanders, "Remembering Dr. King," *Where We Go from Here*, p. 174.

Dr. King led in 1963 was called the March for Jobs and Freedom. For *Jobs* and Freedom."[29] What it meant at bottom was that the fight for civil rights was not only a racial issue; it was an economic, class issue: "As [Martin Luther King] often reminded the country, desegregating a restaurant meant nothing if a black worker didn't have the money to pay for the meal being served."[30] And the figure of Martin Luther King was instrumental in Sanders's strategy to build on the specific context of the 1960s to legitimize a democratic socialist roadmap to provide relief, recovery and reform for America in the twenty-first century.

LBJ for Better or for Worse

The U.S. Congress recorded that the primary policy area across all of Bernie Sanders's bill proposals was health care,[31] which was consistent with the presence of another figure in Bernie Sanders's political pantheon: "Thirty years [after the New Deal], in the 1960s, President Johnson passed Medicare and Medicaid."[32] Lyndon B. Johnson was certainly a controversial figure for Bernie Sanders who praised Martin Luther King Jr. for speaking out, "in an act of incredible courage,"[33] on the war in Vietnam:

> In 1964, President Lyndon B. Johnson cited an attack on a U.S. ship in the Gulf of Tonkin as a pretext for escalating the U.S. intervention in Vietnam. We now know from declassified recordings that Johnson himself doubted that the USS *Maddox* had come under fire on August 4, 1964, but he still used that alleged attack to push for the Gulf of Tonkin Resolution, which authorized him to escalate U.S. military involvement in Vietnam. Johnson's administration consistently misled both Congress and the American people into that war, just as the Bush administration misled us into the war in Iraq.[34]

---

[29] Ibid., p. 175.

[30] Sanders, *Our Revolution*, p. 20.

[31] Library of Congress, *op. cit.*, p. 103.

[32] Sanders, "Democratic Socialism in the U.S.A.," *Bernie Speaks*, p. 76.

[33] Id., *Where We Go from Here*, p. 174.

[34] Ibid., p. 170.

Such criticism, notably putting the Lyndon B. Johnson and George W. Bush administrations on an equal footing for consistently misleading the U.S. Congress and the American people into war, was extremely scathing on the part of Bernie Sanders. But the ideologically elastic and eruptive context of the 1960s, the social movements that traversed them, were harbingers of progress for a radical like Sanders, even if that meant overlooking a number of contradictions. Sanders highlighted Lyndon B. Johnson's decisive implication to pass Medicaid and Medicare in the 1960s as an example of what democratic socialism was and could be all about: "How many seniors would not have health insurance today if President Lyndon Baines Johnson had opposed a payroll tax increase to fund Medicare in the 1960s?"[35] Interestingly, Sanders made numerous references to Lyndon B. Johnson's "War on Poverty" but not explicitly to the "Great Society" although the two expressions are used interchangeably, most likely to defuse criticisms that the Great Society fueled a conservative backlash and arguably undermined faith in liberalism itself. As an expression, "War on Poverty" was somewhat less ideologically charged and could be endorsed by successive generations of liberal progressives. Sanders's reference, therefore, was usually to Lyndon B. Johnson's January 8, 1964 State of the Union address.[36]

A whole page is devoted to Johnson's War on Poverty address on Senator Bernie Sanders's official website, and the argument runs that "[o]ut of that speech came a series of programs that transformed America and made life better for millions of our fellow citizens,"[37] including "Medicare," "Medicaid," "food stamps," "Head Start,"[38] "community health centers," "the Older Americans Act,"[39] etc. Johnson was committed to completing the unfinished legacy of the New Deal,

[35] Id., *Our Revolution*, p. 239.

[36] Lyndon B. Johnson, "Annual Message to the Congress on the State of the Union," January 8, 1964, The American Presidency Project, https://www.presidency.ucsb.edu/node/242292.

[37] Sanders, "War on Poverty," Bernie Sanders U.S. Senator for Vermont website, https://www.sanders.senate.gov/buzz/war-on-poverty.

[38] A program of the U.S. Department of Health and Human Services to support comprehensive early childhood education, health, nutrition, and parent involvement services to low-income children and families.

[39] *Older Americans Act*, Pub.L. 89–73, July 14, 1965. The law provided comprehensive services for older people.

including measures to alleviate poverty, from the moment his presidency began. So the filiation from Johnson to Sanders was not illegitimate, although it was a distinctively "liberal" one, one that belonged with the Democratic Party: a host of Democratic figures like Barack Obama, Hillary Clinton, and others revisited Johnson's ideas, including a number of proposals, like the guaranteed family income, which Johnson himself eventually discarded. Because they were typically aired in the immediate context of elections, either to attract liberal voters or for political damage control after electoral defeats, such proposals contributed to the demonetization of the Democratic Party's voice. In *What Happened*, her memoir about her experiences as the Democratic Party's nominee and general election presidential candidate in the 2016 election, Hillary Clinton wrote about the universal basic income:

> I was fascinated by this idea, as was my husband, and we spent weeks working with our policy team to see if it could be viable enough to include in my campaign. [...] Unfortunately, we couldn't make the numbers work. To provide a meaningful dividend each year to every citizen, you'd have to raise enormous sums of money, and that would either mean a lot of new taxes or cannibalizing other important programs. We decided it was exciting but not realistic, and left it on the shelf. That was the responsible decision. I wonder now whether we should have thrown caution to the wind and embraced [it] as a long-term goal and figured out the details later.[40]

Barack Obama was asked about the universal basic income, in June 2016, during an interview with three reporters from *Bloomberg Businessweek*. The exchange was reported by the Basic Income Earth Network (BIEN) under the title: "President Obama Discusses Basic Income Without Clearly Endorsing or Opposing It."[41] Obama became more explicit in July 2018, at the Nelson Mandela Annual Lecture in South Africa, two years into the Trump presidency and a few months before the 2018 midterm elections:

---

[40] Hillary Clinton, *What Happened*, New York, Simon & Schuster, 2017, p. 239.

[41] Josh Martin, "United States: President Obama Discusses Basic Income Without Clearly Endorsing or Opposing It," Basic Income Earth Network, June 24, 2016, https://basicincome.org/news/2016/06/united-states-president-obama-discusses-basic-income-without-either-endorsing-or-opposing-it.

It's not just money that a job provides. It provides dignity and structure and a sense of place and a sense of purpose. So we're going to have to consider new ways of thinking about these problems, like a universal income, review of our workweek, how we retrain our young people, how we make everybody an entrepreneur at some level. But we're going have to worry about economics if we want to get democracy back on track.[42]

The Great Society failed in its promise to erase poverty, but Johnson's War on Poverty considerably reduced it. Joshua Zeitz suggested in *Building the Great Society: Inside Lyndon Johnson's White House* that "LBJ's domestic policy was born of prevailing liberal conviction that experts could grow the economy in perpetuity while sustaining low unemployment and inflation,"[43] and that this belief was no longer tenable after 1973. Then came a decade of runaway inflation due in part to the war in Vietnam as well as to a series of supply shocks in the food and energy sectors. Inflation was accompanied by rising unemployment. "Stagflation," Zeitz concluded, "the combination of high unemployment and inflation [...] was the very antithesis of liberal economics, and it undercut the entire premise of opportunity theory."[44] The liberal premise and its promise had failed the American people. To quote from the lexicon of New Deal liberalism in Sanders's 2015 speech at Georgetown University, poor people needed "decent jobs" and "decent pay,"[45] not assistance to help them capture a prosperity that no longer existed.

6.3   THE LEXICON OF THE 1960S

In terms of a class conception of society, the context, the prism, and the lexicon of the counterculture of the 1960s and 1970s also pervade Bernie Sanders's political rhetoric. There were two major currents in the counterculture movement: one was a profoundly anti-establishment phenomenon fueled by political radicalism, the other was the bohemian lifestyle known

---

[42] Obama, Speech At The 2018 Nelson Mandela Annual Lecture, July 17, 2018, National Public Radio, https://www.npr.org/2018/07/17/629862434/transcript-obamas-speech-at-the-2018-nelson-mandela-annual-lecture?t=1592563071145.

[43] Joshua Zeitz, *Building the Great Society: Inside Lyndon Johnson's White House*, New York, Viking, 2018, p. 312.

[44] Ibid.

[45] Sanders, "Democratic Socialism in the U.S.A.," *Bernie Speaks*, p. 75.

as hippie culture. Hippie culture bore more than a few resemblances with the lifestyle of many early socialists who established utopian communities in nineteenth-century America[46] (Brook Farm, Fruitlands, New Harmony, Oneida, the Shakers, etc.). There were also two major currents in the hippie movement. One was epitomized by the Haight-Ashbury district in San Francisco, with freedom, legendary music bands, drug use, and war resistance. The other was a back-to-the land movement that was more reminiscent of early socialism and of the communes of the nineteenth century. Vermont was one of the favorite destinations of the latter. Writing for the *Burlington Free Press*, Susan Green described a movement that was dubbed "Free Vermont":

> These nonconformists were inspired by anti-establishment militancy, the vision of a rural paradise where artistic and literary pursuits could flourish or a desire for back-to-the-land endeavors. Or all of the above. Differences proved less important than shared objectives. They were able to agree on goals such as a cooperative system for buying food and a clinic to provide free healthcare.[47]

In the summer of 1970, 300 young people living in collectives throughout Vermont gathered at Earthworks, a commune in the town of Franklin. Barbara Nofi, one of the original members of Earthworks explained: "We wanted to make a better life for everyone, make things accessible without bureaucracy, profits and distortion. We were anti-capitalists."[48] Melinda Moulton, who moved to Vermont in 1972, added: "We were really transforming our society. [...] It was a movement of open-minded, radical thinkers."[49] Jackie Calder, a curator for the Vermont Historical Society, narrowed down the period to the 1968–1980 span: "The election of Ronald Reagan was a significant date that signaled the real end of that period. Many social services and federal programs

---

[46] See Robert P. Sutton, *Communal Utopias and the American Experience: Religious Communities, 1732–2000*, Westport, CT, Praeger, 2003.

[47] Susan Green, "Vermont Remains a Hippie Epicenter," *Burlington Free Press*, July 24, 2015, https://eu.burlingtonfreepress.com/story/news/local/vermont/2015/07/24/vermont-remains-hippie-epicenter/30564907.

[48] Ibid.

[49] Ibid.

dried up."[50] The landmark of Reagan's election was significant in that Bernie Sanders moved permanently from Brooklyn to Vermont during the tumultuous year of 1968 and was elected mayor of Burlington, Vermont, in 1981, less than three months after Reagan's inaugural. In the meantime, Sanders did a series of odd jobs and became active in politics as a member of the Liberty Union Party. Later in the 1970s, he took a steady job with a Liberty Union friend and made filmstrips about important events in American history, selling them to schools. This was when he produced a half-hour film about his hero, Eugene V. Debs.[51]

Bernie Sanders was obviously attracted to the aspirations and lifestyle of Vermont utopians, and it reminded him of something he had experienced in Israel where he had traveled after his graduation from the University of Chicago in 1964. Sanders spent six months working and living on an Israeli kibbutz:

> It was a unique experience and a very different type of culture than I was used to. I enjoyed picking grapefruits, netting fish on the "fish farm," and doing other agricultural work. Mostly, however, it was the structure of the community that impressed me. People there were living their democratic values. The kibbutz was owned by the people who lived there, the "bosses" were elected by the workers, and the overall decisions for the community were made democratically.[52]

That was shortly after Sanders had become politically active, after leaving Brooklyn to attend the University of Chicago, when the civil rights movement hit, after he traveled to D.C. to attend the March for Jobs and Freedom in August 1963. Was Sanders really a former hippie? Was hippiedom the path to express his political convictions and to experiment his aspirations? Certainly in part. But Sanders was already extremely atypical, as he himself explained during an interview with Mark Jacobson in 2014: "My hair was long, but not long for the times. I smoked marijuana, but was never part of the drug culture. That wasn't me."[53]

Contrary to many members of the hippie culture, Bernie Sanders was not a rebel without a cause during the 1960s and 1970s. He was indeed

---

[50] Ibid.

[51] Sanders, *Eugene V. Debs, op. cit.*, p. 3.

[52] Id., *Our Revolution*, pp. 21–22.

[53] Jacobson, *op. cit.*, p. 32.

a rebel with a cause, but a cause he was unable to detonate politically. In 1969, in an article entitled "Reflections on a Dying Society," he painted a socially and politically apocalyptic portrait of the United States, one that resembled the writings of the muckrakers at the turn of the twentieth century:

> The food that the population eats is generally unnutricious if not positively dangerous. [...] Ecologically, the people of the United States and the planet Earth are wreaking havoc on their home terrain. [...] The threat of nuclear annihilation or death by poison gas hovers close to every heart. [...] The circle is a vicious one. Society breeds misery, and the sons and daughters of misery give forth the new society.[54]

A few months later, Sanders wrote "Revolution is Life versus Death," and the diagnosis, once again, was appalling: "The years come and go, suicide, nervous breakdown, cancer, sexual deadness, heart attack, alcoholism, senility at 50. Slow, death, fast Death. DEATH."[55] But the utopia of a revolutionary cure offered an alternative course:

> The Revolution is coming and it is a very beautiful revolution. It is beautiful because, in its deepest sense, it is quiet, gentle, and all pervasive. IT KNOWS. [...] The revolution comes when two strangers smile at each other, when a father refuses to send his child to school because schools destroy children, when a commune is started and people begin to trust each other, when a young man refuses to go to war, and when a girl pushes aside all that her mother has "taught" her and accepts her boyfriend's love.[56]

As of 1969, Sanders's utopian revolution was not radically subversive. He was a socialist, but not enough of a socialist; he was a radical, but never radically outside of the mainstream of American politics.[57] The only

---

[54] Sanders, "Reflections on a Dying Society," *Vermont Freeman*, August 1–3, 1969, p. 8. Available via the Vermont State Library, https://www.documentcloud.org/docume nts/2157596-sanders-reflection.html.

[55] Id., "The Revolution Is Life Versus Death," *Vermont Freeman*, November 14–17, 1969, p. 9. Available via the Vermont State Library, https://www.documentcloud.org/documents/2157415-sanders-revolution.html.

[56] Ibid., p. 9.

[57] Jacobson, *op. cit.*, p. 32.

way to channel his own activism with reasonable hopes for a measure of agency was through the liberal matrix. Part of Sanders's more personal motivation had always been to affirm that he was a different kind of politician, and this is also, arguably, what his socialism was all about. He spent his whole political career trying to differentiate himself from what he regarded as conventional establishment politicians. But Bernie Sanders's radicalism lacked agency. American society was highly explosive, but there was no social detonator likely to trigger any form of substantial, let alone socialist, reform.

REFERENCES

Altman, Jake. *Socialism before Sanders: The 1930s Movement from Romance to Revisionism*. Cham, Switzerland: Palgrave Macmillan, 2019.

Belafonte, Harry, Michael Shnayerson. *My Song: A Memoir of Art, Race, and Defiance*. New York: Vintage, 2012.

Clinton, Hillary. *What Happened*. New York: Simon & Schuster, 2017.

Green, Susan. "Vermont Remains a Hippie Epicenter." *Burlington Free Press* (July 24, 2015), https://eu.burlingtonfreepress.com/story/news/local/vermont/2015/07/24/vermont-remains-hippie-epicenter/30564907.

Hines, Nico. "Bernie Sanders's Brother: He Backs 'Class Warfare,' Bill Clinton Was Worse Than Bush." The Daily Beast, February 19, 2016, https://www.thedailybeast.com/bernie-sanderss-brother-he-backs-class-warfare-bill-clinton-was-worse-than-bush.

Hoover, Herbert. "Rugged Individualism." Campaign Speech (October 22, 1928). Digital History, http://www.digitalhistory.uh.edu/disp_textbook_print.cfm?smtid=3&psid=1334.

Jacobson, Mark. "Bernie Sanders for President? Why Not Try a Real Socialist for a Change?" *New York* (December 28, 2014), http://nymag.com/intelligencer/2014/12/bernie-sanders-for-president-why-not.html.

Johnson, Lyndon B. "Annual Message to the Congress on the State of the Union" (January 8, 1964). The American Presidency Project, https://www.presidency.ucsb.edu/node/242292.

Maney, Patrick J. *The Roosevelt Presence: The Life and Legacy of FDR*. Berkeley: University of California Press, 1998.

Martin, Josh. "United States: President Obama Discusses Basic Income Without Clearly Endorsing or Opposing It." Basic Income Earth Network (June 24, 2016), https://basicincome.org/news/2016/06/united-states-president-obama-discusses-basic-income-without-either-endorsing-or-opposing-it.

Medina, Jennifer, Lisa Lerer. "Too Far Left? Some Democratic Candidates Don't Buy Obama's Argument." *New York Times* (November 22, 2019), https://www.nytimes.com/2019/11/16/us/obama-left-democrats-2020.html.

Obama, Barack H. Speech at the 2018 Nelson Mandela Annual Lecture (July 17, 2018), National Public Radio, https://www.npr.org/2018/07/17/629862434/transcript-obamas-speech-at-the-2018-nelson-mandela-annual-lecture?t=1592563071145.

Sanders, Bernard. "Reflections on a Dying Society," *Vermont Freeman* (August 1–3, 1969) p. 8. Available via the Vermont State Library, https://www.documentcloud.org/documents/2157596-sanders-reflection.html.

———. "The Revolution is Life versus Death," *Vermont Freeman* (November 14–17, 1969), p. 9. Available via the Vermont State Library, https://www.documentcloud.org/documents/2157415-sanders-revolution.html.

———. *Eugene V. Debs: Trade Unionist, Socialist, Revolutionary, 1855–1926.* New York: Folkways Records, 1979.

———, with Huck Gutman. *Outsider in the House: A Political Autobiography.* New York: Verso, 1997. Rpt. *Outsider in the White House,* 2015.

———. *Our Revolution: A Future to Believe In.* New York: Thomas Dunne Books, 2016.

———. *Bernie Speaks: Speeches by Bernie Sanders,* compiled by David Cane. CreateSpace Independent Publishing Platform: Greenbridge Publishing, 2017.

———. *Where We Go from Here: Two Years in the Resistance.* New York: Thomas Dunne Books, 2018.

Steffens, Lincoln J. *The Letters of Lincoln Steffens,* vol. 1, edited by Ella Winter and Granville Hicks. New York: Harcourt, Brace & Co., 1938.

Sutton, Robert P. *Communal Utopias and the American Experience: Religious Communities, 1732–2000.* Westport, Conn.: Praeger, 2003.

Thomas, Norman. *The New Deal: A Socialist Analysis.* Chicago, IL: Socialist Party of America, Committee on Education and Research, 1934, https://digital.library.pitt.edu/islandora/object/pitt%3A31735061544668.

Zeitz, Joshua. *Building the Great Society: Inside Lyndon Johnson's White House.* New York: Viking, 2018.

PART III

99 Percent

CHAPTER 7

Hegemony

In January 2020, during an interview with Lacey Rose for the *Hollywood Reporter*, Hillary Clinton lashed out at Bernie Sanders, now a candidate for the 2020 presidential election: "Nobody likes him, nobody wants to work with him, he got nothing done. He was a career politician. It's all just baloney and I feel so bad that people got sucked into it."[1] However, Clinton also indicated in *What Happened*, that "Bernie Sanders and [herself] wrote the 2016 platform together," that they "share[d] many of the same values," and that "most of [their] differences over policy [were] relatively minor."[2] One is indeed bound to wonder "what happened." Part of the answer is to be found in other sections of Clinton's memoir, when she explains that "[s]ome on the left, including Bernie Sanders, argue that working-class whites have turned away from Democrats because the party became beholden to Wall Street donors and lost touch with its populist roots."[3] Here again, one is bound to wonder: "on the left" of what? On the left the American political mainstream? Or on the left of the Democratic Party? And Clinton added: "After all, by

---

[1] Hillary Clinton, quoted in Lacey Rose, "Hillary Clinton in Full: A Fiery New Documentary, Trump Regrets and Harsh Words for Bernie: 'Nobody Likes Him,'" Hollywood Reporter, January 21, 2020, https://www.hollywoodreporter.com/features/hillary-clinton-full-a-fiery-new-documentary-trump-regrets-harsh-words-bernie-1271551.

[2] Hillary Clinton, *What Happened*, p. 422.

[3] Ibid., p. 276.

© The Author(s), under exclusive license to Springer Nature Switzerland AG 2021
N. Gachon, *Bernie Sanders's Democratic Socialism*,
https://doi.org/10.1007/978-3-030-69661-0_7

nearly every measure, the Democratic Party has moved to the left over the past fifteen years, not to the right."[4] That Hillary Clinton referred to the "populist roots" of the Democratic Party, rather than to the grassroots for example, is significant in that it implicitly tended to ideologize and marginalize what she indistinctly referred to as "the left." Her argument that the Democratic Party moved to the left over the previous fifteen years, "not the right," referred to the Obama presidency but Clinton also wrote that: "President Obama had raised more money from Wall Street than anyone in history, and that didn't stop him from imposing tough new rules to curb risk and prevent future financial crashes."[5] And elsewhere in *What Happened*, Clinton argued against moving left: "Some supporters of Bernie Sanders have argued that if I had veered further left and run a more populist campaign we would have done better in the Rust Belt. I don't believe it."[6] The ideological compass of the Democratic Party was obviously disoriented as of 2016, for a number of reasons. First among these was the intense polarization of American politics, a phenomenon extensively analyzed since the end of the twentieth century,[7] with the corollary caveat that political parties, in such a highly polarized environment, did indeed need to be perceived as radically different from one another. But Clinton's argument—and even the Obama presidency at large—arguably told a sensibly different story. Another factor lay in the fact that Sanders's candidacy constituted a disorienting factor for having introduced an additional pole in an already polarized political environment. With the recent emergence of a number of movements—the Tea Party, Black Lives Matter, Occupy Wall Street—that also concurred to destabilize the two-party system, at stake was whether the whole political map was still relevant in twenty-first-century America, whether the traditional political parties had not become empty voices of a bygone era, institutional channels to political power rather than forums of intellectual ferment. Updating the political map entailed questioning the norms

[4] Ibid.

[5] Hillary Clinton, *What Happened*, p. 97.

[6] Ibid, p. 411.

[7] See, for example: Daniel J. Hopkins, John Sides, eds. *Political Polarization in American Politics*, New York, Bloomsbury, 2015; Thomas Carothers, Andrew O'Donohue, eds., *Democracies Divided: The Global Challenge of Political Polarization*, Washington, DC, Brookings, 2019.

Americans consensually lived by and challenging the cultural hegemony of neoliberal economics.

7.1 Gramscian Hegemony

In the introduction to the documentary he devoted to Eugene Debs in 1979, Bernie Sanders argued with almost Gramscian overtones that the capitalist hegemony of material culture in the United States blocked access to ideas outside of the political mainstream, in particular to ideas diverging from the interests of the dominant group:

> It is very probable, especially if you are a young person, that you have never heard of Eugene Victor Debs. If you are the average American who watches television 40 h a week you have probably heard of such important people as Kojack and Wonder Woman, have heard about dozens of different kinds of underarm spray deodorants, every hack politician in your state, and the latest game between the Boston Red Sox and the New York Yankees. Strangely enough, however, nobody has told you much about Gene Debs—one of the most important Americans of the 20th century. Why? Why haven't they told you about Gene Debs and the ideas he fought for? The answer is simple. More than a half century after his death the handful of people who own and control this country—including the mass media and the educational system—still regard Debs and his ideas as dangerous—as a threat to their stability and class rule—and as someone best forgotten about.[8]

Antonio Gramsci's reflections on the structural force of capitalism led him to develop a class-based approach of the concept of hegemony. Gramsci was the General Secretary of the Italian Communist Party when Mussolini's government dissolved the Italian Parliament and all opposition organizations in November 1926. He was arrested on November 9, 1926, at age thirty-five, and sentenced to twenty years in prison in June 1928. It was during his confinement, between 1929 and 1935, that Gramsci wrote some 3000 pages of history and political analysis in his *Prison Notebooks*, thirty notebooks that contain a major contribution to

---

[8] Sanders, *Eugene V. Debs*, band 1, "Introduction."

Marxist thought and to twentieth-century political theory, including his theory of hegemony.[9]

For Gramsci, the supremacy of the dominant class in society was not a simple question of domination; it was not a simple question of coercion either. The supremacy of the dominant class was also, and primarily so, a question of intellectual and moral supremacy, the two core components of the concept of hegemony. The equation, therefore, was more complex. From there, Gramsci wrote, "one might say that State = political society + civil society, in other words hegemony protected by the armour of coercion."[10] On the basis of its cultural hegemony, therefore, the dominant class found itself in a position from which it could breed subjects who would accept and support the ideology of the system that exploited and oppressed them, a position from which it could also co-opt opposition movements and blend them into the mainstream of the dominant thought:

> The formation of this class involved the gradual but continuous absorption, achieved by methods which varied in their effectiveness, of the active elements produced by allied groups-and even of those which came from antagonistic groups and seemed irreconcilably hostile. In this sense political leadership became merely an aspect of the function of domination- in as much as the absorption of the enemies' *élites* means their decapitation, and annihilation often for a very long time.[11]

Co-opting revolutionary impulses into the dominant mainstream turned potentially active revolutions into what Gramsci described as "passive" revolutions: "The thesis alone in fact develops to the full its potential for struggle, up to the point where it absorbs even the so-called representatives of the antithesis: it is precisely in this that the passive revolution or revolution/restoration consists."[12] State or class domination might indeed ultimately end up in a dictatorship, but there was another form of domination: hegemonic domination. Hegemonic domination is obtained

---

[9] Joseph V. Femia, *Gramsci's Political Thought: Hegemony, Consciousness, and the Revolutionary Process*, Oxford, Clarendon Press, 1981, p. 12.

[10] Gramsci, p. 263.

[11] Ibid., pp. 58–59.

[12] Ibid., p. 110.

by the consent of the dominated through the diffusion and populariza-
tion of the worldviews of the ruling class. Gramsci regarded hegemony
and dictatorship as mutually dependent phenomena, the length of dictatorship depending on the ability of the dictatorship to promote general
acceptance of the economic structure and worldviews of the ruling class,
and on the consensual aspect of political control.

Marxist thought holds that society functions through structures: the
base (the infrastructure) and the superstructure.[13] While the "infrastructure" is made up of the forces, means, and relations of production,
the "superstructure" includes the culture, ideology, norms, and identities that people endorse. Marx claimed that the superstructure grows
out of the infrastructure as a reflection of the interests of the dominant
class. Gramsci's contribution to Marxist thought lay in its focus on the
superstructure:

> What we can do, for the moment, is to fix two major superstructural
> "levels": the one that can be called "civil society", that is the ensemble of
> organisms commonly called "private" and that of "political society" or "the
> State." These two levels correspond on the one hand to the function of
> "hegemony" which the dominant group exercises throughout society and
> on the other hand to that of "direct domination" or command exercised
> through the State and "juridical" government. The functions in ques-
> tion are precisely organizational and connective. The intellectuals are the
> dominant group's "deputies" exercising the subaltern functions of social
> hegemony and political government.[14]

Joseph V. Femia explained in *Gramsci's Political Thought: Hegemony,
Consciousness, and the Revolutionary Process* (1981) that Antonio Gramsci
was aware of the tendency toward increased state intervention in civil
society, notably in the realm of culture and education.[15] He understood
perfectly, Femia wrote, the manipulative potential of the media (the radio
and the press), whether or not the said media had direct ties with the
government:

---

[13] Michael Heinrich, *An Introduction to the Three Volumes of Karl Marx's Capital*, New
York, Monthly Review Press, 2004, p. 200.

[14] Ibid., p. 12.

[15] Femia, p. 28.

The crucial point, to [Gramsci's] mind, was that governments can often mobilize the support of the mass media and other ideological instruments, partly because the various elites, political or otherwise, share similar world-views and life-styles, and partly because the institutions of civil society, whether or not they are directly controlled by the state, must operate within a legal framework of rules and regulations.[16]

In his 1979 explanation of the reasons why young Americans had no access to the political ideas of Eugene Debs, Bernie Sanders made a similar point: "the handful of people who own and control this country— including the mass media and the educational system—still regard Debs and his ideas as dangerous—as a threat to their stability and class rule— and as someone best forgotten about."[17] The same argument was further developed in *Outsider in the White House*:

The paramount issue is the movement of this country toward what I call an oligarchic form of society—where you have a small number of people owning and controlling not only our economy, not only our media (the means by which people get their information) but increasingly, and especially as a result of Citizens United, our political process.[18]

Intellectuals, in the Gramscian sense of the term, are not only thinkers. They may also be political leaders, civil servants, clerics, etc. Their significance does not lie in their specific occupation but in the role they fulfill in society. Gramsci distinguished between two types of intellectuals: "organic" intellectuals and "traditional" intellectuals. Organic intellectuals, "those [...] who come into existence on the same industrial terrain as the economic group,"[19] were directly tied to the class they represented, giving it "homogeneity and an awareness of its own function not only in the economic but also in the social and political fields."[20] Gramsci takes the example of "[t]he capitalist entrepreneur [who] creates alongside himself the industrial technician, the specialist in political economy,

---

[16] Ibid, pp. 27–28.

[17] Sanders, *Eugene V. Debs*, band 1, "Introduction."

[18] Id., *Outsider in the White House*, p. 334.

[19] Gramsci, p. 18.

[20] Ibid., p. 5.

the organizers of a new culture, of a new legal system, etc."[21] Traditional intellectuals, on the other hand, regroup pre-existing categories of intellectuals, for example vestiges of organic intellectuals from previous social groups, and that seem to represent "historical continuity uninterrupted even by the most complicated and radical changes in political and social forms."[22] Gramsci mentions "the ecclesiastics" and adds that "traditional intellectuals experience through an *'esprit de corps'* their uninterrupted historical continuity and their special qualification, they thus put themselves forward as autonomous and independent of the dominant social group."[23] In contemporary society, the equivalent of Gramsci's traditional intellectuals would be lawyers, journalists, doctors, professors, businessmen, etc. Traditional intellectuals tend to believe that they are independent of the dominant social group in society, but Gramsci describes this belief as a "social utopia by which the intellectuals think of themselves as 'independent,' autonomous, endowed with a character of their own, etc."[24] While they may not always share the views of the dominant class, they eventually compromise with those views, because of institutional pressures or financial inducements, and end up propagating ideas and ways of thinking that are essentially conservative.[25] From that angle, in the Gramscian sense of the term, Bernie Sanders can be regarded as an "organic" intellectual, an intellectual seeking to give his class "an awareness of its own function not only in the economic but also in the

---

[21] Ibid.

[22] Ibid., p. 7.

[23] Ibid.

[24] Ibid., p. 8.

[25] For a comparative approach to Bourdieu's theory of symbolic domination and Gramsci's theory of hegemony, see Michael Burawoy: "Gramsci and Bourdieu may appear convergent at one level, but at a deeper level they are mirror opposites: Bourdieu attacks Gramsci's organic intellectual as mythical, while Gramsci attacks Bourdieu's traditional intellectual as self-deluding. At bottom, the divergence rests on claims about the (in)ability of the dominated to understand the world and the (in)ability of intellectuals to transcend their corporate class interests. To these two questions, Gramsci and Bourdieu have opposite answers: Gramsci claims the dominated can have a partial insight into their worlds and organic intellectuals exist to elaborate that insight; Bourdieu, by contrast, claims the dominated cannot comprehend their subjugation, while intellectuals, so long as they are autonomous from classes, can see and represent the truth through the fog of cultural domination." Michael Burawoy "Cultural Domination: Gramsci Meets Bourdieu," *Symbolic Violence: Conversations with Bourdieu*, Durham, NC, Duke University Press, 2019, pp. 74–75.

social and political fields."[26] At stake behind Bernie Sanders's democratic socialism was the cultural hegemony at work in the United States.

7.2   Americanism

From a strictly Marxist perspective, capitalism was the dictatorship of the bourgeoisie, a dictatorship maintained by coercion and violence in class warfare. The conflict between oppressors and oppressed, as Lenin observed,[27] was therefore endemic to capitalism. Gramsci, however, claimed that class warfare did not simply develop, and arguably not primarily, within this generic framework. The ultimate end of capitalism, Gramsci argued, was to secure capitalist domination but also to conceal class antagonisms and, ideally, to wrap them in the garb of consensus. Besides, for Gramsci, the situation in the United States was not quite similar to the situation in Europe, the reason being that the superstructure was historically much more important in Europe than it was in the United States: "Structures and superstructures form an 'historical bloc.' That is to say the complex, contradictory and discordant *ensemble* of the superstructures is the reflection of the ensemble of the social relations of production."[28] Europe, in other words, had more "traditional intellectuals" than the United States:

> European "tradition," European "civilization," is, conversely, characterised precisely by the existence of such classes, created by the "richness" and "complexity" of past history. This past history has left behind a heap of passive sedimentations produced by the phenomenon of the saturation and fossilization of civil-service personnel and intellectuals, of clergy and landowners, piratical commerce and the professional (and later conscript, but for the officers always professional) army.[29]

---

[26] Gramsci, p. 18. See also Jan Rehmann, "Bernie Sanders and the Hegemonic Crisis of Neoliberal Capitalism: What Next?" *Socialism and Democracy*, vol. 30, n° 3, 2016, pp. 1–11, https://doi.org/10.1080/08854300.2016.1228874

[27] Femia, p. 34.

[28] Gramsci, p. 366.

[29] Ibid., p. 281.

Gramsci regarded this condition as what made it possible, in the United States, to apply Frederick W. Taylor's "principles of scientific management"[30] to a new but not so new model of society:

Taylor is in fact expressing with brutal cynicism the purpose of American society—developing in the worker to the highest degree automatic and mechanical attitudes, breaking up the old psycho-physical nexus of qualified professional work, which demands a certain active participation of intelligence, fantasy and initiative on the part of the worker, and reducing productive operations exclusively to the mechanical, physical aspect. But these things, in reality, are not original or novel: they represent simply the most recent phase of a long process which began with industrialism itself.[31]

The Taylorist project was thus realized in the United States by suppressing the critical faculties of workers. Gramsci notably mentioned the image of the "trained gorilla," a cynical metaphor by which Taylor argued that "it would be possible to train an intelligent gorilla so as to become a more efficient pig-iron handler than any man could be."[32] The ultimate division and individualization of labor also undermined any inclination toward collective organization.

"Hegemony" in the United States, Gramsci wrote, "is born in the factory and requires for its exercise only a minute quantity of professional political and ideological intermediaries."[33] However, the intellectual capacities of man were not totally wiped out:

[T]he process of adaptation has been completed, what really happens is that the brain of the worker, far from being mummified, reaches a state of complete freedom. The only thing that is completely mechanicised is the physical gesture [...]. American industrialists have understood all too well this dialectic inherent in the new industrial methods. They have understood that "trained gorilla" is just a phrase, that "unfortunately" the worker remains a man and even that during his work he thinks more, or at least has greater opportunities for thinking, once he has overcome the crisis of

[30] Frederick W. Taylor, *The Principles of Scientific Management*, New York, Harper & Brothers, 1911.

[31] Gramsci., p. 382.

[32] Ibid.

[33] Ibid., p. 285.

adaptation without being eliminated: and not only does the worker think, but the fact that he gets no immediate satisfaction from his work and realizes that they are trying to reduce him to a trained gorilla, can lead him into a train of thought that is far from conformist.[34]

Gramsci understood Fordism as a consent-making device that utilized wages, because coercion had to be "ingenuously combined with persuasion and consent," an effect that could be achieved "by higher remuneration such as to permit a particular living standard which can maintain and restore the strength that has been wore down by the new form of toil."[35] High wages, in other words, could be distributed to buy off and silence workers. That process of "rationalization" was still in its initial phase, as Gramsci himself remarked in his *Notebooks*, and was "still idyllic," "still at the stage of psycho-physical adaptation to the new industrial structure, aimed for through high wages." And he observed that "[u]p to the present (until the 1929 crash) there ha[d] not been, except perhaps sporadically, any flowering of the 'superstructure.' In other words, the fundamental question of hegemony has not yet been posed."[36] The hegemony of the superstructure would be built somewhat later as a cultural rather than economic phenomenon, in the wake of the New Deal and on the ashes of World War II, with the emergence of the so-called consumer society, a modern avatar of what Gramsci described as "the so-called 'high wages' paid by Fordised and rationalised industry."[37] Consumption was more effective in occupying the thinking minds of workers. It succeeded where mechanization in the form of Taylorism and Fordism had fallen short by the early 1930s.

Hence, therefore, Bernie Sanders's argument that "the average American who watches television 40 h a week" heard of "such important people as Kojack and Wonder Woman," about "dozens of different kinds of underarm spray deodorants," etc., but was certainly not exposed to the political thought of such personalities as Eugene V. Debs.[38] In *Outsider in the House*, Sanders explicitly extended the consumption metaphor to

[34] Ibid., pp. 309–310.
[35] Ibid., p. 310.
[36] Ibid., p. 286.
[37] Ibid., p. 180.
[38] Sanders, *Eugene V. Debs*, band 1, "Introduction."

denounce a mechanism of "public consumption" orchestrated to promote political adhesion by the public—against the public's own interests:

> Given that their real ideology—not the sham philosophy of "states' rights" or "personal responsibility" created for public consumption—reflects the interests of a tiny and very privileged segment of the population, Republicans are faced with the same dilemmas that vexed the ruling elites of the South: How to convince working people and the middle class to vote against their own best interests. [...] Further, how to deflect attention away from the issues that affect the vast majority of people and around which they could unite.[39]

Gramsci's major contribution to Marxist thought lay in his focus on the superstructure while Marx was more focused on the infrastructure, or base. By inverting the Marxian model, Gramsci also accorded primacy to culture rather than to economic determinism. He envisioned the diminution of revolutionary possibilities under cultural hegemony, an aspect of his political thought that was largely embraced by the Frankfurt School of social research in the 1930s, when Max Horkheimer[40] became Head of the *Institut für Sozialforschung* and was surrounded by such intellectuals as Theodor W. Adorno,[41] Erich Fromm,[42] and Herbert Marcuse.[43,44] Fromm, in particular, was one of the writers Sanders had read when he

---

[39] Sanders, *Outsider in the House*, pp. 128–129.

[40] Max Horkheimer notably published *Eclipse of Reason*, Oxford, Oxford University Press, 1947, in which he discusses how the Nazis were able to project their agenda as "reasonable," and, together with Theodor W. Adorno, *Dialectic of Enlightenment* (1947, rpt., New York, Verso, 2016).

[41] Theodor W. Adorno was the leading figure of the Frankfurt School of critical theory. See, notably: Theodor W. Adorno *Negative Dialectics*, trans. E. B. Ashton, London, Routledge & Kegan Paul, 1973.

[42] See *supra*, p. 20.

[43] Herbert Marcuse notably published *Soviet Marxism: A Critical Analysis*, New York, Columbia University Press, 1958 to criticize the ideology of the Communist Party of the Soviet Union. He worked for the Office of Strategic Services (OSS), the U.S. wartime intelligence agency and the forerunner of the CIA. He also authored *One-Dimensional Man: Studies in the Ideology of Advanced Industrial Society*, New York, Beacon Press, 1964.

[44] See: Peter E. Gordon, Espen Hammer, Alex Honneth, eds., *The Routledge Companion to the Frankfurt School*, New York, Routledge, 2019.

was a student in the 1960s.[45] Both Gramsci and the Frankfurt School were interested in how mass-produced culture could end up limiting the potential for human agency. In other words, how could people escape normative discourses if representations, texts, literature, film, music, etc. all reflected the dominant ideology? Gramsci's distinctive contributions lay in the realm of political-cultural ideology to explore the neo-Marxist dilemma. At stake, to quote from Walter Lippmann, who started his career as an assistant to muckraking journalist Lincoln Steffens, was the issue of the "manufacture" of consent in the United States, which he described in 1922 in *Public Opinion*: "That the manufacture of consent is capable of great refinements no one, I think, denies. [...] The creation of consent is not a new art. It is a very old one which was supposed to have died out with the appearance of democracy. But it has not died out."[46] Beyond, as Bernie Sanders put it in *Our Revolution*:

> Media shapes our very lives. It tells us what products we need to buy and, by the quantity and nature of coverage, what is "important" and what is "unimportant." Media shapes our political consciousness, and informs us as to the scope of what is "realistic" and "possible." [...] Media is not just about what is covered and how it is covered. More importantly, it is about what is not covered. And those decisions, of what is and is not covered, are not made in the heavens. They are made by human beings who often have major conflicts of interest.[47]

7.3   CONSENT AND CONSENSUS

Gramsci explained that hegemony is "protected by the armour of coercion,"[48] that capitalism rests on a "passive revolution"[49] by which subjects are led to believe that no alternative course is possible and to

---

[45] See *supra*, p. 17.

[46] Water Lippmann, *Public Opinion*, New York, Macmillan, 1922. Rpt. New Brunswick, NJ, Transaction Publishers, 1988, p. 248. The expression "manufacturing consent" was later used in 1988 by Edward S. Herman and Noam Chomsky in the title of their book, *Manufacturing Consent: The Political Economy of the Mass Media*, New York, Pantheon Books, 1988.

[47] Sanders, *Our Revolution*, pp. 420–421.

[48] Gramsci, p. 263.

[49] Ibid., p. 110.

eventually accept and embrace the system that oppresses them. The intellectuals of the "superstructure" play a decisive instrumental role as "the dominant group's 'deputies' exercising the subaltern functions of social hegemony and political government."[50] Consent is manufactured along two principal lines:

> The "spontaneous" consent given by the great masses of the population to the general direction imposed on social life by the dominant fundamental group; this consent is "historically" caused by the prestige (and consequent confidence) which the dominant group enjoys because of its position and function in the world of production.
>
> The apparatus of state coercive power which "legally" enforces discipline on those groups who do not "consent" either actively or passively. This apparatus is, however, constituted for the whole of society in anticipation of moments of crisis of command and direction when spontaneous consent has failed.[51]

Manufacturing consent is akin to manufacturing consensus; it is not only a temporary agreement around a divisive issue but rather what Gramsci referred to as "common sense," the largely unconscious way and therefore uncritical way of perceiving and understanding the world that has become "common" in any given period of history. Kate Crehan points out that Gramscian "common sense" is the sum of "heterogeneous beliefs people arrive at not through critical reflection, but encounter as already existing, self-evident truths," and added that "the Italian *senso comune* is a far more neutral term than the English *common sense*."[52] Gramsci distinguished "good sense" from "common sense" and described "good sense" as "more unitary and coherent," as "the healthy nucleus that exists in 'common sense.'"[53] "Good sense," in other words, was meant in the English sense of the term as practical empirical common sense. This question has far-reaching implications in the perimeter of Bernie Sanders's social diagnosis and proposed cure in the form of democratic socialism. As previously mentioned, the fuel of social suffering and discontent was

[50] Ibid., p. 12.

[51] Ibid.

[52] Kate Crehan, *Gramsci's Common Sense: Inequality and Its Narratives*, Durham, NC, Duke University Press, 2016, p. x.

[53] Gramsci, p. 328.

certainly everywhere in American society, but there was no detonator to start off a radical movement. From what would be a Gramscian perspective of mainstream politics, the mechanism to translate the social crisis into popular "common sense" was either non-existent or had been stifled by a cultural hegemony.

As someone born in 1941,[54] during the Roosevelt administration, Bernie Sanders grew up and came of age during the so-called liberal consensus, when the "liberal" ideology was intellectually dominant in the United States. In December 1949, in *The Liberal Imagination*, Lionel Trilling described what, by all standards, could be regarded as a form of hegemony:

> In the United States at this time liberalism is not only the dominant but even the sole intellectual tradition. For it is the plain fact that nowadays there are no conservative or reactionary ideas in general circulation. This does not mean, of course, that there is no impulse to conservatism or to reaction. Such impulses are certainly very strong, perhaps even stronger than most of us know. But the conservative impulse and the reactionary impulse do not, with some isolated and some ecclesiastical exceptions, express themselves in ideas but only in action or in irritable mental gestures which seek to resemble ideas.[55]

In the wake of the New Deal and of World War II, the liberal "consensus" seemed there to stay. Patrick Garry defined liberalism as a "broad, inclusive concept," or, in the words of Arthur Schlesinger Jr., "an expression of the total national experience."[56] While "classical" (or "economic") liberalism is based on competitive individualism, laissez-faire, the right to private property, limited government, and a free market, an ideology that took hold in the eighteenth century and that can be regarded as the dominant doctrine in the United States, the liberal consensus was around "modern liberalism," a pragmatic, progressive, but never radical, form of social liberalism whose belief in the individual required a belief in social justice and in a mixed economy. Modern liberalism started with

---

[54] See *supra*, p. 32.

[55] Lionel Trilling, *The Liberal Imagination*, New York, Harcourt, Brace, Jovanovich, 1950, p. vii.

[56] Patrick M. Garry, *Liberalism and American Identity*, Kent, OH, Kent State University Press, 1992, p. 37.

the New Deal, whose aim, according to the Democrats, was to help the individual in the face of an economy that had gone out of control and was impoverishing the individual. The new dominant doctrine was hybrid in that it brought together "modern" liberals but eventually also "modern" conservatives. The liberal consensus did not erase the capitalist relations of production nor did it evacuate the basic values of the classic liberal ideas, but there was a fusion: modern liberals and modern conservatives rallied in sustaining the capitalist economic development, in defending the interests of multinational corporations and banks, in promoting the government's active role in the economy and society in an effort to expand capitalism. The liberal consensus was also labeled "corporate liberalism" to describe a consensus position facilitated by a growing economy, an expanding state, and the global hegemony of the United States after World War II. With the adoption of positive state-interventionism, the social welfare system gradually became indispensable to the macro-economic regulation of the economy.

The liberal consensus lasted until the late 1960s, until the election of Richard Nixon to the White House in 1968, and arguably even until the election of Ronald Reagan in 1980. It was then supplanted by a new ideology, neoliberalism, a "conservative" consensus that arose in place of the liberal consensus. Neoliberalism's rise to prominence—or to "common sense" status in the Gramscian sense of the term—was evident in that it had conquered both major political parties, as testified by Bill Clinton's 1996 State of the Union address:

> We know big Government does not have all the answers. We know there's not a program for every problem. We know, and we have worked to give the American people a smaller, less bureaucratic Government in Washington. And we have to give the American people one that lives within its means. The era of big Government is over.[57]

The liberal consensus had failed to transform American society in the long term in the wake of the New Deal and of a number of advances in terms of civil rights and health care in the 1960s To use James MacGregor's

---

[57] William J. Clinton, Address Before a Joint Session of the Congress on the State of the Union, January 23, 1996, The American Presidency Project, https://www.presidency.ucsb.edu/node/223046.

theory of leadership,[58] only Franklin D. Roosevelt and Ronald Reagan were genuinely transformational leaders in the twentieth century. Other presidents were what Burns described as "transactional" leaders whose leadership is based on an exchange (economic, political) between leaders and followers but in which the motivations of constituents remained unchanged. Transformational leadership, on the other hand, was moral leadership combined with a fusion of purpose and vision between leaders and followers: "Such leadership comes when one or more persons engage with others in such a way that leaders and followers raise one another to higher levels of motivation and morality."[59] Transactional leaders, therefore, usually did not strive to change the cultural hegemony:

> [T]ransactional leaders work within their organizational cultures following existing rules, procedures, and norms; transformational leaders change their culture by first understanding it and then realigning the organization's culture with a new vision and a revision of its shared assumptions, values, and norms.[60]

On the campaign trail for the 2008 Democratic presidential nomination, for example, then-Senator Barack Obama acknowledged that Ronald Reagan had been a transformational president:

> I don't want to present myself as some sort of singular figure. I think part of what's different are the times. I do think that, for example, the 1980 election was different. I think Ronald Reagan changed the trajectory of America in a way that, you know, Richard Nixon did not and in a way that Bill Clinton did not. He put us on a fundamentally different path because the country was ready for it.[61]

Both Roosevelt and Reagan were transformational presidents in that they succeeded in forcing realignments that built long-lasting majority coalitions. Dwight Eisenhower, a Republican, succeeded Franklin D. Roosevelt and Harry Truman but did not challenge the liberal consensus.

---

[58] James MacGregor Burns, *Leadership*, New York, Harper & Row, 1978.

[59] Ibid., p. 6.

[60] Bernard M. Bass, Bruce J. Avolio, "Transformational Leadership and Organizational Culture," *Public Administration Quarterly*, vol. 17, n° 1, Spring 1993, p. 112.

[61] Obama, Interview with the Editorial Board of the *Reno Gazette-Journal*, January 14, 2008, https://www.youtube.com/watch?v=HFLuOBsNMZA

Bill Clinton, a Democrat, succeeded Ronald Reagan and George H. W. Bush but proposed a "third way" that still embraced a significant part of the legacy of the Reagan revolution.[62] As Bernie Sanders put it in *Outsider in the House* in 1997, "President Clinton, like Bush and Reagan before him, is supporting a trade policy that protects the interests and profits of multinational corporations, while compromising the interests of American workers."[63]

For Bernie Sanders, the Reagan revolution had shown that the transformation of society attempted by the New Deal remained an unfinished business:

> Over 80 years ago, Franklin Delano Roosevelt helped create a government that made transformative progress in protecting the needs of working families. Today, in the second decade of the 21st century, we must take up the unfinished business of the New Deal and carry it to completion. This is the unfinished business of the Democratic Party and the vision we must accomplish.[64]

What was lacking to carry the New Deal to completion was agency, a social movement, a political infrastructure that the Democratic Party seemed unable to provide, even, as Sanders remarked, when Bill Clinton was campaigning for reelection in 1996:

> No. I do not want Bob Dole to be president. I'm voting for Bill Clinton.
> Do I have confidence that Clinton will stand up for the working people of this country—for children, for the elderly, for the folks who are hurting? No, I do not. But a Clinton victory could give us some time to build

---

[62] Stephen Skowronek's "political time" theory holds that the possibilities for presidential leadership are in fact shaped by each president's relationship to the political regime in which he or she is elected: "American political history has been punctuated by many beginnings and many endings. Periods are marked by the rise to power of an insurgent political coalition that secures its dominance over national affairs for an extended period of time. The dominant coalition perpetuates its position by gearing the federal government to favor a particular approach to public policy questions. The political-institutional regimes they establish tend to have staying power because the Constitution, with its separation of powers and checks and balances, makes concerted change of the sort needed to dislodge these arrangements difficult and rare." Stephen Skowronek, *Presidential Leadership in Political Time*, Lawrence, University of Kansas Press, 2008. Rpt. 2020, p. 28.

[63] Sanders, *Outsider in the House*, p. 237

[64] Id., "Sanders Calls For 21st Century Bill of Rights," op. cit, p. 65.

a movement, to develop a political infrastructure to protect what needs protecting, and to change the direction of the country. This is more than utopian fantasy.[65]

Bernie Sanders voted for Bill Clinton, as he would vote for Barack Obama in 2008. Still, the ideal of America as a classless society remained a utopian one.

REFERENCES

Adorno, Theodor W. *Negative Dialectics*. Trans. E. B. Ashton. London: Routledge & Kegan Paul, 1973.

———, Max Horkheimer. *Dialectic of Enlightenment*, 1947. Rpt., New York: Verso, 2016.

Bass, Bernard M., Bruce J. Avolio, "Transformational Leadership and Organizational Culture." *Public Administration Quarterly*, vol. 17, n° 1 (Spring 1993), pp. 112–121.

Burawoy, Michael. *Symbolic Violence: Conversations with Bourdieu*. Durham, NC: Duke University Press, 2019.

Burns, James MacGregor. *Leadership*. New York: Harper & Row, 1978.

Carothers, Thomas, Andrew O'Donohue, eds. *Democracies Divided: The Global Challenge of Political Polarization*, Washington, DC: Brookings, 2019.

Clinton, Hillary. *What Happened*. New York: Simon & Schuster, 2017.

Clinton, William J. Address Before a Joint Session of the Congress on the State of the Union (January 23, 1996). The American Presidency Project, https://www.presidency.ucsb.edu/node/223046.

Crehan, Kate. *Gramsci's Common Sense: Inequality and Its Narratives*. Durham, NC: Duke University Press, 2016.

Femia, Joseph V. *Gramsci's Political Thought: Hegemony, Consciousness, and the Revolutionary Process*. Oxford: Clarendon Press, 1981.

GARRY, Patrick M. *Liberalism and American Identity*. Kent, OH: Kent State University Press, 1992.

GORDON, Peter E., et al., eds. *The Routledge Companion to the Frankfurt School*. New York: Routledge, 2019.

Gramsci, Antonio. *Selections from the Prison Notebooks of Antonio Gramsci*, edited and translated by Quintin Hoare and Geoffrey N. Smith. New York: International Publishers, 1971.

Heinrich, Michael. *An Introduction to the Three Volumes of Karl Marx's Capital*. New York: Monthly Review Press, 2004.

[65] Id., *Outsider in the House*, p. 25.

Herman, Edward S., Noam Chomsky. *Manufacturing Consent: The Political Economy of the Mass Media.* New York: Pantheon Books, 1988.

Hopkins, Daniel J., John Sides, eds. *Political Polarization in American Politics.* New York: Bloomsbury, 2015.

Horkheimer, Max. *Eclipse of Reason.* Oxford: Oxford University Press, 1947.

Lippmann, Walter. *Public Opinion.* New York: Macmillan, 1922. Rpt. New Brunswick, NJ: Transaction Publishers, 1988.

Marcuse, Herbert. *Soviet Marxism: A Critical Analysis.* New York: Columbia University Press, 1958.

———. *One-Dimensional Man: Studies in the Ideology of Advanced Industrial Society.* New York: Beacon Press, 1964.

Obama, Barack H. Interview with the Editorial Board of the *Reno Gazette-Journal* (January 14, 2008), https://www.youtube.com/watch?v=HFLuOBsnMZA.

Rehmann, Jan. "Bernie Sanders and the Hegemonic Crisis of Neoliberal Capitalism: What Next?" *Socialism and Democracy*, vol. 30, n° 3 (2016), pp. 1–11, https://doi.org/10.1080/08854300.2016.1228874.

Rose, Lacey. "Hillary Clinton in Full: A Fiery New Documentary, Trump Regrets and Harsh Words for Bernie: 'Nobody Likes Him.'" *Hollywood Reporter* (January 21, 2020), https://www.hollywoodreporter.com/features/hillary-clinton-full-a-fiery-new-documentary-trump-regrets-harsh-words-bernie-1271551.

Sanders, Bernard. *Eugene V. Debs: Trade Unionist, Socialist, Revolutionary, 1855–1926.* New York: Folkways Records, 1979.

———, with Huck Gutman. *Outsider in the House: A Political Autobiography.* New York: Verso, 1997. Rpt. *Outsider in the White House*, 2015.

———. *Our Revolution: A Future to Believe In.* New York: Thomas Dunne Books, 2016.

———. *Bernie Speaks: Speeches by Bernie Sanders*, compiled by David Cane. CreateSpace Independent Publishing Platform: Greenbridge Publishing, 2017.

Skowronek, Stephen. *Presidential Leadership in Political Time.* Lawrence: University of Kansas Press, 2008. Rpt. 2020.

Taylor, Frederick. *The Principles of Scientific Management.* New York: Harper & Brothers, 1911.

Trilling, Lionel. *The Liberal Imagination.* New York: Harcourt, Brace, Jovanovich, 1950.

CHAPTER 8

Hope

As he was running for presidential office in 2008, Barack Obama, then still the junior senator from Illinois, made a number of rousing promises to the American people along the campaign trail, often in proverbial—if not quasi messianic— rhetoric:

> I am absolutely certain that generations from now, we will be able to look back and tell our children that this was the moment when we began to provide care for the sick and good jobs to the jobless; this was the moment when the rise of the oceans began to slow and our planet began to heal; this was the moment when we ended a war and secured our nation and restored our image as the last, best hope on Earth. This was the moment— this was the time—when we came together to remake this great nation so that it may always reflect our very best selves, and our highest ideals.[1]

Compelling catchwords and phrases such as "Hope" and "Change we can believe in" became indelible slogans. They carried a sense of empowerment, of agency, and spread the belief that political willpower would now, at long last, effectively drive out prejudices and build a more peaceful and inclusive society. Barack Obama arguably sealed his legacy

[1] Id., Remarks in St. Paul, Minnesota Claiming the Democratic Presidential Nomination, June 3, 2008, The American Presidency Project, https://www.presidency.ucsb.edu/node/277836.

© The Author(s), under exclusive license to Springer Nature Switzerland AG 2021
N. Gachon, *Bernie Sanders's Democratic Socialism*,
https://doi.org/10.1007/978-3-030-69661-0_8

the moment he sealed victory in the 2008 election: now a black man was running the White House, a house that was "built by slaves" as First Lady Michelle Obama emotionally reminded the audience at the 2016 Democratic National Convention in Philadelphia.[2] Barack Obama, however, did not win the presidential election because he was a black man. The reason was primarily because the country was facing a major economic crisis, was still embroiled in two unpopular wars, and was crying out for change. Barack Obama answered the aspirations of a majority of Americans by promising "[c]hange [they could] believe in." His election was soon termed "historic" while a dominant discourse was already holding that the new president embodied the end of racism in the United States.

8.1   A Post-American Promise

While the expression "post-America" was often used by political opponents to discredit Barack Obama's posture and policies, to denounce a "war on America"[3] that he allegedly waged, our argument here is that Barack Obama's campaign rhetoric was designed to rouse the spirits of the American people by projecting a better image of themselves, by holding up a mirror to America's better nature,[4] to point toward the direction of a future that Obama said he could envision and that could eventually work.[5] To be sure, Barack Obama's America could be perceived as a most desirable utopia, a vision of America that even the Nobel Prize Committee, for example, immediately bought as it awarded Obama the Nobel Prize for Peace in 2009, largely on the promise that he would transform America's relations with the world. During the presidential campaign, Obama had vowed to end the war in Iraq, to heal the breach with the Islamic world, and to reset relations with Russia. During his Nobel Prize lecture, however, the president was significantly more cautious:

[2] Michelle Obama, "Speech at the 2016 Democratic National Convention," PBS News, July 25, 2016, https://www.youtube.com/watch?v=zHnJ2sTIVUI.

[3] See, for example, Pamela Geller, Robert Spencer, *The Post-American Presidency: The Obama Administration's War on America*, New York, Threshold Editions, 2010.

[4] The image is borrowed from William Shakespeare, *Hamlet*, III, iii., 16–23.

[5] Steffens, Letter to Marie Howe, op. cit., p. 198.

I receive this honor with deep gratitude and great humility. It is an award that speaks to our highest aspirations—that for all the cruelty and hardship of our world, we are not mere prisoners of fate. Our actions matter, and can bend history in the direction of justice. And yet I would be remiss if I did not acknowledge the considerable controversy that your generous decision has generated. In part, this is because I am at the beginning, and not the end, of my labors on the world stage. [...] But perhaps the most profound issue surrounding my receipt of this prize is the fact that I am the Commander-in-Chief of the military of a nation in the midst of two wars. One of these wars is winding down. The other is a conflict that America did not seek; one in which we are joined by 42 other countries—including Norway—in an effort to defend ourselves and all nations from further attacks. Still, we are at war, and I'm responsible for the deployment of thousands of young Americans to battle in a distant land. Some will kill, and some will be killed.[6]

So much for imminent peace, therefore, and for the implementation of a much-hoped-for Obama doctrine in the immediate present. Still, the attractiveness of Obama's promise of a post-America, an America ready to address and transcend its besetting sins, seemed irresistible.

On the home front, Obama's post-America bore the promise to bridge the political polarization which had been ripping the country apart for the past two decades. He expressed his vision most eloquently in the landmark address he gave at the July 2004 Democratic National Convention in Boston, when John Kerry was nominated to challenge George W. Bush in the upcoming presidential election:

There's not a liberal America and a conservative America; there's the United States of America. [...] The pundits, the pundits like to slice and dice our country into red states and blue states: red states for Republicans, blue States for Democrats. But I've got news for them, too. [...] We are one people, all of us pledging allegiance to the stars and stripes, all of us defending the United States of America.[7]

---

[6] Obama, "Nobel Prize Lecture, Oslo," The Nobel Prize, December 10, 2009, https://www.nobelprize.org/prizes/peace/2009/obama/26183-nobel-lecture-2009.

[7] Id., "Address at the 2004 Democratic National Convention," The American Presidency Project, July 27, 2004, https://www.presidency.ucsb.edu/node/277378.

And Obama conjured up Martin Luther King Jr.'s famous phrase "the fierce urgency of now"[8] to stress the importance of his own candidacy in a series of speeches starting in 2007:

> I chose to run in this election—at this moment—because of what Dr. King called "the fierce urgency of now." Because we are at a defining moment in our history. Our nation is at war. Our planet is in peril. Our health care system is broken, our economy is out of balance, our education system fails too many of our children, and our retirement system is in tatters.[9]

Such references most likely fell on the receptive ears of Bernie Sanders who placed his own democratic socialism under the umbrella of Martin Luther King Jr.'s radical vision of a country that had cynically implemented "socialism for the rich" and "rugged individualism for the poor."[10] However, in 2004, four years prior to the 2008 presidential election, Barack Obama's proposed vision of a reconciled post-partisan America was not one that explicitly expanded the scope and limits of government intervention to correct social evils. With hindsight, the picture was even somewhat confusing in that Obama's rousing rhetoric placed both strains of liberalism, economic and political, on an equal footing:

> Don't get me wrong. The people I meet in small towns and big cities, in diners and office parks, they don't expect government to solve all their problems. [...] No, people don't expect government to solve all their problems. But they sense, deep in their bones, that with just a change in priorities, we can make sure that every child in America has a decent

---

[8] "We have also come to this hallowed spot to remind America of the fierce urgency of Now. This is no time to engage in the luxury of cooling off or to take the tranquilizing drug of gradualism. Now is the time to make real the promises of democracy." Martin Luther King Jr., "I Have a Dream," Address delivered at the March on Washington for Jobs and Freedom, August 28, 1963, The Martin Luther King Jr. Research and Education Institute (Stanford University), https://kinginstitute.stanford.edu/king-papers/documents/i-have-dream-address-delivered-march-washington-jobs-and-freedom.

[9] Obama, "Remarks in Des Moines, Iowa," The American Presidency Project, December 19, 2007, https://www.presidency.ucsb.edu/node/277494.

[10] See *supra*, p. 116. The title of Bernie Sanders's *Where We Go from Here* was also inspired by the title of a book by Martin Luther King Jr. See: Martin Luther King Jr., *Where Do We Go from Here: Chaos or Community?* New York, Beacon Press, 1968.

shot at life, and that the doors of opportunity remain open to all. They know we can do better. And they want that choice.[11]

In fact, Barack Obama's highly effective campaign and high-flown rhetoric left unclear what kind of change he was exactly proposing. To a large extent, Obama ran an idealistic campaign that sought to reinvent the modern president's role as a transcendent leader, one who would seek to govern independently of political parties. He pledged to bring Americans together, to restore the authority of the Constitution, to overcome the raw partisanship that had polarized the Washington community for two decades and divided the country during George Bush's eight years in office. The danger, however, with such a posture was that it could also turn into a plebiscitary form of politics that might promise more than a president could—or should—assume.

Obama's promise to transform America lay most conspicuously on the prospect of a post-racial society, of finally reaching the historic turning point in the troubled racial history of the United States. After centuries of slavery, racial discrimination, and segregation, Americans finally chose a man of African ancestry to become their president and commander-in-chief in 2008. As he was the first black president in American history, Barack Obama's election and presidency were de facto historic and transformational, whatever might happen later with the obstructionism of the Republicans in Congress. In a sense, the very fact of being elected to the highest office will probably remain as Barack Obama's most significant achievement. The hope he promised, however, was set to collide with two immediate realities. One, as Ta-Nehisi Coates put it, had to do with the racial tensions still inherent to American society:

> Only Obama, a black man who emerged from the best of white America, and thus could sincerely trust white America, could be so certain that he could achieve broad national appeal. And yet only a black man with that same biography could underestimate his opposition's resolve to destroy him.[12]

---

[11] Obama, Address at the 2004 Democratic National Convention, op. cit., p. 147.

[12] Ta-Nehisi Coates, "My President Was Black: A history of the first African American White House—And of What Came Next," *The Atlantic*, January/February 2017, https://www.theatlantic.com/magazine/archive/2017/01/my-president-was-black/508793.

The other was conjunctural. Barack Obama was elected on November 6, 2008, in the context of the worst economic crisis since the Great Depression. The crisis that he had inherited was soon to be regarded by more and more people, opponents and supporters alike, as his own—Obama's own—problem. As a consequence, his presidency was ultimately to be defined by the long, slow, and uncertain process of economic recovery. The crisis soon came to be known as the Great Recession, therefore as the worst period since the Great Depression of the 1930s. And it was largely expected that the liberal Obama administration, like Franklin Roosevelt's New Deal, would approach such a serious economic downturn as the result of misconduct and greed inherent in a competitive capitalist system.

8.2   THE GREAT RECESSION

In his April 25, 2009 Weekly Address, President Obama reminded his listeners that his administration had come into office facing a budget deficit of $1.3 trillion for 2009 alone and that the cost of facing the economic crisis was high:

> But we can't settle for a future of rising deficits and debt that our children can't pay. All across America, families are tightening their belts and making hard choices. Now, Washington must show that same sense of responsibility. [...] So much of our Government was built to deal with different challenges from a different era. Too often the result is wasteful spending, bloated programs, and inefficient results. It's time to fundamentally change the way we do business in Washington.[13]

Barack Obama's calls for fiscal responsibility may have sounded wise but were quite different from the way Franklin Roosevelt had handled the Great Depression. In his first days and weeks in office, Roosevelt declared a four-day bank holiday that kept all banks shut until Congress could act,[14] abandoned the international gold standard, delinking the value of

---

[13] Obama, The President's Weekly Address, April 25, 2009, *Public Papers of the Presidents of the United States: Barack Obama, 2009*, Washington, DC, U.S. Government Printing Office, 2010, p. 554.

[14] Eliot A. Rosen, *Roosevelt, the Great Depression, and the Economics of Recovery*, Charlottesville, University of Virginia Press, 2005, p. 25.

the dollar to gold,[15] and pursued a policy of reflation that raised the prices of American commodities like wheat and cotton, returning them to their 1926 pre-contraction level, in order to counteract the deflation that had dragged the economy into the abyss.[16] Barack Obama did not engage in any comparably radical policy. His approach was typically more incremental. Obama's response to the Great Recession often inspired criticism, because of the timidity of his stimulus plan, of his failure to provide broad support to struggling homeowners, and of the premature shift to deficit cutting he announced in his April 25, 2009 Weekly Address.[17] This criticism was largely due to the parallel between the Great Recession and the Great Depression, and to the implicit comparison between Barack Obama and Franklin D. Roosevelt.

Obama's strategy seemed controversial to many liberals from the moment he started appointing his economic team shortly after the November 4, 2008 election. Writing for the *Times* in London, Gerard Baker dubbed Obama's economic team "the Robert Rubin Memorial All Stars,"[18] after Robert Rubin, the former Goldman Sachs vice-chairman (1987–1990), then co-chairman (1990–1992), Bill Clinton named as his Treasury Secretary in 1995. Tim Geithner, a former protégé of Rubin's, was handpicked to become Barack Obama's nominee to the Treasury Department. And Robert Rubin himself, along with Larry Summers[19]—who was Treasury Secretary in the final year and a half of the Clinton administration—would serve as Obama's chief economic advisers. Robert Rubin, as well as John Podesta, Hillary Clinton's future campaign manager, were among the persons many liberals, including Bernie Sanders, blamed for Bill Clinton's pro-business, anti-regulation

---

[15] Ibid., pp. 67–68.

[16] Ibid., p. 42.

[17] Obama, The President's Weekly Address, April 25, 2009, op. cit., p. 150.

[18] Gerard Baker, "Why Barack Obama Picked a Political Who's Who," *The Times*, December 5, 2008, https://www.thetimes.co.uk/article/why-barack-obama-picked-a-pol itical-whos-who-mjc76tgzm6t.

[19] Larry Summers was also one of the economic advisers to Joe Biden's 2020 campaign, which caused several progressive groups to ask Joe Biden on Wednesday to remove former Treasury Secretary Larry Summers from his campaign and to promise not to include him in any future Biden administration. See: Jennifer Epstein, "Biden Feels Heat from Left to Drop Larry Summers as an Adviser," *Fortune*, May 6, 2020, https://fortune.com/2020/05/06/joe-biden-larry-summers-advisor-activi sts-working-families-party-greenpeace-moveon.

policies and for the 1999 repeal of the New Deal's *Glass-Steagall Act*[20] which had separated investment and commercial banking activities since 1932. In the words of Bernie Sanders:

> The Clinton administration worked closely with Wall Street and Republicans to repeal the Glass-Steagall Act and deregulate the major financial institutions in the country. This initiative, pushed by Clinton's secretary of the treasury, Robert Rubin, a top Wall Street executive, unleashed the greed of the major financial institutions and their contempt for the law. It allowed large commercial banks to merge with investment banks and insurance companies. In my view, and in the view of many financial experts, that decision led to the 2008 Wall Street crash and the worst economic downturn since the Great Depression of 1929. A Democratic president should not be in bed with Wall Street.[21]

Many argued that Barack Obama had chosen the wrong persons, that the members of his economic team all shared some responsibility in the current financial crisis. Yet Obama selected them because they were three of the top minds in economic and financial policy, offering "not just extensive experience shaping economic policy and managing financial markets" but also "an unparalleled understanding of [the] current economic crisis in all of its depth, complexity, and urgency,"[22] a crisis they had arguably let happen. He was clearly not taking an all-out liberal approach to the economic crisis. Tim Geithner's nomination, in particular, was intended as a sign of continuity to reassure markets and lawmakers, Geithner having "served with distinction," in the president-elect's own words, "under both Democrats and Republicans," and having "a long history of working comfortably and as an honest broker on both sides of the aisle."[23] Tim Geithner came to epitomize an Obama economic team that was viewed as too close to Wall Street.

---

[20] *Glass-Steagall Act*, Pub.L. 72-44, February 27, 1932.

[21] Sanders, *Our Revolution*, p. 51.

[22] Obama, "Remarks in Chicago Announcing Members of the Economic Team," The American Presidency Project, November 24, 2008, https://www.presidency.ucsb.edu/node/216777.

[23] Ibid.

The unemployment rate was at 7.6% on the day Obama was inaugurated and climbed to more than 10% by the end of 2009.[24] The president realized that he needed to increase the $190 billion fiscal stimulus he had promised during his campaign[25] to stop the bleeding. He signed the *American Recovery and Reinvestment Act* into law on February 17, 2009,[26] less than a month later. The challenge was to create a stimulus strong enough to soften the recession, but not so strong as to raise doubts about the ballooning debt. Unfortunately, Obama's strategy was blamed for doing both. Although jobs were created, it failed to initially reduce unemployment below 9% and added to the debt. Many were disappointed that the stimulus was "only" $787 billion under the *Recovery Act* and believed it needed to be higher. While it seemed likely that a bigger stimulus would have provided a bigger economic jolt and accelerated the recovery, it was most unlikely that Barack Obama would be allowed any more public money by the U.S. Congress. The bill needed 60 votes in the Senate to overcome a Republican filibuster, and the three Republican moderates who supported it[27] insisted that it could not possibly exceed $800 billion.[28] Finally, everyone involved in the negotiations, including the liberals who favored a larger stimulus, agreed that Barack Obama obtained as much as he could. And, as implicitly confirmed in his April 25, 2009 Weekly Address,[29] the president was not too willing to push for a bigger stimulus because he wanted, and had promised to, take a historic step in the field of health care reform. Obama needed to keep political credit and to appear as reasonably fiscally conservative if he was to ever have a chance to earn bipartisan support for the upcoming *Patient Protection and Affordable Care Act*.[30] In the end, the Great Recession

---

[24] Pew Research Center, "Unemployment vs. Obama Disapproval," January 26, 2010, https://www.pewresearch.org/2010/01/26/its-all-about-jobs-except-when-its-not.

[25] "Obama Expected to Offer Stimulus Package," Reuters, November 5, 2008, https://www.reuters.com/article/us-usa-election-stimulus-1/factbox-obama-expected-to-offer-stimulus-package-idUSTRE4A43FH20081105.

[26] American Recovery and Reinvestment Act, Pub.L. 111-5, February 17, 2009.

[27] The bill did not receive a single Republican vote in the House of Representatives.

[28] David M. Herszenhorn, "Recovery Bill Gets Final Approval," *New York Times*, February 13, 2009, https://archive.nytimes.com/www.nytimes.com/2009/02/14/us/politics/14web-stim.html.

[29] Obama, The President's Weekly Address, April 25, 2009, p. 103.

[30] Patient Protection and Affordable Care Act, Pub.L. 111–148, March 23, 2010.

did not turn out to be another Great Depression. From a strictly quantitative standpoint, Obama's stimulus did indeed succeed in launching a weak recovery. In July 2010, using statistics provided by the Council of Economic Advisors, the nonpartisan, non-profit Committee for a Responsible Federal Budget reported that "the 2009 stimulus ha[d] boosted GDP by 2.7% and raised employment by 2.5 million jobs since February 2009, relative to what would have occurred absent the stimulus."[31] Yet, in January 2010, a CNN survey indicated that 63% of the public thought that the projects in the *Recovery Act* had been included for purely political reasons and that they would have no economic benefit, with only 36% saying that those projects would benefit the economy. 45% of respondents thought that "nearly all" or "most" of the money had been wasted.[32] The reason was that the choices made by Barack Obama were confusing as to what his economic policy actually was to help those who were suffering from the recession.

On March 23, 2009, Treasury Secretary Tim Geithner unveiled a plan aimed at freeing the nation's banks from up to $1 trillion in toxic assets that were seen as roadblocks to economic recovery.[33] The so-called bailouts were immensely unpopular, although Barack Obama was only partially responsible. Most of them had been passed after a bipartisan vote in October 2008, before he was elected, through the "Troubled Asset Relief Program" created under the *Emergency Economic Stabilization Act*.[34] Bernie Sanders had addressed the Senate on October 1, 2008, in the final weeks of the Bush administration, to oppose what he called "the Wall Street bailout":

> If a bailout is needed, if taxpayer money must be placed at risk, if we are going to bail out Wall Street, it should be those people who have caused the problem, those people who have benefited from President Bush's tax

---

[31] "Measuring the Effects of ARRA," Committee for a Responsible Federal Budget, July 15, 2010, https://www.crfb.org/blogs/measuring-effects-arra.

[32] CNN Opinion Research Poll, January 25, 2010, http://i2.cdn.turner.com/cnn/2010/images/01/25/rel1g.pdf.

[33] Edmund L. Andrews, Eric Dash, "U.S. Expands Plan to Buy Banks' Troubled Assets," *New York Times*, March 23, 2009, https://www.nytimes.com/2009/03/24/business/economy/24bailout.html.

[34] *Emergency Economic Stabilization Act*, Pub.L. 110–343, October 3, 2008.

breaks for millionaires and billionaires, those people who have taken advantage of deregulation who should pick up the tab, not ordinary working people.[35]

Barack Obama did not change course after his election. And public opinion largely resented the bailouts after a financial crisis that had been caused by reckless bankers. Tim Geithner explained in 2014 that there was no alternative:

> As much as the public hated bailouts, we were pretty sure people would hate the consequences of uncontrolled default even more. And I had learned during the nineties that the kind of actions that solve financial crises are never popular, that it wasn't worth trying too hard to make them popular.[36]

The same thing happened, Geithner wrote, when the Obama administration took measures to save the automobile industry by rescuing General Motors and Chrysler:

> Once again, we hit the political sweet spot where the right, the left, and much of the middle disapproved of our actions. Most of the country saw the GM and Chrysler rescues as new big-government bailouts for mismanaged firms. But the industry and its Democratic defenders saw the stringent conditions as a betrayal, especially compared to our approach to the financial industry. Bankruptcy would mean haircuts for creditors—as well as hardships for autoworkers, retired autoworkers, and auto dealers—that we hadn't imposed during our bank rescues.[37]

More and more liberals were lamenting an economic team that was viewed as too close to Wall Street. On March 22, 2009, Nobel Prize-winning economist Paul Krugman published a scathing criticism of the Obama administration, and more particularly of Tim Geithner: "if asset values go up, the investors profit, but if they go down, the investors can

---

[35] Sanders, "Wall Street Bailout," U.S. Senator for Vermont website, October 1, 2008, https://www.sanders.senate.gov/newsroom/press-releases/2008/10/01/wall-street-bailout.

[36] Timothy F. Geithner, *Stress Test: Reflections on Financial Crises*, New York, Crown Publishing Group, 2014, p. 201.

[37] Ibid., p. 338.

walk away from their debt. So this isn't really about letting markets work. It's just an indirect, disguised way to subsidize purchases of bad assets."[38]

Even the *Dodd–Frank Wall Street Reform and Consumer Protection Act*,[39] which the president signed into law on July 21, 2010, failed to earn the trust of liberals. As had been the case with the *Recovery Act of 2009*, the law was voted on party lines, without a single Republican vote in the House and only 4 in the Senate. The aim of the *Dodd–Frank Act* was to regulate the financial markets and to protect consumers to prevent a repeat of the 2008 crisis. *Dodd-Frank* is generally regarded as one of the most significant laws enacted during the presidency of Barack Obama. And it happened to be the most comprehensive financial reform since the *Glass-Steagall Act*[40] of 1933, which had regulated banks after the 1929 stock market crash until the *Gramm-Leach-Bliley Act*[41] repealed it in 1999, a deregulation that contributed to the 2008 recession. Republicans argued that the *Dodd-Frank Act* was "big-government liberalism run amok, an assault on free enterprise" while the Democrats "dismissed it as fake reform, a triumph for too-big-to-fail Wall Street banks."[42] As Tim Geithner himself acknowledged, the law was not perfect: "Dodd-Frank was messy and complicated. It occupied that shrinking pragmatic center of the American political system," but it kept Obama's promise to make the American "Wild West financial system much safer."[43] Still, Barack Obama's ambivalent strategy did not allow him to strengthen his political position. Rather than consolidating the coalition that brought him to victory in 2008, Barack Obama often found himself vilified across the board even when the economic situation of the country improved. He eventually lost the House of Representatives in 2010, then both the House and the Senate in 2014. Looking back to that sequence of events, Bernie Sanders wrote in *Our Revolution*:

---

[38] Paul Krugman, "Financial Policy Despair," *New York Times*, March 22, 2009, https://www.nytimes.com/2009/03/23/opinion/23krugman.html.

[39] Dodd–Frank Wall Street Reform and Consumer Protection Act, Pub.L. 111–203, July 21, 2010.

[40] *Glass Steagall Act*, op. cit., p. 151.

[41] *Gramm-Leach-Bliley Act*, Pub.L. 106-102, November 12, 1999.

[42] Geithner, p. 424.

[43] Ibid.

Yes. The economy was better than it had been when President Bush left office. Yes. There had been major troop withdrawal from Iraq. Yes. President Obama was doing a number of things that were right. But, despite that, something was deeply wrong in the country, and people felt it. Millions of workers were falling further and further behind. The gap between the rich and everyone else was growing wider. The political system was increasingly corrupt and the economic and political establishment was far removed from the lives of ordinary Americans.[44]

Barack Obama was no Franklin Roosevelt. To many liberals, "Recovery" and "Reinvestment," the two Rs of the *American Recovery and Reinvestment Act*, were only pale reflections of the three Rs of the New Deal—Relief, Recovery, and Reform.

8.3   A DREAM DEFERRED[45]

On May 14, 2008, while still on the campaign trail and as he was being endorsed by former Senator John Edwards (D-N.C.), Barack Obama promised to "change things around [...] to lift up every American out of poverty," and added that John Edwards's "campaign to cut poverty in half over the next 10 years" was a goal he would "set as president of the United States."[46] In December 2013, almost a year into his second presidential term, Obama was still calling poverty "the defining challenge of our time"[47] and insisted that poverty was his central preoccupation: "Making sure our economy works for every working American. It's why I ran for President. It was at the center of last year's campaign. It drives everything I do in this office."[48] And in May 2015, during a speech at Georgetown University, Obama used the "red states" v. "blue states" rhetoric again, the one he had deployed at the 2004 Democratic National

---

[44] Sanders, *Our Revolution*, p. 78.

[45] Langston Hughes, "Harlem," in *the Collected Poems of Langston Hughes*, edited by Arnold Rampersad, New York, Vintage, 1995, p. 426.

[46] Obama, Remarks following endorsement by John Edwards, in "Edwards Endorses Obama," May 14, 2008, Real Clear Politics, https://www.realclearpolitics.com/articles/2008/05/edwards_endorses_obama.html.

[47] Id., Remarks by the President on Economic Mobility, December 4, 2013, The White House, Office of the Press Secretary, https://obamawhitehouse.archives.gov/the-press-off ice/2013/12/04/remarks-president-economic-mobility.

[48] Id.

Convention[49] to decry what he considered to be a stereotype regarding poverty:

> The stereotype is that you've got folks on the left who just want to pour more money into social programs, and don't care anything about culture or parenting or family structures, and that's one stereotype. And then you've got cold-hearted, free market, capitalist types who are reading Ayn Rand and [laughter] think everybody are moochers. And I think the truth is more complicated.[50]

In typical fashion, Barack Obama was seeking a middle-of-the-road incremental approach rather than a markedly ideological approach which, he believed, would have brought his policies to a deadlock. The signature achievement of his presidency and the centerpiece of his plan to fight poverty in the United States was the 2010 *Patient Protection and Affordable Care Act*.[51] Obama sought to fight poverty with a social policy that aimed to improve the lives of all Americans, including the poorest, including African Americans, by providing economic and educational opportunities, and by improving health care coverage. And he held a similar position on reparations for slavery, as in this December 2016 remark to Ta-Nehisi Coates:

> I have much more confidence in my ability [...] to mobilize the American people around a multiyear, multibillion-dollar investment to help every child in poverty in this country than I am in being able to mobilize the country around providing a benefit specific to African Americans as a consequence of slavery and Jim Crow.[52]

The Obama administration did not seek to develop a specific public policy program to end poverty. As he celebrated the fiftieth anniversary of Lyndon Johnson's declaration of an "unconditional War on Poverty in

---

[49] Id., Address at the 2004 Democratic National Convention, op. cit., p. 147.

[50] Id., Remarks by the President in Conversation on Poverty at Georgetown University, May 12, 2015, https://obamawhitehouse.archives.gov/realitycheck/the-press-office/2015/05/12/remarks-president-conversation-poverty-georgetown-university.

[51] Obama, Address at the 2004 Democratic National Convention, op. cit., p. 147.

[52] Coates, op. cit., p. 102.

America" [53] in April 2014, Obama did not explicitly promise to engage in any similar effort.[54] His language was more about the economy as a whole, emphasizing the plight of the middle class rather than the poor specifically. When it came to the poor specifically, Obama preferred to use already existing programs. However, the deadlock he was seeking to avoid through consensus policies seemed to be hitting his administration with a vengeance.

Compromises are not always workable solutions—let alone change people can believe in—when all parties involved end up being disappointed. Outside of the Republican ranks, one of the most vocal critics of Barack Obama turned out to be Cornel West, the black intellectual who believed in Obama's potential for change and had done sixty-five campaign events for him in 2008. As early as May 2011, only two years into Barack Obama's first term, Cornel West expressed his disappointment in an interview with Pulitzer Prize-winning journalist Chris Hedges during which he bitterly described Obama as "a black mascot of Wall Street oligarchs and a black puppet of corporate plutocrats [who now] has become head of the American killing machine and is proud of it."[55] Cornel West explained that Barack Obama had unfortunately revealed his true face when he appointed his economic team during the presidential transition period in 2008:

> It became very clear to me as the announcements were being made that this was going to be a newcomer, in many ways like Bill Clinton, who wanted to reassure the Establishment by bringing in persons they felt comfortable with and that we were really going to get someone who was using intermittent progressive populist language in order to justify a centrist, neoliberalist policy that we see in the opportunism of Bill Clinton. It was very much going to be a kind of black face of the DLC [Democratic Leadership Council].[56]

[53] Johnson, op. cit., p. 118.

[54] Obama, Remarks by the President at LBJ Presidential Library Civil Rights Summit, April 10, 2014, The White House, Office of the Press Secretary, https://obamawhitehouse.archives.gov/the-press-office/2014/04/10/remarks-president-lbj-presidential-library-civil-rights-summit.

[55] Cornel West, quoted in Chris Hedges," "The Obama Deception: Why Cornel West Went Ballistic," Truthdig, May 16, 2011, https://www.truthdig.com/articles/the-obama-deception-why-cornel-west-went-ballistic.

[56] Ibid.

West lamented Obama's about-face in economic terms as the loss of "America's last chance to fight back against the greed of the Wall Street oligarchs and corporate plutocrats," as well as in racial terms to denounce the post-racial illusion behind the Obama presidency, and Obama's refusal to use his position as president to intervene on behalf of African Americans:

> [H]e's always had to fear being a white man with black skin. All he has known culturally is white. [...] Obama, coming out of Kansas influence, white, loving grandparents, coming out of Hawaii and Indonesia, when he meets these independent black folks who have a history of slavery, Jim Crow, Jane Crow and so on, he is very apprehensive. He has a certain rootlessness, a deracination. It is understandable.[57]

Bernie Sanders, for his part, has always been hesitant to talk about race and showed a certain disdain for identity politics, seeing the plight of underprivileged African Americans primarily as a class-based issue. The class-centric rhetoric cost Sanders the black vote in the 2016 Democratic primaries.[58] In March 2019, during the campaign for the 2020 Democratic nomination, Sanders admitted that his 2016 campaign had been "too white" and pledged to change that, yet he failed to earn the support of black voters once again[59] and eventually dropped out the race on April 8, 2020. Bernie Sanders insufficiently took into account the fact that, from the point of view of black voters, the economy is structured by race, not only by class. It was certainly a political miscalculation, if only because no candidate ever received the Democratic nomination without the black vote. What Sanders can be reproached with here is what the early-twentieth-century muckrakers, for example, were also reproached with. The muckrakers aimed to reform American society along transversal lines that were exclusively political and economic, and social. Except for

---

[57] Ibid.

[58] 58% of Black Democratic and Democratic-leaning voters supported Hillary Clinton as of March 2016 while only 34% supported Bernie Sanders. See: "Perceptions of the Presidential Candidates, and Primary Preferences," Pew Research Center, March 31, 2016, https://www.pewresearch.org/politics/2016/03/31/4-perceptions-of-the-pre sidential-candidates-and-primary-preferences.

[59] Adam Harris, "Bernie Sanders Reached Out to Black Voters. Why Didn't It Work?" *The Atlantic*, March 10, 2020, https://www.theatlantic.com/politics/archive/2020/03/ bernie-sanders-black-voters/607789.

Ray Stannard Baker 's *Following the Color Line*[60] (1908), for example, the muckrakers hardly ever tackled racial issues. Eugene Debs, Sanders's political hero, was a man of that era,[61] and Sanders's political vision calls for a paradigm shift that, from the outset, aimed to reform America following a utopian model, to rebuild the relation between the individual and society, with an underlying class prism. Richard Rorty explains in *Achieving Our Country* (1998) that, before the 1960s, the American left was largely reformist in its orientation to politics and that it then ceased to be political and instead became a cultural movement, with the prevailing view was that equality and social justice could no longer be promoted within the system. The cultural left (multiculturalism) "[taught] Americans to recognize otherness,"[62] as Rorty puts it. There was nothing morally objectionable about that from Sanders's point of view but, as a political strategy, however, it was problematic. It reinforced sectarian impulses and detracted from coalition-building. Bernie Sanders, therefore, from that angle, is a man of the early twentieth century: hence the multi-faceted reflection over utopianism, and about "holding utopia accountable," developed in this volume. By refusing to explicitly acknowledge the racial and gender dimensions of social interactions, Sanders also aimed to evacuate culturalism from the inquiry of social science and ultimately from the reality of public policy. The underlying fear here was that cultural variables may eventually disarm socio-economic (i.e., class) struggles and blur what Sanders perceived as the bedrock reality of unequal wealth distribution. His positions considerably evolved after he admitted that his 2016 campaign had been "too white" and pledged to change that.

On January 9, 2017, eleven days before Donald Trump was sworn in, Cornel West published an article entitled "Pity the sad legacy of Barack Obama" in which he scathingly denounced the "Obama cheerleaders who

---

[60] Baker, op. cit., p. 50.

[61] In 1903, Eugene Debs famously wrote "We have nothing special to offer the Negro, and we cannot make separate appeals to all the races. Debs, "The Negro in the Class Struggle." *International Socialist Review*, vol. IV, n° 5, November 1903, https://www.marxists.org/archive/debs/works/1903/negro.htm.

[62] Rorty, p. 79.

refused to make him accountable"[63] and their "responsibility" in the fact that, since day one, his administration had stood for the wrong cause:

> A few of us begged and pleaded with Obama to break with the Wall Street priorities and bail out Main Street. But he followed the advice of his "smart" neoliberal advisers to bail out Wall Street. In March 2009, Obama met with Wall Street leaders. He proclaimed: I stand between you and the pitchforks. I am on your side and I will protect you, he promised them.[64]

Cornel West accordingly decided to support Bernie Sanders in the 2016 presidential election. In the face of a dawning Trump presidency, his article was already seeking accountability for the electoral debacle: "Bernie Sanders gallantly tried to generate a leftwing populism but he was crushed by Clinton and Obama in the unfair Democratic party primaries. So now we find ourselves entering a neofascist era."[65] For West and left-wing liberals, the Obama presidency deferred the liberal dream and arguably failed the legacies of Franklin Roosevelt and Lyndon Johnson: "The president's greatest legislative achievement was to provide healthcare for over 25 million citizens," West wrote in 2017, "even as another 20 million are still uncovered. But it remained a market-based policy."[66]

The Sanders candidacy certainly rocked the Democratic establishment in 2016 in that the emerging accountability motif in left-wing liberal discourse marked a change in the political map. It seemed that the mainstream, the center, could no longer hold unless it could be held politically accountable. It seemed that the fuel of social discontent had found its detonator in the early years of the Obama presidency. When he opposed the bank bailouts in the final weeks of the Bush administration in October 2008, before Barack Obama was even elected, Bernie Sanders made an almost prophetic statement on the Senate floor:

> In our country today, we have the most unequal distribution of income and wealth of any major country on earth, with the top 1 percent earning

---

[63] West, "Pity the Sad Legacy of Barack Obama," *The Guardian*, January 9, 2017, https://www.theguardian.com/ commentisfree/2017/jan/09/barack-obama-legacy-presidency.

[64] Ibid.

[65] Ibid.

[66] Ibid.

more income than the bottom 50 percent and the top 1 percent owning more wealth than the bottom 90 percent. [...]

The time has come to assure our constituents in Vermont and all over this country that we are listening and understand their anger and their frustration. The time has come to say that we have the courage to stand up to all of the powerful financial institution lobbyists who are running amok all over the Capitol building [...].[67]

REFERENCES

Andrews, Edmund L., Eric Dash. "U.S. Expands Plan to Buy Banks' Troubled Assets." *New York Times* (March 23, 2009), https://www.nytimes.com/2009/03/24/business/economy/24bailout.html.

Baker, Gerard. "Why Barack Obama Picked a Political Who's Who." *The Times* (December 5, 2008), https://www.thetimes.co.uk/article/why-barack-obama-picked-a-political-whos-who-mjc76tgzm6t.

Coates, Ta-Nehisi. "My President Was Black: A History of the First African American White House—And of What Came Next." *The Atlantic* (January/February 2017), https://www.theatlantic.com/magazine/archive/2017/01/my-president-was-black/508793.

Epstein, Jennifer. "Biden Feels Heat from Left to Drop Larry Summers as an Adviser," *Fortune* (May 6, 2020), https://fortune.com/2020/05/06/joe-biden-larry-summers-advisor-activists-working-families-party-greenpeace-moveon.

Geithner, Timothy F. *Stress Test: Reflections on Financial Crises.* New York: Crown Publishing Group, 2014.

Geller, Pamela, Robert Spencer. *The Post-American Presidency: The Obama Administration's War on America.* New York: Threshold Editions, 2010.

Harris, Adam. "Bernie Sanders Reached Out to Black Voters. Why Didn't It Work?" *The Atlantic* (March 10, 2020), https://www.theatlantic.com/politics/archive/2020/03/bernie-sanders-black-voters/607789.

Hedges, Chris. "The Obama Deception: Why Cornel West Went Ballistic." Truthdig (May 16, 2011), https://www.truthdig.com/articles/the-obama-deception-why-cornel-west-went-ballistic.

Herszenhorn, David M. "Recovery Bill Gets Final Approval." *New York Times* (February 13, 2009), https://archive.nytimes.com/www.nytimes.com/2009/02/14/us/politics/14web-stim.html.

[67] Sanders, "Wall Street Bailout," op. cit., p. 153.

Johnson, Lyndon B. "Annual Message to the Congress on the State of the Union." The American Presidency Project (January 8, 1964), https://www.presidency.ucsb.edu/node/ 242292.

King, Martin Luther, Jr. "I Have a Dream," Address delivered at the March on Washington for Jobs and Freedom (August 28, 1963). The Martin Luther King Jr. Research and Education Institute (Stanford University), https://kinginstitute.stanford.edu/king-papers/documents/i-have-dream-address-delivered-march-washington-jobs-and-freedom.

———. *Where Do We Go from Here: Chaos or Community?* New York: Beacon Press, 1968.

Krugman, Paul. "Financial Policy Despair." *New York Times* (March 22, 2009), https://www.nytimes.com/2009/03/23/opinion/23krugman.html.

Obama, Barack H. "Address at the 2004 Democratic National Convention." The American Presidency Project (July 27, 2004), https://www.presidency.ucsb.edu/node/277378.

———. "Remarks in Des Moines, Iowa." The American Presidency Project (December 19, 2007), https://www.presidency.ucsb.edu/node/277494.

———. "Remarks Following the New Hampshire Primary." The American Presidency Project (January 8, 2008), https://www.presidency.ucsb.edu/node/276824.

———. Remarks Following Endorsement by John Edwards, in "Edwards Endorses Obama." Real Clear Politics (May 14, 2008), https://www.realclearpolitics.com/articles/2008/05/edwards_endorses_obama.html.

———. "Remarks in St. Paul, Minnesota Claiming the Democratic Presidential Nomination." The American Presidency Project (June 3, 2008), https://www.presidency.ucsb.edu/node/277836.

———. "Remarks in Chicago Announcing Members of the Economic Team." The American Presidency Project (November 24, 2008), https://www.presidency.ucsb.edu/node/216777.

———. The President's Weekly Address (April 25, 2009). *Public Papers of the Presidents of the United States: Barack Obama, 2009.* Washington, DC: U.S. Government Printing Office, 2010, p. 554.

———. "Nobel Prize Lecture, Oslo." The Nobel Prize (December 10, 2009), https://www.nobelprize.org/prizes/peace/2009/obama/26183-nobel-lecture-2009.

———. "Remarks by the President on Economic Mobility." The White House, Office of the Press Secretary (December 4, 2013), https://obamawhitehouse.archives.gov/the-press-office/2013/12/04/remarks-president-economic-mobility.

———. "Remarks by the President at LBJ Presidential Library Civil Rights Summit." The White House, Office of the Press Secretary (April 10, 2014), https://obamawhitehouse.archives.gov/the-press-office/2014/04/10/remarks-president-lbj-presidential-library-civil-rights-summit.

———. "Remarks by the President in Conversation on Poverty at Georgetown University" (May 12, 2015), https://obamawhitehouse.archives.gov/realitycheck/the-press-office/2015/05/12/remarks-president-conversation-poverty-georgetown-university.

Obama, Michelle. "Speech at the 2016 Democratic National Convention." PBS News (July 25, 2016), https://www.youtube.com/watch?v=zHnJ2sTIVUI.

Rosen, Eliot A. Roosevelt, the Great Depression, and the Economics of Recovery. Charlottesville: University of Virginia Press, 2005.

Sanders, Bernard. "Wall Street Bailout." U.S. Senator for Vermont website (October 1, 2008), https://www.sanders.senate.gov/newsroom/press-releases/2008/10/01/wall-street-bailout.

———. Our Revolution: A Future to Believe In. New York: Thomas Dunne Books, 2016.

———. Where We Go from Here: Two Years in the Resistance. New York: Thomas Dunne Books, 2018.

Steffens, Lincoln J. The Letters of Lincoln Steffens, vol. 1, edited by Ella Winter and Granville Hicks. New York: Harcourt, Brace & Co., 1938.

West, Cornel. "Pity the Sad Legacy of Barack Obama." The Guardian (January 9, 2017), https://www.theguardian.com/commentisfree/2017/jan/09/barack-obama-legacy-presidency.

CHAPTER 9

Occupying Wall Street

One striking, arguably paradoxical consequence of the 2008 Great Recession, which by all accounts marked a breakdown of neoliberalism, was that it seemed to result in more neoliberalism, with bailouts for banks, bailouts for large corporations, and austerity for the people. Another surprising consequence was that there seemed be little if any popular reaction, no spontaneous social movement to decry the inequity of the American economy, nothing likely to ignite the fuel of popular discontent. The only reaction resembling a "movement" was initially the emergence of the Tea Party in 2009, which, if it was challenging neoliberalism at all, was challenging it from the right. The Tea Party movement had ties to Wall Street, called for more austerity, and voiced anxious concerns about tax increases[1] should the Obama administration seek to address the roots of economic imbalances in American society and to provide remedies. More than anything else, the Tea Party movement expressed violent resentment over the recent election of Barack Obama and spread the idea that a dangerous liberal—if not socialist—takeover of government was under way, which spoke volumes on the ambivalence of Barack Obama's handling of public policy.

---

[1] Beyond the obvious reference to the 1773 Boston Tea Party, "Tea" was an acronym for "Taxed Enough Already."

© The Author(s), under exclusive license to Springer Nature   165
Switzerland AG 2021
N. Gachon, *Bernie Sanders's Democratic Socialism*,
https://doi.org/10.1007/978-3-030-69661-0_9

9.1   A Bipolar Political Spectrum

The Republicans were quick to turn the context of the Great Recession into a debate on state intervention and on big government. In a book entitled *The Forgotten Man: A New History of the Great Depression*, Amity Shlaes held that "government intervention helped to make the Depression Great," in other words that Franklin Roosevelt's New Deal had actually made the Great Depression worse:

> The period was not one of a moral battle between a force for good—the Roosevelt presidency—and forces for evil, those who opposed Roosevelt. It was a period of a power struggle between two sectors of the economy, both containing a mix of evil and virtue. The public sector and the private sector competed relentlessly for advantage. At the beginning, in the 1920s, the private sector ruled. By the end, when World War II began, it was the public sector that was dominant.[2]

One favorite target of the Republicans was John Maynard Keynes: "Roosevelt happened on an economic theory that validated his politics and his moral sense: what we now call Keynesianism," Shlaes added, "emphasized consumers, who were also voters."[3] The ultimate target, of course, was Barack Obama, a Democrat who, after "liberal," was now showcased as being "Keynesian," and even "socialist." True to their belief in Ronald Reagan's famous 1981 inaugural statement that "government is not the solution to our problem; government is the problem,"[4] the Republicans insisted that recessions generally are the result of bad government policies leading to fundamental and unsustainable economic imbalances.[5] In a fascinating turn of events, the debate over the causes of economic crisis totally shifted. At stake were no longer the excesses of unregulated financial institutions. The economic crisis, so the argument went, had been caused by big government, by the excesses of state intervention. The current government, in other words, was indeed the problem, not the

---

[2] Amity Shlaes, *The Forgotten Man: A New History of the Great Depression*, New York, Harper Collins, 2007, pp. 9–10.

[3] Ibid., p. 11.

[4] Ronald W. Reagan, Inaugural Address, January 20, 1981, The American Presidency Project, https://www.presidency.ucsb.edu/node/246336.

[5] Llewellyn H. Rockwell Jr., "Obama and the Economy," Mises Institute, August 6, 2009, https://mises.org/print/5661.

solution. The confusion between the bailouts and the stimulus in the public eye made it even easier for the Republicans to add fuel to the fire against Barack Obama.

On February 18, 2009, Obama gave a speech in Phoenix, Arizona about the mortgage crisis. The plan he announced focused "on rescuing families who've played by the rules and acted responsibly, by refinancing loans for millions of families in traditional mortgages who are underwater or close to it."[6] Although the president insisted that the plan would "not rescue the unscrupulous or irresponsible by throwing good taxpayer money after bad loans,"[7] Rick Santelli, reporting the next day from the floor of the Chicago Board of Trade for CNBC, engaged in a rant against Barack Obama's economic policies, against the newly announced housing bailout plan to help certain homeowners refinance mortgages and avoid foreclosure. The clip became viral and provoked intense reaction that broke along partisan lines:

> The government is promoting bad behavior. [...] How about this, President and new administration? Why don't you put up a website to have people vote on the Internet as a referendum to see if we really want to subsidize the losers' mortgages [...]. We're thinking of having a Chicago Tea Party in July.[8]

That particular event was widely regarded as the birth of the Tea Party movement, a movement consisting of conservative grassroots activists and Washington insiders who were angry in the aftermath of George W. Bush's financial bailout of Wall Street, who believed that the Republican president had betrayed libertarian principles by using government to save wealthy financial interests as well as homeowners from their own mistakes. But the new target was obviously President Obama himself. Some Tea Party activists were motivated by unhappiness about having an African American president, but most of them were simply furious that a liberal Democrat had been victorious over John McCain and Sarah Palin.

---

[6] Obama, Remarks by the President on the Mortgage Crisis, February 18, 2009, The White House, Office of the Press Secretary, https://obamawhitehouse.archives.gov/the-press-office/remarks-president-mortgage-crisis.

[7] Id.

[8] Eric Etheridge, "Rick Santelli: Tea Party Time," *New York Times*, February 20, 2009, https://opinionator.blogs.nytimes.com/2009/02/20/rick-santelli-tea-party-time.

The Tea Party, the first movement to take shape in the wake of the Great Recession, emerged as a conservative, populist branch of the Republican Party, one that opposed government spending, taxation, and regulation, and that had come together as a reaction to Barack Obama's stimulus package. Yet the president also resorted to a rhetoric that could be regarded as anti-Keynesian, as in his April 25, 2009, Weekly Address— "American families are tightening their belts and making hard choices. Now, Washington must show that same sense of responsibility"[9]—or in this remark reported by Michael Grunwald: "Look, I get the Keynesian thing. But it's not where the electorate is."[10] Barack Obama was certainly not into Keynesian politics. As Paul Krugman concluded in 2011, "the Obama administration [...] accepted the Republican claim that stimulus failed, and should never be tried again."[11] Krugman added that "everyone [was] drawing the wrong lesson. Fiscal policy didn't fail; it wasn't tried."[12]

On December 10, 2010, Bernie Sanders took the Senate floor in opposition to one of Barack Obama's policies—the extension of some of Bush's tax breaks for the wealthiest Americans. He began his speech at 10:30 a.m. and ended it eight and a half hours later. It was the longest filibuster on the Senate floor in many years. Sanders's bold gesture drew considerable attention nationwide. Michael Tomasky, editor in Chief of *Democracy*, a quarterly journal of progressive and liberal politics, who would later endorse Hillary Clinton in the 2016 presidential election, wrote as he watched:

> Independent Bernie Sanders of Vermont is not a Democrat but a socialist. However, he does caucus with the Democrats, and he has been mainly an Obama supporter. But there he is, as I write, finishing his fifth hour of filibustering the tax deal.
>
> I admire Sanders, and although I think the deal is pretty good, under the circumstances, and should pass, I do take my hat off to the guy. It's

---

[9] Obama, The President's Weekly Address, April 25, 2009, op. cit., p. 149.

[10] Michael Grunwald, *The New New Deal: The Hidden Story of Change in the Obama Era*, New York, Simon & Schuster, 2012, p. 338.

[11] Krugman, "The Great Abdication," *New York Times*, February 14, 2011, https://krugman.blogs.nytimes.com/2011/02/14/the-great-abdication.

[12] Ibid.

just nice to see someone taking a stand for the view that upper-income households don't need a tax cut [...].[13]

Four days earlier, on December 6, 2010, President Obama had announced a tentative deal with Congressional Republicans to extend the Bush-era tax cuts at all income levels for two years, including for wealthier families, as part of a package that would also renew unemployment benefits for another thirteen months and cut payroll taxes for all workers for a year.[14] In the introduction to the book edition of his entire filibuster speech by Nation Books a few months later, Sanders explained that one reason why he went to the Senate floor was clearly political:

> At a time when this country has a $13.8 trillion dollar national debt and the most unequal distribution of wealth and income of any major country, it seemed to me totally absurd to provide hundreds of billions in tax breaks for millionaires and billionaires. Further, by confirming—under a Democratic president, a Democratic House, and a Democratic Senate—the basic tenets of Bush's horrendous trickle-down economic theory, this agreement was laying the groundwork for more bad decisions in the future.[15]

The other reason was about redressing social and moral wrongs:

> Second, more tax breaks for the very rich is only one symptom of an economic and political system that is grotesquely failing the average American. [...] What does it mean, morally and economically, that in 2007 the top one percent earned over 23 percent of all income in this country, more than the bottom fifty percent? Or that the top one percent owns more wealth than the bottom 90 percent? Given the enormous political power that goes with this concentration of wealth, in terms of lobbying capabilities, campaign contributions, and media ownership, is the United

---

[13] Michael Tomasky, "The Significance of Bernie Sanders' Filibuster," *The Guardian*, December 10, 2010, https://www.theguardian.com/commentisfree/michaeltomasky/2010/dec/10/bernie-sanders-filibuster-tax-cuts.

[14] Obama, Statement by the President on Tax Cuts and Unemployment Benefits, December 6, 2010, The White House, Office of the Press Secretary, https://obamawhitehouse.archives.gov/the-press-office/2010/12/06/statement-president-tax-cuts-and-unemployment-benefits.

[15] Sanders, *The Speech: A Historic Filibuster on Corporate Greed and the Decline of Our Middle Class*, New York, Nation Books, 2011, p. 9.

States on its way to becoming an oligarchic form of society with almost all power resting in the hands of a tiny few?[16]

The rhetoric of the top 1% earning more than the bottom 90% was beginning to sink in and to be appropriated by public opinion as a counter-neoliberal response. As Sanders later put it in *Our Revolution*, "[m]y ideas were beginning to generate more interest."[17] It seemed as if the fuel of social discontent was now likely to ignite.

Less than a year later, "99%" became the simple and powerful slogan of the Occupy Wall Street movement, which emerged at the opposite end of the political spectrum from the Tea Party movement. Blair Taylor claimed that while "[t]he 'greed' of the economic '1%,' counterpoised to the hardworking, rule-abiding 99%," emerged as a dominant political frame, the slogan "conceal[ed] as much as it reveal[ed]" in that there was "confusion as to whether the current crisis [was] in fact the exception or the rule."[18] From Bernie Sanders's standpoint, the crisis was systemic and it was the rule. What was the exception was in fact the gathering of public opinion around the 99% slogan and the emergence of a social movement. Bernie Sanders had fought his entire political life against inequality in American society, following in the ideological footsteps of Debsian socialism and early twentieth-century reformers like Lincoln Steffens, and had been explicitly hammering against "the top one percent" at least since 2008 when he had opposed the bank bailouts in the final weeks of the Bush administration.[19] Something, however, changed radically in the context of the Obama administration: once the president had come under attack from the left for not moving aggressively against Wall Street, social discontent explicitly targeted the top 1%. The introspection and self-incrimination that underlay Lincoln Steffens's social consciousness in his 1904 *Shame of the Cities* were no longer on the plate.[20] Now was the time for agency. Now was the time to occupy Wall Street.

---

[16] Ibid.

[17] Sanders, *Our Revolution*, p. 47.

[18] Blair Taylor, "From Alterglobalization to Occupy Wall Street: Neoanarchism and the New Spirit of the Left," *City: Analysis of Urban Trends, Culture, Theory, Policy, Action*, vol. 17, n° 6, December 11, 2013, p. 742, http://dx.doi.org/10.1080/13604813.2013.849127.

[19] Sanders, "Wall Street Bailout," op. cit., p. 153.

[20] See *supra*, p. 51.

9.2   CONTENT AND FORM

On February 15, 2010, cyber activist and writer David DeGraw posted the first issue of a six-part series entitled "The Economic Elite vs. the People of the United States" on a website named AmpedStatus.com. The first line read: "It's time for 99% of Americans to mobilize and aggressively move on common sense political reforms."[21] When AmpedStatus came under a number of cyber-attacks and was mysteriously knocked offline, the Anonymous "hacktivist" group launched a new platform called A99. On March 23, 2011, A99 called for the occupation of Liberty Park (later named Zuccotti Park), two blocks from Wall Street, on June 14. The event soon fizzled out, but the organizers came together with another group, the New York City General Assembly, which had been opposing budget cuts in New York City, and started planning a new occupation for the fall. In this context, citing the success of the Egyptian demonstrations in Tahrir Square in January 2011, the Canadian Vancouver-based anti-capitalist website Adbusters issued a call to show up at Wall Street on September 17 and to "bring a tent."[22] Soon, a new website named "Occupy Wall Street" posted a simple slogan borrowed from David DeGraw's original AmpedStatus post, "We are the 99 percent that will no longer tolerate the greed and corruption of the 1 percent."[23] A thousand demonstrators showed up on September 17 and about three hundred ended up camping out on Zuccotti Park. It seemed that social discontent had found its detonator. Over the next month, the movement attracted thousands in New York and spread across the country while similar protests emerged in major cities, including Los Angeles, Chicago, Boston, and others.[24] Many protesters were college-educated young people (reducing or writing off student debts was a prominent demand) and also from veterans of past anti-globalization

---

[21] David DeGraw, "The Economic Elite vs. the People of the United States," Amped-Status, February 15–27, 2010, https://daviddegraw.org/the-economic-elite-vs-the-peo ple-%EF%BB%BF%EF%BB%BForiginal-99-movement-call-to-action.

[22] Sarah Van Gelder, *This Changes Everything: Occupy Wall Street and the 99% Movement*, San Francisco, CA, Berrett-Koehler, 2011, p. 1.

[23] Occupy Wall Street, http://occupywallst.org.

[24] Pew Research Center, "Occupy Wall Street Drives Economic Coverage," October 9, 2011, https://www.journalism.org/2011/10/09/pej-news-coverage-index-october-39-2011.

struggles, like the demonstrations in Seattle in 1999 against the World Trade Organization.[25]

The movement captured and occupied the attention of the nation. The Pew Research Center indicated that the news coverage of Occupy Wall Street amounted to roughly 7% of the overall newshole between October 3–9, 2011, nearly four times the amount of protest coverage from the week before.[26] Occupy Wall Street was speaking, and the nation was listening. The nation was listening to a movement whose focus was on lower Manhattan—Wall Street—as the location and symbol of power. The movement reintroduced words like "class" and "capitalism" into the political discourse and in political debates across the country. Issues that were typically regarded as marginal, if not extremist or even taboo, in mainstream politics, such as corporate greed, higher taxes on the wealthy, or capping the cost of higher education, were suddenly given central attention. One consequence of the Great Recession, therefore, was that the left (and arguably also the right through the Tea Party movement) was brought back to confronting financial and corporate elites as well as their increasing influence over elections in the United States, which, as Heather Gautney explains, provided a sort of echo chamber for Bernie Sanders's democratic socialism:

> The constituency for Bernie's rails against Wall Street and big money in politics was broadening thanks to Occupy Wall Street, especially after he filed a constitutional amendment to overturn *Citizens United* and filibustered on the Senate floor for nine hours after Obama cut a deal with the GOP to extend the Bush tax cuts.[27]

Social discontent literally exploded two years into the Obama administration. By October 5, 2011, most progressives—Bernie Sanders, major unions,[28] students, key Democrats, MoveOn.org, Democracy for

---

[25] John B. Judis, *The Populist Explosion: How the Great Recession Transformed American and European Politics*, New York, Columbia Global Reports, 2016, p. 61.

[26] Pew Research Center, "Occupy Wall Street Drives Economic Coverage," op. cit., p. 169.

[27] Gautney, p. 4.

[28] Steven Greenhouse, and Cara Buckley, "Seeking Energy, Unions Join Protest Against Wall Street," *New York Times*, October 5, 2011, https://www.nytimes.com/2011/10/06/nyregion/major-unions-join-occupy-wall-street-protest.html.

America, etc.—had already endorsed Occupy Wall Street while Obama still remained silent. On October 28, during an interview with Jake Tapper on ABC News, Barack Obama finally argued that he understood "the frustrations being expressed in those protests" and awkwardly remarked that Occupy Wall Street was not too different from the Tea Party movement: "In some ways, they're not that different from some of the protests that we saw coming from the Tea Party. Both on the left and the right, I think people feel separated from their government. They feel that their institutions aren't looking out for them."[29] In fact, Barack Obama's argument acknowledged, if not officialized, the importance of Occupy Wall Street, not only as a counterweight to the Tea Party movement but also as a significant political force per se. In the following weeks and months, Obama tried to embrace the Occupy vocabulary and to add his own spin to it. On December 6, 2011, in Osawatomie, Kansas, the president said: "Look at the statistics. In the last few decades, the average income of the top 1% has gone up by more than 250% to $1.2 million per year. I'm not talking about millionaires, people who have a million dollars. I'm saying people who make a million dollars every single year."[30] In the same speech, Obama also tried to blend the Occupy lexicon into his own 2004 "red states and blue states"[31] rhetoric: "These aren't Democratic values or Republican values. These aren't 1% values or 99% values. They're American values. And we have to reclaim them."[32] Obama's attempts to appropriate the rhetoric of Occupy were hardly successful. Occupy Wall Street's message was hitting home. In January 2012, a Pew Research Center survey indicated that about two-thirds of the public (66%) believed there were "very strong" or "strong" conflicts between the rich and the poor (a 19% increase since 2009), and that three-in-ten Americans (30%) said there were "very strong conflicts"

---

[29] Devin Dwyer, "Obama: Occupy Wall Street 'Not That Different' From Tea Party Protests," *ABC News*, October 18, 2011, https://abcnews.go.com/blogs/politics/2011/10/obama-occupy-wall-street-not-that-different-from-tea-party-protests.

[30] Obama, "Remarks by the President on the Economy in Osawatomie, Kansas," December 6, 2011, The White House, Office of the Press Secretary, https://obamawhitehouse.archives.gov/the-press-office/2011/12/06/remarks-president-economy-osawatomie-kansas.

[31] Id., Address at the 2004 Democratic National Convention, op. cit., p. 147.

[32] Id., Remarks by the President on the Economy in Osawatomie, Kansas, op. cit., p. 170.

between poor people and rich people.[33] As Todd Gitlin put it in *Occupy Nation*, "[u]nlike any other movement on the American left in at least three-quarters of a century, this movement began with a majority base of support. [...] What it stood for—economic justice and curbs on the wealthy—was popular."[34]

The Occupy Wall Street community was extremely diverse and tended to be interconnected by logistics and organization more than it was by ideology or by a clear or definite political agenda. Anna Szolucha saw Occupy's "non-hierarchical ways" and rejection of any set blueprint for "grand social change" as intrinsic openness to the diversity of the 99% but also to what direct democracy is all about.[35] Occupy Wall Street was highly significant in that the movement questioned the viability of people's "blind attachment to representative, party democracy."[36] Yet Occupy's non-hierarchical ways and rejection of any blueprint for grand social change were eventually also obstacles to the further development of the movement. By practicing direct democracy, Occupy Wall Street revealed the hidden complexity and essentially ambiguous nature of all concepts of democracy.[37] Szolucha compared Occupy Wall Street to Jacques Derrida's "democracy-to-come," which, in Derridean thinking, was not simply a regulative idea but involved an urgent task that people "inherit as a promise."[38] In the words of Derrida:

> At stake here is the very concept of democracy as concept of a promise that can only arise in such a *diastema* (failure, inadequation, disjunction, disadjustment, being 'out of joint'). That is why we always propose to speak of a democracy *to come*, not of a *future* democracy in the future

---

[33] Pew Research Center, "Rising Share of Americans See Conflict Between Rich and Poor," January 11, 2012, https://www.pewsocialtrends.org/2012/01/11/rising-share-of-americans-see-conflict-between-rich-and-poor.

[34] Todd Gitlin, *Occupy Nation: The Roots, the Spirit, and the Promise of Occupy Wall Street*, New York, It Books, 2012, p. 33.

[35] Anna Szolucha, *Real Democracy in the Occupy Movement: No Stable Ground*, New York, Routledge, 2017, p. 170.

[36] Ibid., p. 174.

[37] Id.

[38] Ibid., p. 170.

present, not even of a regulating idea, in the Kantian sense, or of a utopia [...].[39]

In the forming of "a more Perfect Union,"[40] the U.S. Constitution postulates the perpetual perfectibility of democracy, and Martin Luther King Jr.'s resounding calls for "the fierce urgency of now"[41] also fit under the philosophical umbrella of Derrida's "democracy-to-come," as well as Barack Obama's frequent use of "the fierce urgency of now" motif during his campaign for the 2008 presidential election.[42] However, should democracy abdicate its own ideals, should "democracy-to-come" be perpetually deferred, should inequality no longer be the exception but the rule, then democratic ideals arguably become utopia.

In his 2013 study of the shift from alterglobalization to Occupy Wall Street, Blair Taylor pointed out to a conflation of form and content, a fusion of means and ends, in the Occupy movement, by which form became content, by which political goals became synonymous with and indistinguishable from movement form.[43] The fusion of form and content, Taylor wrote, circumvented the need for ideology as well as the sectarianism and squabbles it entailed:

> In the early days of OWS, discussion of contentious political questions had already proven to immediately shatter any consensus among the 99%, which further incentivized the reduction of politics to tactics. Thus the importance of maintaining the self-organized encampments: they neatly fill this ideological vacuum and suspend the need for further discussion; form—and the continuous demands of householding—stands in for and evacuates political content. Listening to the general assemblies held in Zuccotti Park, one hears little discussion of political vision, policy measures, the feasibility of socialism in one country or even the Tobin Tax. Instead, most discussion centers on the logistics of maintaining the

---

[39] Jacques Derrida, Spe*cters of Marx: The State of the Debt, the Work of Mourning and the New International*, New York, Routledge, 2006, p. 81. Ibid., p. 171.

[40] U.S. Constitution, op. cit., p. 61.

[41] King, op. cit., p. 147.

[42] Obama, *op. cit*, p. 147.

[43] Taylor, "From Alterglobalization to Occupy Wall Street," p. 739.

occupation: feeding people, noise issues [...], keeping warm and sleeping arrangements.[44]

What Taylor described as a conflation of form and content also had to do with what utopia entails more generally. Nineteenth- and twentieth-century utopian communities, for example, already distinctively conflated content and form. Living in a commune was an experiment in an alternative model, therefore in social disruption. From that angle, a historical and cultural icon like the American dream can also be regarded as the conflation of form and content. The American dream is in fact a dream of America, a utopia. Beyond that, the content escapes all form of consensus. If, as Taylor argues, conflating content and form makes it possible to "circumvent the need for ideology,"[45] then a form is always likely to be emptied of its ideological content.

9.3   NEOANARCHISM

In political terms, Occupy Wall Street made a breakthrough when the leaders of the Congressional Progressive Caucus,[46] which Bernie Sanders had co-founded, and also the Congressional Black Caucus, joined Sanders in endorsing the movement on October 5, 2011.[47] Jimmy Hoffa, the general president of the Teamsters Union,[48] also supported the movement:

> No one should be surprised that Occupy Wall Street is gaining support and spreading quickly around the country. The American Dream has

---

[44] Ibid.

[45] Ibid.

[46] See *supra*, p. 81.

[47] John Nichols, "Occupy Wall Street: Bernie Sanders, Progressives, Big Unions Endorse; Obama's Silent," *Nation*, October 5, 2011, https://www.thenation.com/art icle/archive/politics-occupy-wall-street-bernie-sanders-progressives-big-unions-endorse-obamas-silent.

[48] The International Brotherhood of Teamsters was founded in 1903 by the merger of The Team Drivers International Union and The Teamsters National Union. It now represents a diverse membership of blue-collar and professional workers in both the public and private sectors.

disappeared for students, whose reality is debt and unemployment. The dream disappeared for workers forced to take wage cuts by employers sitting on billions of dollars in profits. The dream disappeared for working families who paid too steep a price for Wall Street's greed, stupidity and fraud. [...] We stand in solidarity with Americans who want better lives for themselves and for future generations.[49]

Bernie Sanders was even more explicit:

We have the crooks on Wall Street, and I use that word advisedly—don't misquote me, the word is 'crooks'—whose greed, whose recklessness, whose illegal behavior caused this terrible recession with so much suffering. We believe in this country; we love this country; and we will be damned if we're going to see a handful of robber barons control the future of this country. [...] I applaud those protesters who are out there, who are focusing attention on Wall Street, but what we've got to do is put meat on that bone. We've got to make demands on Wall Street [and] break those institutions up.[50]

Sanders's rhetoric clearly advocated for the redress of wrongs perpetrated by those whom he called "robber barons," a reference to prominent businessmen in the late nineteenth century who made fortunes through ruthless and unscrupulous business practices. Occupy Wall Street was a *protest* movement that had made a political breakthrough but it was not a *political* movement, and Sanders "knew that a progressive agenda could never be implemented without the efforts of a strong and successful political movement."[51] Hence his intention to "put meat on that bone." Another question, beyond "mak[ing] demands on Wall Street," resided in Sanders's apparent intention "to break those institutions up," which resonated with what many organizers, but few participants of the Occupy

---

[49] James P. Hoffa, "Hoffa Says Teamsters Stand with Occupy Wall Street Movement," Teamsters.org, October 5, 2011, https://teamster.org/blog/2015/11/breaking-hoffa-says-teamsters-stand-occupy-wall-street-movement-0.

[50] Sanders, *Outsider in the White House*, p. 332.

[51] Ibid., op. cit., p. 80.

Wall Street movement, seemed to want. As Mark Bray remarked in *Translating Anarchy*, "while most Occupy participants wanted to reform capitalism, most organizers wanted to destroy it (78% were anti-capitalist)."[52] For Alexandre Carvalho, an anarchist Occupy Wall Street organizer:

> Capital is directly and indirectly responsible for the violent dehumanization of people. Its violence is political, economic, physical, moral. It is a violence that extracts and steals time from people, robs us of space; it coerces and forces people to produce, consume or die. Capital is the ultimate mechanism for mass dehumanization.[53]

Anarchism and the desire to destroy capitalism were inherent to the organization of the movement.

Blair Taylor defined neoanarchism as "an attempt to revive the revolutionary project in the wake of the authoritarian legacy of twentieth-century Marxism, while addressing the expanded terrains of power and struggle initiated by the New Left."[54] There were strong anarchist currents in the New Left of the 1960s, even stronger than the socialist current, according to Todd Gitlin, in spite of all the efforts made by Marxists to organize the student movement in class categories.[55] Gitlin explained that participatory democracy, "a phrase that Students for a Democratic Society originally used for a system of self-government both as an end-goal and as a means to achieve it,"[56] also conflated content and form.[57] Occupy Wall Street was a happening that impersonated an alternative to the status quo through the occupation of space.[58] Hence, for example, the endless general assemblies where every participant had a chance to talk, where frustration was also frequent because of perceptions of inefficiency. Occupy would probably have needed to "move on," which

[52] Mark Bray, *Translating Anarchy: The Anarchism of Occupy Wall Street*, Winchester, Zero Books, 2013, p. 4.

[53] Ibid., p. 60.

[54] Taylor, "From Alterglobalization to Occupy Wall Street," p. 734.

[55] Gitlin, p. 81.

[56] Gitlin, *op. cit.*, p. 171.

[57] Taylor, op. cit., p. 167.

[58] Marco Briziarelli, and Susana Martinez Guillem, "The Counter-Hegemonic Spectacle of Occupy Wall Street: Integral State and Integral Struggle," *Revista Científica de Información y Comunicación*, 2014, p. 151.

was incidentally the name of the MoveOn community, "a force social justice and political progress" formed in 1998.[59] In March 2012, Jeffrey Juris, an associate professor of anthropology at Northeastern University, warned about the danger inherent to the fetishization of occupation: "It's critical to broaden tactics," he said. "But how do you do that when the movement is called Occupy?"[60] That limitation largely contributed to the short lifespan of the mobilization. Another limitation that had to do with the inherent anarchism of the movement was the absence of leadership. Cornel West addressed this issue in the *Occupied Wall Street Journal* of November 18, 2011:

> Our movement—leaderless and leaderful—is a soulful expression of a moral outrage at the ugly corporate greed that pushes our society and world to the brink of catastrophe. [...] We refuse to be mere echoes of the vicious lies that support an illegitimate status quo. Our deep democratic awakening takes the form of we everyday people raising our individual and collective voices to tell the painful truths about unjust systems and unfair structures that yield unnecessary social misery.[61]
>
> Distrust of outside authority was dominant. As Gitlin put it in *Occupy Nation*: "Demands conferred legitimacy on the authorities. Demand-lessness, in other words, was the movement's culture, its identity."[62] "Demandlessness" did not mean that no demands were ever voiced, but that the state was not envisioned as a plausible interlocutor, or as the likely recipient of progressive demands.

Occupy's distrust of outside authority and characteristic "demandless-ness" seem at odds with Gramsci's conception of the role of the state: "In politics the error occurs as a result of an inaccurate understanding of what the State (in its integral meaning: dictatorship+hegemony) really

---

[59] "What is MoveOn?" MoveOn.org, https://front.moveon.org/about.

[60] Jennifer Schuessler, "Academia Occupied by Occupy," *New York Times*, April 30, 2012, https://www.nytimes.com/2012/05/01/books/academia-becomes-occupied-with-occupy-movement.html.

[61] West, "A Love Supreme," *The Occupied Wall Street Journal*, November 18, 2011, p. 1.

[62] Gitlin, p. 110.

is."[63] For Gramsci, only "an integral state" possesses "all the intellectual and moral forces [...] needed to organize and perfect society."[64] The anarchism inherent to the Occupy Wall Street seemingly placed it in a position from which, from a Gramscian perspective, constructing a counter-hegemony would be impossible:

> In the modern world, a party is such integrally, and not, as happens, a fraction of a larger party—when it is conceived, organized and led in ways and in forms such that it will develop integrally into a State (an integral State, and not into a government technically understood) and into a conception of the world.[65]

Occupy Wall Street was not only a leaderless movement, it was also structureless since the state was apprehended as an antagonistic model of structuration. While neoliberal ideology seeks to represent the state as a neutral observer that guarantees the self-corrective mechanism of the market, most leftist reform movements claim that the state typically operates to preserve and defend the interests of the dominant group or class. Then, if the Gramscian "integral State" was technically the ally of capital and corporate greed, then the advent of a counter-hegemony de facto required confronting it, confronting the "integral State." The 99% slogan may be regarded as a missed opportunity to appeal to the people's "good sense" to radically transform the hegemonic "common sense" (*senso comune*).[66] Transient progress was achieved, as testified by public opinion polls,[67] but without radically transforming society: economic inequality was not erased, nor was the functioning of Wall Street even disrupted. Gramsci defined hegemony as the combination of force and consent. Earning the consent of the people, even ideally uniting 99% of the people, was unlikely to bring about a new hegemonic order without engaging the "integral State," without translating the people's "good sense" into the political power to reform the state.

---

[63] Gramsci, p. 239.

[64] Ibid., p. 271.

[65] Ibid., p. 267.

[66] See *supra*, p. 139.

[67] Pew Research Center, "Rising Share of Americans See Conflict Between Rich and Poor," op. cit., p. 171.

The Occupy Wall Street movement was highly significant in that its success lay in the symbolic order. It was the detonator that propelled Bernie Sanders to boldly run in the 2016 presidential election. Sanders sought to engage the "integral State," to translate the people's "good sense" into the political power to reform the government. Occupy was a brief detonator of social discontent whose fire Bernie Sanders seized. While Occupy Wall Street was a protest movement that aimed to change American society without taking power, Sanders aimed to take power to change American society in the wake of Occupy Wall Street. On January 21, 2016, in issue zero of the newly launched *International Times*, Marisa Holmes published an article entitled "Bernie Sanders swallows Occupy's microphone" to discuss his presidential run:

> Bernie Sanders is running for president. He talks a good game, and, just like De Blasio, he uses the rhetoric of OWS in his speeches. In his announcement that he was running he stated, "Let me be very clear. There is something profoundly wrong when the top one-tenth of 1 percent owns almost as much wealth as the bottom 90 percent, and when 99 percent of all new income goes to the top 1 percent."[68]

Bernie Sanders's 2016 presidential run was in fact Act Two of the movement that had started in Zuccotti Park, New York City, five years earlier. Sanders was to engage the American utopia to which every American was entitled but that seemed to have been perpetually deferred. At that point, utopian radicalism was being upended by demands for state and corporate accountability.

References

Bray, Mark. *Translating Anarchy: The Anarchism of Occupy Wall Street*. Winchester: Zero Books, 2013.
Briziarelli, Marco, and Susana Martinez Guillem. "The Counter-Hegemonic Spectacle of Occupy Wall Street: Integral State and Integral Struggle." *Revista Científica de Información y Comunicación* (2014), pp. 145–166, https://idus.us.es/bitstream/handle/11441/33199/The%20Counter-Hegemonic%20Spectacle%20of%20Occupy%20Wall%20Street.pdf.

---

[68] Marisa Holmes, "Mic Check! Bernie Sanders Swallows Occupy's Microphone," *International Times: The Newspaper of Resistance*, January 21, 2016, http://internationaltimes.it/mic-check-bernie-sanders-swallows-occupys-microphone.

Degraw, David. "The Economic Elite vs. the People of the United States." AmpedStatus.com (February 15–27, 2010), https://daviddegraw.org/the-economic-elite-vs-the-people-%EF%BB%BF%EF%BB%BForiginal-99-movement-call-to-action.

Derrida, Jacques. *Specters of Marx: The State of the Debt, the Work of Mourning and the New International.* New York: Routledge, 2006.

Dwyer, Devin. "Obama: Occupy Wall Street 'Not That Different' from Tea Party Protests." *ABC News* (October 18, 2011), https://abcnews.go.com/blogs/politics/2011/10/obama-occupy-wall-street-not-that-different-from-tea-party-protests.

Etheridge, Eric. "Rick Santelli: Tea Party Time." *New York Times* (February 20, 2009), https://opinionator.blogs.nytimes.com/2009/02/20/rick-santelli-tea-party-time.

Gitlin, Todd. *Occupy Nation: The Roots, the Spirit, and the Promise of Occupy Wall Street.* New York: It Books, 2012.

Gramsci, Antonio. *Selections from the Prison Notebooks of Antonio Gramsci,* edited and translated by Quintin Hoare and Geoffrey N. Smith. New York: International Publishers, 1971.

Greenhouse, Steven, and Cara Buckley. "Seeking Energy, Unions Join Protest Against Wall Street." *New York Times* (October 5, 2011), https://www.nytimes.com/2011/10/06/nyregion/major-unions-join-occupy-wall-street-protest.html.

Grunwald, Michael. *The New New Deal: The Hidden Story of Change in the Obama Era.* New York, Simon & Schuster, 2012.

Hoffa, James P. Hoffa. "Hoffa Says Teamsters Stand with Occupy Wall Street Movement." Teamsters.org (October 5, 2011), https://teamster.org/blog/2015/11/breaking-hoffa-says-teamsters-stand-occupy-wall-street-movement-0.

Holmes, Marisa. "Mic Check! Bernie Sanders Swallows Occupy's Microphone." *International Times: The Newspaper of Resistance* (January 21, 2016), http://internationaltimes.it/mic-check-bernie-sanders-swallows-occupys-microphone.

Judis, John B. *The Populist Explosion: How the Great Recession Transformed American and European Politics.* New York: Columbia Global Reports, 2016.

King, Martin Luther Jr. "I Have a Dream." Address delivered at the March on Washington for Jobs and Freedom (August 28, 1963). The Martin Luther King Jr. Research and Education Institute (Stanford University), https://kinginstitute.stanford.edu/king-papers/documents/i-have-dream-address-delivered-march-washington-jobs-and-freedom.

Krugman, Paul. "The Great Abdication." *New York Times* (February 14, 2011), https://krugman.blogs.nytimes.com/2011/02/14/the-great-abdication.

Nichols, John. "Occupy Wall Street: Bernie Sanders, Progressives, Big Unions Endorse; Obama's Silent." *Nation* (October 5, 2011), https://www.thenat ion.com/article/archive/politics-occupy-wall-street-bernie-sanders-progressi ves-big-unions-endorse-obamas-silent.

Obama, Barack H. Obama. Address at the 2004 Democratic National Convention (July 27, 2004). The American Presidency Project, https://www.presid ency.ucsb.edu/node/277378.

———. Remarks in Des Moines, Iowa (December 19, 2007). The American Presidency Project, https://www.presidency.ucsb.edu/node/277494.

———. Remarks by the President on the Mortgage Crisis (February 18, 2009). The White House, Office of the Press Secretary, https://obamawhitehouse. archives.gov/the-press-office/remarks-president-mortgage-crisis.

———. Statement by the President on Tax Cuts and Unemployment Benefits (December 6, 2010), The White House, Office of the Press Secretary, https://obamawhitehouse.archives.gov/the-press-office/2010/12/06/ statement-president-tax-cuts-and-unemployment-benefits.

———. Remarks by the President on the Economy in Osawatomie, Kansas (December 6, 2011), The White House, Office of the Press Secretary, https://obamawhitehouse.archives.gov/the-press-office/2011/12/06/ remarks-president-economy-osawatomie-kansas.

Reagan, Ronald W. Inaugural Address (January 20, 1981). The American Presidency Project, https://www.presidency.ucsb.edu/node/246336.

Rockwell, Llewellyn H. Jr. "Obama and the Economy." Mises Institute (August 6, 2009), https://mises.org/print/5661.

Sanders, Bernard, with Huck Gutman. *Outsider in the House: A Political Autobiography*. New York: Verso, 1997. Rpt. *Outsider in the White House*, 2015.

———. "Wall Street Bailout." U.S. Senator for Vermont website (October 1, 2008), https://www.sanders.senate.gov/newsroom/press-releases/2008/ 10/01/wall-street-bailout.

———. *The Speech: A Historic Filibuster on Corporate Greed and the Decline of Our Middle Class*. New York: Nation Books, 2011.

———. *Our Revolution: A Future to Believe In*. New York: Thomas Dunne Books, 2016.

Schuessler, Jennifer. "Academia Occupied by Occupy." *New York Times* (April 30, 2012), https://www.nytimes.com/2012/05/01/books/academia-bec omes-occupied-with-occupy-movement.html.

Shlaes, Amity. *The Forgotten Man: A New History of the Great Depression*. New York: Harper Collins, 2007.

Szolucha, Anna. *Real Democracy in the Occupy Movement: No Stable Ground*. New York: Routledge, 2017.

Taylor, Blair. "From Alterglobalization to Occupy Wall Street: Neoanarchism and the New Spirit of the Left." *City: Analysis of Urban Trends, Culture, Theory, Policy, Action*, vol. 17, n° 6 (December 11, 2013), pp. 729–747, http://dx. doi.org/10.1080/13604813.2013.849127.

Tomasky, Michael. "The Significance of Bernie Sanders' Filibuster." *The Guardian* (December 10, 2010), https://www.theguardian.com/commentis free/michaeltomasky/2010/dec/10/bernie-sanders-filibuster-tax-cuts.

Van Gelder, Sarah. *This Changes Everything: Occupy Wall Street and the 99% Movement*. San Francisco, CA: Berrett-Koehler, 2011.

West, Cornel. "A Love Supreme." *The Occupied Wall Street Journal* (November 18, 2011), p. 1.

PART IV

Democratic Socialism as Reparative Justice

CHAPTER 10

Enduring Injustice

Representative Alexandria Ocasio-Cortez (D-NY), who gained national recognition by winning the Democratic Party's primary election for New York's 14th Congressional district on June 26, 2018,[1] defeating Joseph Crowley, the fourth-ranking Democrat in Congress, and who was among the first female members of the Democratic Socialists of America elected to serve in Congress, worked as an organizer during the primary for Bernie Sanders's 2016 presidential campaign. Just forty-eight hours after leaping into the national spotlight, Alexandria Ocasio-Cortez was interviewed by Stephen Colbert on "The Late Show," and asked what democratic socialism meant for her, to which she answered: "So, for me, Democratic Socialism is about—really the value for me is that I believe that in a modern, moral and wealthy society, no person in America should be too poor to live. That's what I feel."[2] Ocasio-Cortez added that it meant "every child, no matter where you are born, should have access to a college or trade-school education, if they so choose it," and that "no person should be homeless, if we can have public structures and public

---

[1] "N.Y. District 14 Race," November 6, 2018, Our Campaigns, https://www.ourcampaigns.com/RaceDetail.html?RaceID=832978.

[2] Giovanni Russonello, "Ocasio-Cortez Tells Colbert: 'We Changed Who Turns Out,'" *New York Times*, June 29, 2018, https://www.nytimes.com/2018/06/29/arts/television/alexandria-ocasio-cortez-interview-stephen-colbert.html.

© The Author(s), under exclusive license to Springer Nature   187
Switzerland AG 2021
N. Gachon, *Bernie Sanders's Democratic Socialism*,
https://doi.org/10.1007/978-3-030-69661-0_10

policy to allow for people to have homes and food and lead a digni-
fied life in the United States."[3] Ocasio-Cortez was building on Bernie
Sanders's conception of "a modern, moral and wealthy society," which
he had exposed in previous speeches like in this address he gave before
12,000 students at Liberty University on September 14, 2015: "Now,
when we talk about morality, and when we talk about justice, we have to,
in my view, understand that there is no justice when so few have so much
and so many have so little." As of 2015, however, Sanders's rhetoric had
evolved from denouncing the excesses of capitalism and corporate greed
to one that held the American idea accountable for allowing enduring
injustice:

> There is no justice, and I want you to hear this clearly, when the top one-
> tenth of 1 percent—not 1 percent, the top one-tenth of 1 percent—today
> in America owns almost as much wealth as the bottom 90 percent. And
> in your hearts, you will have to determine the morality of that, and the
> justice of that.[4]

Bernie Sanders's democratic socialism had evolved into a plea for
economic reparative justice.

10.1   Historicism and Collective Memory

In a chapter to *Street Politics in the Age of Austerity: From the Indignados to Occupy*, Jackie Smith argued that one major shortcoming of
Occupy Wall Street was its lack of a sense of history and of a connection to existing movements in the United States and abroad, even while
participants were responding to the same economic and political pressures that motivated other movements. Most importantly, Smith added,
this lack of historical and global perspective made it hard for Occupy Wall
Street to bridge the racial and class hierarchies that divide people and

---

[3] Ibid.
[4] Sanders, *Our Revolution*, p. 151.

movements in the United States.[5] In *Enduring Injustice*, Jeff Spinner-Halev argued that "the pedigree" of an injustice does indeed matter and that it helps define "enduring" injustice. Contrary to historical injustice, "[e]nduring injustice has roots in the past, and continues into the present day; an enduring injustice endures over time and over space as well."[6] All enduring injustices are also historical injustices, but not all historical injustices are enduring injustices. What makes an injustice enduring is notably how difficult it is to repair. History is often linked to responsibility in terms of repairing injustices, but many enduring injustices remain beyond repair. Instead of looking at history as a way to assign responsibility, Spinner-Halev suggested using history to understand why the injustice persists, which leads very quickly to issues of collective memory, which Spinner-Halev also called "collective narrative."[7] Injustice lies at the core of Bernie Sanders's rhetoric and political message, as in this speech at Liberty University on September 14, 2015: "In the United States of America today, there is massive injustice in terms of income and wealth inequality. Injustice is rampant."[8] Beyond, Sanders acknowledged that the intention behind his 2016 presidential campaign was not simply to elect a president of the United States, that the campaign was about "transforming America," by which he meant building a sense of collective memory:

> That's what the history of the trade union movement is about. That's what the history of the women's movement is about. That's what the history of the civil rights movement is about. That's what the history of the gay rights movement is about. That's what the history of the environmental movement is about. That's what any serious movement for justice is about. That's what the political revolution is about.[9]

---

[5] Jackie Smith, "Social Movements and Political Moments: Reflections on the Intersections of Global Justice Movements & Occupy Wall Street," *Street Politics in the Age of Austerity: From the Indignados to Occupy*, edited by Marcos Ancelovici, Pascale Dufour, and Héloïse Nez, Amsterdam, Amsterdam University Press, 2016, p. 206.

[6] Jeff Spinner-Halev, *Enduring Injustice*, Cambridge, Cambridge University Press, 2012, p. 56.

[7] Ibid., p. 57.

[8] Sanders, *Our Revolution*, p. 150.

[9] Ibid., p. 4.

In other words, to use Jackie Smith's argument again, for lack of a historical perspective, Occupy Wall Street participants were rebels without a definite cause, hence the movement's almost necessary conflation of form and content.[10] Building on the Occupy Wall Street movement, however, Bernie Sanders sought to place present-day injustices in historical perspective, as when he concluded his speech to Liberty University students in September 2015:

> Throughout human history, there has been endless discussion. It is part of who we are as human beings, people who think and ask questions, endless discussion and debate about the meaning of justice and about the meaning of morality. […] I would hope, and I conclude with this thought, I would hope very much that as part of that discussion and part of that learning process, some of you will conclude that if we are honest in striving to be a moral and just society, it is imperative that we have the courage to stand with the poor, to stand with working people and when necessary, take on very powerful and wealthy people whose greed, in my view, is doing this country enormous harm.[11]

What Sanders referred to as a "learning process" was not unlike Spinner-Halev's intellectual approach to injustice, whose aim is "to call attention to the way in which we should begin with present injustices, trace them backward and then project them forward."[12] As the introduction to Sanders's *Our Revolution* reads: "This book describes the history-making campaign that we ran. But more important, it looks to the future. It lays out a new path for America based on principles of economic, social, racial, and environmental justice."[13] Historicism was therefore central to Sanders's democratic socialism. It was the learning path in a learning process.

Jeff Spinner-Halev made a strong statement in claiming that "[t]ying past injustices to present injustices, however, does not say how things would have been different."[14] Our argument here is that utopia precisely

---

[10] See *supra*, p. 172.

[11] Sanders, *Our Revolution*, p. 152.

[12] Spinner-Halev, p. 56.

[13] Sanders, *Our Revolution*, p. 4.

[14] Spinner-Halev, p. 59.

plays that function, telling or showing how things could be different, literally envisioning an alternative course or future for society. This is what
turn-of-the-twentieth-century utopian radicalism was all about. Edward
Bellamy retrospectively "looked backward" from the future while Lincoln
Steffens "saw" a future that worked.[15] Bernie Sanders is extremely wary
in using the term "utopia." In *Our Revolution*, he referred to the years
between 1947 and 1973, a period when "the rich were doing well, the
middle class was expanding, and fewer people were living in poverty,"[16]
an argument that may sound contradictory with Sanders's classic—historicized—argument of enduring economic injustice in the United States. In
this instance, Sanders was in fact describing the post-New Deal society,
which he saw as a model to be carried to completion,[17] but immediately
stepped back from claiming that those years were a utopian time:

> Look, I am not suggesting it was a utopian time. There were also great
> struggles. [...] No, it was certainly not a utopian time. But it was a time
> of enormous economic growth, and while there was income and wealth
> inequality, the benefits of the economy were far more equitably shared
> with the working families that made up the broad middle.[18]

As a presidential candidate, and in both *Our Revolution* (2016) and *Where
We Go from Here* (2018), Sanders almost systematically distanced himself
from the word "utopia" and its potentially negative charge:

> [*Our Revolution*] Our goal should be to cut U.S. carbon pollution by at
> least 40 percent by 2030 and 80 percent by 2050, compared with where
> we were in 1990. These are not some unachievable, utopian goals. We can
> make it happen [...].[19]
> [*Where We Go from Here*] A full-employment economy is not some
> wild utopian proposal. The truth is that in this country today there is an
> enormous amount of work to be done.[20]

---

[15] See *supra*, pp. 46, p. 50.

[16] Sanders, *Our Revolution*, p. 209.

[17] Sanders, "Sanders Calls For 21st Century Bill of Rights," op. cit., p. 65.

[18] Id., *Our Revolution*, pp. 209–210.

[19] Ibid., p. 364.

[20] Sanders, *Where We Go from Here*, p. 260.

Utopianism could not transcend the Occupy Wall Street dynamic and would most certainly be perceived as a badge of inefficiency in a society which called for "the fierce urgency of now" after Barack Obama's unachieved promise.[21] Radical utopianism was now a potential liability. In *Radical Utopianism and Cultural Studies: On Refusing to be Realistic,* John Storey defined radical utopianism in these terms:

> Radical utopianism allows us to dare to dream that the way things are is not inevitable—that is, a world arranged in the interest of the powerful few. It broadens our vision of the world and opens up new ways of seeing. As the familiar is defamiliarized, what we learned to think of as immutable suddenly looks changeable and the capitalist dogma *There Is No Alternative* can begin to give way to the enabling slogan *Another World Is Possible.* It allows us to anticipate the possibility of a world in which the words of Percy Bysshe Shelley, to slightly misquote them, have a revolutionary insistence: "We are many, they are few."
>
> Radical utopianism seeks to free imagination from the limits placed on it by a society run in the interests of the powerful few and to know that these limits are *historical.* While we seem able to see the past as historical and the future as history waiting to happen, the present seems outside history: in a word, "natural." Radical utopianism makes the present historical.[22]

Bernie Sanders sought to demonstrate that the limits were "enduring"[23] rather than "historical," but there is no fundamental contradiction between Sanders's posture and Storey's arguments that radical utopianism "makes the present historical," which could even be assimilated to "the fierce urgency of now."[24] This explains why Bernie Sanders's posture regarding was sometimes perceived as ambivalent, if not hesitant, in the wake of the Occupy Wall Street movement. With Occupy, social discontent detonated in the present. Sanders did not explicitly discard utopianism per se, but he now sought to hold utopianism accountable in

---

[21] Obama, Remarks in Des Moines, Iowa, December 19, 2007, op. cit., p. 147.

[22] John Storey, *Radical Utopianism and Cultural Studies: On Refusing to be Realistic,* New York, Routledge, 2019, p. xi–xii.

[23] Spinner-Halev, op. cit., p. 184.

[24] Luther King Jr., "I Have a Dream," op. cit., p. 147.

the present, if only to fend off attacks on his credibility, as when Ivanka Trump was reported to admire the "utopian" Bernie Sanders.[25]

Jeff Spinner-Halev raised another significant issue pertaining to historicism and collective memory. He expressed his skepticism about the idea that a group can "acquire memories" but conceded that "people can and do identify with a collective past."[26] Collective narratives are extremely important in shaping identities, both individual and collective. Belonging to a group situates people in the world, gives them a point of reference. The corollary, as Spinner-Halev wrote, is that "to call a group a victim of enduring injustice is to render a judgment that the group has a collective narrative that dominates other narratives" and also that "there is good reason to think the group will continue to feel the effects of the injustice without some change of course."[27] Spinner-Halev was primarily interested in the cases of African and Native Americans but extended his reflection to the case of workers to argue that "[c]lass lines are often permeable" and to wonder whether workers can really be said to be victims of injustice:

> Some certainly are, but others may not be; if their wages, benefits, and working hours are reasonable, then it may be hard to call them victims of injustice. Further, if they are victims of injustice, it is not clear if they view themselves as an intergenerational group with a collective narrative.[28]

We believe that this was precisely the function of Bernie Sanders's "democratic socialism," a doctrine that resisted definition because it brought a number of utopian, radical, if not subversive overtones into the political mainstream to try to historicize economic injustice and to federate an intergenerational group: "On behalf of our children and grandchildren, it is a path that must be followed and a fight that must be won. The struggle continues [...]," [29] Sanders wrote in *Our Revolution*, and "[u]nless we change the trajectory of our economy, the country's younger

[25] Ana Veciana-Suarez, "Who, Exactly, Is Ivanka Trump? We're Just Scratching Our Heads for Now," *Miami Herald*, May 2, 2017, https://www.miamiherald.com/living/liv-columns-blogs/ana-veciana-suarez/article148013744.html.

[26] Spinner-Halev, p. 60.

[27] Ibid., p. 63.

[28] Id.

[29] Sanders, *Our Revolution*, p. 4.

generation will be the first in modern history to have a lower standard of living than their parents."[30] Bernie Sanders himself acknowledged this effort to create an intergenerational dynamic. In the introduction to *Our Revolution*, he mentioned a poll conducted by the Harvard Institute of Politics that was reported by the *Washington Post* on April 25, 2016:

> "The data, collected by researchers at Harvard University, suggest that not only has Sanders's campaign made for an unexpectedly competitive Democratic primary, he has also changed the way millennials think about politics," said polling director John Della Volpe. "He's not moving a party to the left. He's moving a generation to the left," Della Volpe said of the senator from Vermont. "Whether or not he's winning or losing, it's really that he's impacting the way in which a generation—the largest generation in the history of America—thinks about politics."[31]

Economic inequality, class warfare, exploitation, corruption, etc. had always underlain socialism. But now, in the wake of the Occupy Wall Street movement and as Bernie Sanders was about to launch his first presidential campaign, the keyword was *accountability*:

> Our country can no longer afford to tolerate the culture of fraud and corruption on Wall Street. The people responsible for illegal behavior must be held accountable. Unfortunately, that has not been the case so far. [...] We are supposed to be a country of laws and equal justice. There is not supposed to be one standard for Wall Street executives and another for everybody else. Wall Street caused incalculable harm to our country, and the people who were responsible must be held to account.[32]

America had evolved into a capitalist utopia. The original American promise had to be held accountable.

---

[30] Ibid., p. 192.

[31] Ibid., pp. 2–3. See also: Max Ehrenfreund, "Bernie Sanders Is Profoundly Changing How Millennials Think About Politics, Poll Shows," *Washington Post*, April 25, 2016, https://www.washingtonpost.com/news/wonk/wp/2016/04/25/bernie-sanders-is-profoundly-changing-how-millennials-think-about-politics-poll-shows.

[32] Ibid., pp. 305–306.

10.2   A Failure of Liberalism

In *A Theory of Justice*, John Rawls exposed two principles of justice. The first was that "each person is to have an equal right to the most extensive basic liberty compatible with a similar liberty for others"; the second that "social and economic inequalities are to be arranged so that they are both (a) reasonably expected to be to everyone's advantage, and (b) attached to positions and offices open to all."[33] Economic injustice, from that perspective, is the consequence of failed redistribution policies and, therefore, testifies to a failure of egalitarian liberalism. Jeff Spinner-Halev argued that "our historical experience gives us reason to believe that the welfare state can solve certain kinds of injustices."[34] Therein lay his argument that workers may indeed be victims of past injustices, but not enduring injustices since the welfare state was designed as a solution to those.[35] However, when they are not rectified by the tools of liberal democracy, injustices become enduring and neither the past nor the present give the victims of the injustice much hope for the future. If liberal egalitarianism fails its own goals, therefore, welfare remains an unfunded mandate and, to many Americans, a utopia. In the opening pages of *Outsider in the White House*, Bernie Sanders stated his belief that "Americans, battered by job losses and wage stagnation, angered by inequality and injustice, have come to this understanding."[36] Welfare, according to Sanders, was hijacked and diverted from its intended recipients:

> [I]f you listen closely you will never hear much talk about the largest welfare recipient in America: the Walton family, the owners of Wal-Mart. The Walton family is the wealthiest family in the country, with a net worth of more than $130 billion. This one family owns more wealth than the bottom 42 percent of Americans—130 million people. They also receive more welfare than anybody else.[37]

---

[33] John Rawls, *A Theory of Justice*, Cambridge, MA: Harvard University Press, 1971, p. 60.

[34] Spinner-Halev, p. 64.

[35] Ibid., op. cit., p. 188.

[36] Sanders, *Outsider in the White House*, p. xvii.

[37] Id., *Our Revolution*, p. 223.

This is exactly what Martin Luther King Jr. depicted as "socialism for the rich and rugged individualism for the poor" in 1963, a phrase that was subsequently used by Bernie Sanders on many occasions to spread his own message.[38] Sanders's intention was to bring allegedly utopian ideals—"dreams deferred"[39]—into the mainstream of U.S. politics:

> Raising the minimum wage to $15 an hour may have been a fringe idea a few years ago, but now it is a mainstream idea whose time has come. This legislation would also end an outrageous aspect of corporate welfare. Today, many workers in large and profitable corporations, some of which are owned by multibillionaires, earn wages that are so low that they are forced to rely on publicly funded programs like Medicaid, food stamps, and public housing in order to survive.[40]

While Sanders's constant denunciation of "corporate welfare"[41] was extremely telling, his argument was not that egalitarian liberalism cannot function. By referring to existing publicly funded programs like Medicaid, food stamps, and public housing, Sanders argued that the mechanisms of egalitarian liberalism did not fail but were diverted to exploit workers instead of redistributing wealth. Sanders was not promoting class warfare

[38] Id., "Response to the 2019 State of the Union Address," U.S. Senator for Vermont website, February 5, 2019, https://www.sanders.senate.gov/newsroom/press-releases/sanders-response-to-2019-state-of-the-union-address.

[39] Hughes, op. cit., p. 155.

[40] Sanders, *Where We Go from Here*, p. 81.

[41] On September 5, 2018, Bernie Sanders introduced the *Stop BEZOS Act* in the U.S. Senate. The bill, which aimed to levy a tax on beneficiaries of corporate welfare such as Amazon, Walmart, McDonald's, and Uber, died in committee (S. 3410, *Stop Bad Employers by Zeroing Out Subsidies Act*, 115th Congress, September 5, 2018, GovTrack.us, https://www.govtrack.us/congress/bills/115/s3410). Stephen Moore and Dean Stansel of the libertarian Cato Institute define corporate welfare as "special government subsidies or benefits that are targeted to specific industries or corporations." Consumer and civic advocate Ralph Nader defines it as "the enormous and myriad subsidies, bailouts, giveaways, tax loopholes, debt revocations, loan guarantees, discounted insurance and other benefits conferred by government on business" (quoted in: James T. Bennett, *Corporate Welfare: Crony Capitalism that Enriches the Rich*, New York, Routledge, 2015, pp., 1, 7). From that angle, the 2008 "Troubled Asset Relief Program" created under the *Emergency Economic Stabilization Act* was regarded by many, Sanders included, as corporate welfare, i.e. as tax money given to banks and to corporations—notably the auto industry—in order to avoid a financial meltdown (see *supra*, p. 153).

here, let alone proposing any alternative model, his avowed intention was to hold the existing model accountable:

> The majority of Americans today are outsiders, especially in the halls of power where decisions about our economy are being made. And we will remain outsiders for as long as the political balance is tipped against the great mass of Americans, for as long as the status quo is characterized by inequality and injustice. It will take all the energy of the new movements of this new time to make the change that is needed.[42]

Achieving more inclusive and representative access into the halls of power was certainly a major political, democratic, project indeed.[43] Spinner-Halev, however, considered that there is a gap between democracy and egalitarian liberalism, that democracy "does insist that a standard of individual rights be protected," but that "there is no reason to think that this standard completely coincides with liberal justice. Participatory rights are a subset of liberal rights; they are not the whole of liberal rights."[44] One way of understanding Bernie Sanders's political ideal as expressed in the form of "democratic socialism" is to trace a constant claim that there was—or should be in practice—a perfect overlap between democracy and liberalism. This is to a large extent what made Sanders's brand of socialism "democratic." For Spinner-Halev, on the other hand, "[t]here is no question that a modern minimal democracy will have some overlap between it and liberalism, but there is still a gap between the two."[45]

Jeff Spinner-Halev, whose conception of liberalism was primarily that of "classical" liberalism,[46] saw the failure of liberal practice as proof that

---

[42] Sanders, *Outsider in the White House*, p. xvi.

[43] This is arguably what Bernie Sanders's political trajectory had been all about from the moment he was elected to the mayorship of Burlington, Vermont in 1981: "We were a coalition of ordinary people, none of whom had any real access to power in the conventional scheme of things, but we had contested an important election—and we had won. If an independent progressive movement could win in America's most rural state—and until recently, one of America's most Republican—then it might be possible for progressives to do likewise anywhere in the nation." Ibid., p. 54.

[44] Spinner-Halev, p. 167.

[45] Ibid.

[46] "By liberalism, I mean classical liberalism, the idea that individual rights should be protected, and that government should be limited; the government should be divided so

"justice cannot be achieved even if the state redoubles its efforts at redistributing wealth."[47] The consequence for the victimized group, here the workers, was that the said group would eventually have good reason to mistrust the government, and perhaps even liberal democracy as well. Certain groups mistrust the government for what it has done in the past and because they have little reason to think that it will act otherwise in the present or in the future. Mistrust in government was probably one of the components, and consequences, of Donald Trump's election to the presidency. As early as 2016, in its annual "Democracy Index," *The Economist* reclassified the United States as a "flawed democracy" (as opposed to a "full democracy"), due to eroding public confidence in American political institutions as documented in surveys by Gallup, the Pew Research Center, and others.[48] Robert C. Lieberman et al. linked this question to the issue of populism:

> In comparative perspective, populist figures divide the political arena between a virtuous "people," whom they claim to represent, and a venal or incompetent power elite accused of abandoning or betraying "the people." Like many populist leaders, Trump chafes at institutional constraints on his authority, and he projects the belief that he alone can embody the popular will ("I alone can fix it").[49]

Both Bernie Sanders and Donald Trump were labeled as "populists" in the context of the 2016 election.[50] The argument developed by Lieberman et al. did point to a common feature in that both Sanders and Trump could be said to divide the political arena between a virtuous people and a venal or incompetent power elite they blamed for having abandoned or betrayed the people, but also to differences in that Sanders could not be said to have chafed at institutional constraints on his own authority, or to project the belief that he alone could embody the

---

the power of one branch is circumscribed; liberalism is characterized by the rule of law rather than of men and women." Ibid., p. 12.

[47] Ibid., p. 75.

[48] Robert C. Lieberman, et al., "The Trump Presidency and American Democracy: A Historical and Comparative Analysis," *Perspectives on Politics*, vol. 17, n° 2, June 2019, p. 470.

[49] Ibid., p. 471.

[50] See *supra*, p. 6.

popular will. The "Not me. *Us.*" slogan used during his 2020 presidential campaign was perfectly designed to deflate such accusations of populism. If Sanders ever chafed at institutional constraints, it was at constraints on his chances to be elected, even before the 2016 and 2020 Democratic National Conventions. In 1981, when he was elected mayor of Burlington, Bernie Sanders, the only socialist mayor in America, "was now the only mayor in the country to have bucked the two-party system."[51] Sanders certainly mistrusted the American government, the two-party system, democratic institutions initially designed to represent and enforce the will of the people: "Our democratic institutions are so endangered that a clear-eyed observer might well conclude that we live not in a democracy but an oligarchy."[52] Hence the growing public mistrust in political institutions Sanders accordingly lamented in *Our Revolution*:

> Poll after poll tells us that our citizens no longer have confidence in our political institutions and, given the power of big money in the political process, they have serious doubts about how much their vote actually matters and whether politicians have any clue as to what is going on in their lives.[53]

Bernie Sanders did not so much denounce the failure of egalitarian liberalism as he pleaded for a restoration of discarded egalitarian principles in U.S. politics.

10.3 RESTORING AN EGALITARIAN LIBERAL ORDER

When Donald Trump ran his campaign on the "Make America Great Again" slogan, many wondered what that exactly meant. When had America been great? And for whom? As Trump never explicitly specified the period for which he was expressing nostalgia, his voters were left to decide for themselves.[54] In the case of Bernie Sanders, the historical point of reference was explicitly clear—it was the New Deal.[55] As

---

[51] Sanders, *Our Revolution*, p. 32.

[52] Sanders, *Outsider in the White House*, p. 274.

[53] Sanders, *Our Revolution*, p. 122.

[54] Margot Sanger-Katz, "When Was America Greatest?" *New York Times*, April 26, 2016, https://www.nytimes.com/2016/04/26/upshot/when-was-america-greatest.html.

[55] See *supra*, p. 111.

a landmark, the New Deal was the cornerstone that historicized Bernie Sanders's political message. The New Deal era was the historical moment when the United States broke decisively with its laissez-faire, isolationist, and protectionist past to embrace the principles of what was to become the dominant liberal order of the middle and late twentieth century. The civil rights revolution that took place in the 1960s was the other major building block of the liberal order.[56] Roosevelt never identified as a socialist nor did his administration ever seek to socialize the means of production, yet the New Deal was seen by many, by socialists and by enemies of socialism, as a form of socialism in the running of government. Almost everything Roosevelt proposed was called "socialist," Sanders told his Georgetown University audience on November 19, 2015:

> Social Security, which transformed life for the elderly in this country was "socialist." The concept of the "minimum wage" was seen as a radical intrusion into the marketplace and was described as "socialist." Unemployment insurance, abolishing child labor, the 40-hour work week, collective bargaining, strong banking regulations, deposit insurance, and job programs that put millions of people to work were all described, in one way or another, as "socialist." Yet, these programs have become the fabric of our nation and the foundation of the middle class.[57]

In a politically polarized environment, only Franklin Roosevelt—who could have been eclipsed by Barack Obama had Obama fulfilled more of the expectations raised by his election—really stands as a Democratic icon in the manner that Ronald Reagan stands as a Republican icon. Herein lay much of the ambiguity of Sanders's political posture and much of the tension with the Democratic establishment, as testified by the fact that the Democratic National Committee required Sanders to sign a loyalty pledge before he could run for the 2020 presidential nomination. In an article entitled "The Cosmic Irony of Bernie Sanders's Rise," Seth Ackerman, executive director of *Jacobin*, the democratic socialist quarterly magazine based in New York, wrote in February 2020 that "[w]hat makes

---

[56] As Sanders recalled in his November 19, 2015, address at Georgetown University, in which he aimed to define his democratic socialism, health care is a civil right: "President Johnson passed Medicare and Medicaid to provide health care to millions of senior citizens and families with children, persons with disabilities and some of the most vulnerable people in this county." Sanders, "Democratic Socialism in the U.S.A.," *Bernie Speaks*, p. 75.

[57] Sanders, "Democratic Socialism in the U.S.A.," *Bernie Speaks*, p. 76.

Bernie Sanders so threatening to the Democratic establishment is that he stands for what millions of Democrats thought their party stood for all along."[58] Bernie Sanders's democratic socialism is an elusive doctrine, with variable geometry, which made it all the more difficult for its opponents, especially among the Democratic party, to confront. In a 2019 interview, Seth Ackerman conceded that Bernie Sanders's democratic socialism was not "perfect," not "doctrinally correct," but made sure to historicize the Sanders dynamic as a response to enduring injustice:

> Politics changes over time and so do definitions of socialism. When we look at Bernie's concept of socialism, we should remember that Marx and Engels always said it was more important to have a real movement of workers who understand their real interests than it is to have a perfect, doctrinally correct program. When Engels talked about American politics in the late nineteenth century, he said he much preferred the populistic Knights of Labor or "agrarian reformers" to the hyper-orthodox Marxists of the Socialist Labor Party, who sounded like Marxoid robots when they talked. He much preferred the messy, ideologically incoherent Knights of Labor because they actually represented a real movement of workers fighting for some kind of egalitarian vision in opposition to the established order.[59]

That was variable geometry indeed. The argument was politically pointed in that the Knights of Labor—whom Ackerman significantly called "populistic"—rejected socialism.[60] But they fought for an egalitarian vision of American society. Ackerman's statement meant that Bernie Sanders was standing for the egalitarian liberalism the Democratic establishment had betrayed—and that he was given a socialist blessing for it.

In all of Bernie Sanders's political communications, New Deal liberalism is synonymous with economic justice and emergency action:

[58] Seth Ackerman, "The Cosmic Irony of Bernie Sanders's Rise," *Jacobin*, February 17, 2020, https://www.jacobinmag.com/2020/02/democratic-primary-electability-bernie-sanders.

[59] Micah Uetricht, "What Bernie Sees in the New Deal: An Interview with Seth Ackerman," *Jacobin*, September 7, 2019, https://www.jacobinmag.com/2019/09/bernie-sanders-new-deal-speech-socialism-roosevelt-race-housing-fdr.

[60] See *supra*, p. 78.

> As Franklin Delano Roosevelt reminded us, a nation's greatness is judged not by what it provides to the most well-off, but how it treats the people most in need. And that's the kind of nation we must become.[61]
>
> Way back in 1944, President Franklin Delano Roosevelt talked about the right of every American to have a job. That was true then. It is true today.[62]

The reference was always symbolic and Sanders did not mention any of the ideological debates surrounding the New Deal, such as the difference between the first and the second New Deal, a number of controversies about Roosevelt himself, and even whether it was the New Deal or World War II that eventually pulled the United States out of the Great Depression. What Ackerman said about Sanders and socialism also applied to Sanders and liberalism: his political posture was neither "perfect" nor "doctrinally correct."[63] Sanders's opponents could have argued, not without reason, that there was a certain cult of the leader in Sanders's political thinking. Although Sanders's supporters could have responded that if it existed at all such a cult was a cult of efficiency, Sanders was nonetheless vulnerable to criticism for what may be regarded as a populist posture (which, again, the "Not me. *Us.*" slogan used during his 2020 presidential campaign was designed to counter[64]). Beyond, the fact that Bernie Sanders stressed positive parts of various authoritarian regimes in the course of his political career also exposed him to criticism, from Republicans but also from "fellow" Democrats as in the Democratic presidential primary debate in South Carolina on February 25, 2020, when Pete Buttigieg,[65] tried to put Bernie Sanders and Donald Trump back to back as populists:

---

[61] Sanders, *Our Revolution*, p. 126.

[62] Id., *Where We Go from here*, p. 260.

[63] Ackerman, op. cit., p. 194.

[64] See *supra*, p. 193.

[65] Pete Buttigieg was to quit the presidential race four days later in a move that boosted the candidacy of Joe Biden, Barack Obama's former vice president. President Trump soon reacted to exert pressure on the Democratic camp by reminding them of how Bernie Sanders had lost the 2016 Democratic primary: "Pete Buttigieg is OUT. All of his SuperTuesday votes will go to Sleepy Joe Biden. Great timing. This is the REAL beginning of the Dems taking Bernie out of play—NO NOMINATION, AGAIN!" Donald J. Trump Twitter post, March 2, 2020, https://twitter.com/realDonaldTrump/status/123426303 7110083587.

[...] I am not looking forward to a scenario where it comes down to Donald Trump with his nostalgia for the social order of the 1950s and Bernie Sanders with a nostalgia for the revolution politics of the 1960s. [...] This is about 2020. We are not going to survive or succeed, and certainly not going to win by reliving the Cold War, and we're not going to win these critical House and Senate races if people in those races have to explain why the nominee of the Democratic Party is telling people to look at the bright side of the Castro regime.[66]

The exchange that followed was the perfect illustration of the tensions between Bernie Sanders and the Democratic Party whose nomination he was seeking:

SANDERS: Let us be clear, do we think health care for all, Pete, is some kind of radical communist idea?
BUTTIGIEG: Well, you brought this up, let's talk about that.
SANDERS: Do we think raising the minimum wage to a living wage...
BUTTIGIEG: I'm happy to respond to the question because this is really important...
SANDERS: ... do we think building the millions of units of affordable housing that we need...
BUTTIGIEG: If you're going to ask that rhetorical question, let's...
SANDERS: ... do we think raising taxes on billionaires is a radical idea?
BUTTIGIEG: Let's talk about this. Let's talk about what's radical about that plan.
SANDERS: Do you think criminal justice reform is a radical idea?
BUTTIGIEG: The things you just named are things...
SANDERS: Do you think immigration reform? The truth is, Pete... [...]
SANDERS: ... the American people support my agenda.
BUTTIGIEG: The way you're talking about doing it is radical by...
SANDERS: That is why I am beating Trump in virtually every poll that is done, and why I will defeat him.[67]

"Authoritarians of any stripe is bad,"[68] Sanders finally answered during the debate, but the fact is that he sometimes lowered his critiques of

---

[66] "Read the full transcript of the South Carolina Democratic Debate," *CBS News*, February 25, 2020, https://www.cbsnews.com/news/south-carolina-democratic-debate-full-transcript-text.

[67] Ibid.

[68] Ibid.

autocrats when he considered them to be victims of American imperi-
alism: "Occasionally it might be a good idea to be honest about American
foreign policy, and that includes the fact that America has overthrown
governments all over the world—in Chile, in Guatemala, in Iran."[69] Still
Sanders insisted that he had opposed authoritarianism all over the world
but that some programs, such as Castro's literacy programs, had been
positive:

> SANDERS: I have opposed authoritarianism all over the world and I was
> really amazed at what Mayor Bloomberg just said a moment ago. He
> said that the Chinese government is responsive to the politburo, but
> who the hell is the politburo responsive to? Who elects the politburo?
> You have got a real dictatorship there. Of course you have a dictatorship
> in Cuba. What I said is what Barack Obama said in terms of Cuba, that
> Cuba made progress on education. Yes, I think…
>   [Booing]
> SANDERS: Really? Really? Literacy programs are bad?[70]

Of course there can be no comparison between Fidel Castro, a dictator,
and Franklin Roosevelt, but then there was little comparison either
between President Franklin Roosevelt and Martin Luther King Jr., an
activist, except, from Bernie Sanders's perspective, in their agency, in
their decisiveness, in their capacity to act in the name of the people. In
Our Revolution, Bernie Sanders reproduced part an article published by
Patrick Healy in the *New York Times* on November 19, 2015, the day
Sanders tried to explain what he meant by "democratic socialism" during
a speech at Georgetown University:

> Mr. Sanders, who is hugely popular with liberals but is struggling to attract
> more voters to his Democratic presidential bid against Hillary Rodham
> Clinton, made blunt overtures to the party faithful by presenting himself
> as the heir to the policies and ideals of Franklin Delano Roosevelt and the
> Rev. Dr. Martin Luther King Jr.
>   Invoking the two men several times, Mr. Sanders said that democratic
> socialism was reflected in Roosevelt's priorities like Social Security and
> in Dr. King's call for social and economic justice, contrasting them to

[69] Ibid.
[70] Ibid.

"socialist-communist" caricatures of his thinking put forward by Republicans to tar the Democratic field.[71]

Sanders endorsed the statement that he was presenting himself as the heir of Franklin Roosevelt and Martin Luther King Jr. by adding *"The New York Times* got it right" to introduce Healy's paragraphs in *Our Revolution*.[72] In his quest to restore an egalitarian liberal order, Bernie Sanders was less doctrinaire than many would think. As we saw, his democratic socialism was an elusive doctrine, with variable geometry,[73] and although there were numerous references to "liberals,"[74] "bleeding-heart liberals,"[75] "extreme liberals,"[76] "ultraliberal[s],"[77] "liberal Republican[s],"[78] "liberal Democrat[s],"[79] "moderate-to-liberal Democrat[s],"[80] "party liberals,"[81] "supposedly liberal[s],"[82] etc. the term "liberalism" did not appear once in any of the books published by Bernie Sanders, whether it be *Outsider in the House, Outsider in the White House, Our Revolution*, or *Where We Go from Here*. All the references to "liberals" pointed to individual or group stances that reflected the diversity and polarization of the American political spectrum, most characteristically under the protean banner of liberalism, a "broad, inclusive concept,"[83] which Sanders did not explicitly refer to, preferring

[71] Patrick Healy, "Bernie Sanders, Confronting Concerns, Makes Case for Electability." *New York Times* (November 19, 2015), https://www.nytimes.com/politics/first-draft/2015/11/19/bernie-sanders-defends-democratic-socialism-calling-it-route-to-economic-fairness.

[72] Sanders, *Our Revolution*, p. 166.

[73] See *supra*, p. 195.

[74] Sanders, *Outsider in the White House*, p. 7.

[75] Id., *Our Revolution*, p. 13.

[76] Id., *Outsider in the White House*, p. 55.

[77] Id., *Our Revolution*, p. 168.

[78] Ibid., p. 27.

[79] Id., *Outsider in the White House*, p. 47.

[80] Id., *Outsider in the House*, p. 80.

[81] Id., *Outsider in the White House*, p. 116.

[82] Id., *Outsider in the House*, p. 116.

[83] Garry, op. cit., p. 140.

to advance his democratic socialism to hold the failed liberal utopia accountable for enduring injustice.

References

Ackerman, Seth. "The Cosmic Irony of Bernie Sanders's Rise." *Jacobin* (February 17, 2020), https://www.jacobinmag.com/2020/02/democratic-primary-ele ctability-bernie-sanders.

Bennett, James T. *Corporate Welfare: Crony Capitalism that Enriches the Rich.* New York: Routledge, 2015.

Ehrenfreund, Max. "Bernie Sanders Is Profoundly Changing How Millennials Think About Politics, Poll Shows." *Washington Post* (April 25, 2016), https://www.washingtonpost.com/news/wonk/wp/2016/04/25/bernie-sanders-is-profoundly-changing-how-millennials-think-about-politics-poll-shows.

Garry, Patrick M. *Liberalism and American Identity.* Kent, OH: Kent State University Press, 1992.

Healey, Patrick. "Bernie Sanders, Confronting Concerns, Makes Case for Electability." *New York Times* (November 19, 2015), https://www.nytimes.com/politics/first-draft/2015/11/19/bernie-sanders-defends-democratic-socialism-calling-it-route-to-economic-fairness.

Hughes, Langston. "Harlem." In *The Collected Poems of Langston Hughes*, edited by Arnold Rampersad. New York: Vintage, 1995, p. 426.

King, Martin Luther Jr. "I Have a Dream," Address delivered at the March on Washington for Jobs and Freedom (August 28, 1963). The Martin Luther King Jr. Research and Education Institute (Stanford University), https://kin ginstitute.stanford.edu/king-papers/documents/i-have-dream-address-delive red-march-washington-jobs-and-freedom.

Lieberman, Robert C., et al. "The Trump Presidency and American Democracy: A Historical and Comparative Analysis." *Perspectives on Politics*, vol. 17, n° 2 (June 2019), pp. 470–479.

Obama, Barack H. Remarks in Des Moines, Iowa (December 19, 2007). The American Presidency Project, https://www.presidency.ucsb.edu/node/277494.

Rawls, John. *A Theory of Justice.* Cambridge, MA: Harvard University Press, 1971.

Russonello, Giovanni. "Ocasio-Cortez Tells Colbert: 'We Changed Who Turns Out.'" *New York Times* (June 29, 2018), https://www.nytimes.com/2018/06/29/arts/television/alexandria-ocasio-cortez-interview-stephen-colbert.html.

Sanders, Bernard, with Huck Gutman. *Outsider in the House: A Political Autobiography.* New York: Verso, 1997. Rpt. *Outsider in the White House,* 2015.

———. *Our Revolution: A Future to Believe In.* New York: Thomas Dunne Books, 2016.

———. *Bernie Speaks: Speeches by Bernie Sanders,* compiled by David Cane. CreateSpace Independent Publishing Platform: Greenbridge Publishing, 2017.

———. *Where We Go from Here: Two Years in the Resistance.* New York: Thomas Dunne Books, 2018.

Sanger-katz, Margot. "When Was America Greatest?" *New York Times* (April 26, 2016), https://www.nytimes.com/2016/04/26/upshot/when-was-america-greatest.html.

Smith, Jackie. "Social Movements and Political Moments: Reflections on the Intersections of Global Justice Movements & Occupy Wall Street." *Street Politics in the Age of Austerity: From the Indignados to Occupy,* edited by Marcos Ancelovici, Pascale Dufour, and Héloïse Nez. Amsterdam: Amsterdam University Press, 2016, pp. 205–226.

Spinner-Halev, Jeff. *Enduring Injustice.* Cambridge: Cambridge University Press, 2012.

Storey, John. *Radical Utopianism and Cultural Studies: On Refusing to be Realistic.* New York: Routledge, 2019.

Uetricht, Micah. "What Bernie Sees in the New Deal: An Interview with Seth Ackerman." *Jacobin* (September 7, 2019), https://www.jacobinmag.com/2019/09/bernie-sanders-new-deal-speech-socialism-roosevelt-race-housing-fdr.

Veciana-Suarez, Ana. "Who, Exactly, Is Ivanka Trump? We're Just Scratching Our Heads for Now." *Miami Herald* (May 2, 2017), https://www.miamiherald.com/living/liv-columns-blogs/ana-veciana-suarez/article148013744.html.

CHAPTER 11

State and Corporate Responsibility

The corollary to the concept of enduring injustice is necessarily that of enduring responsibility, with the caveat that most arguments about enduring injustice usually emphasize the continuity of governments, as in the cases of Native and African Americans for example, and suppose that the victims and the perpetrators of an injustice live in the same community—or state—as their ancestors: "The responsibility for the past argument assumes that the state under which a past injustice was committed still exists," Spinner-Halev wrote.[1] In the wake of the Occupy Wall Street movement, in the context of a nation that, according to Bernie Sanders, should have worked for the 99% and not just the 1%, who should be held accountable? Reparations for the descendants of victims of past economic injustices may seem utopian when 99% of Americans remain the victims of economic injustice in the present.

11.1   Enduring Responsibility

Bernie Sanders historicized the concept of enduring responsibility in *Where We Go from Here* by referring to one of the most respected voices in American history, the voice of the Republican president who saved the Union during the American Civil War, Abraham Lincoln:

---

[1] Spinner-Halev, p. 79.

© The Author(s), under exclusive license to Springer Nature
Switzerland AG 2021
N. Gachon, *Bernie Sanders's Democratic Socialism*,
https://doi.org/10.1007/978-3-030-69661-0_11

Standing in Gettysburg in November 1863, soon after that terrible battle that claimed tens of thousands of casualties, Abraham Lincoln reminded his compatriots, and all of us, what [our] "way of life" was, and what our enduring responsibility in a democratic society is. He stated "... that we here highly resolve that these dead shall not have died in vain—that this nation, under God, shall have a new birth of freedom, and that government of the people, by the people, for the people, shall not perish from the earth."

Government of the people, by the people, for the people. Creating a nation that works for all, and not just the few. That was worth fighting for in 1863. It is worth fighting for today.[2]

Historicizing injustice in order to demonstrate its enduring nature certainly helps better understand the form of the injustice and its possible remedy. For Jeff Spinner-Halev, "[j]ustice does not mean that people or communities take responsibility for the past, but rather that political communities take responsibility for the present and the future."[3] That, according to Sanders, was exactly what the profound ideological divide between Republicans and Democrats was—or, for that matter, should have been—all about:

The Republicans have succeeded in convincing Americans that poor people are responsible for the federal deficit, rather than a series of policies over the last twenty years that have given huge tax breaks to the rich and thrown billions of dollars at defense contractors. Not only that. They have also successfully propagated the view that compassion and human sympathy are not the province of government.[4]

The problem here seems inherent to a failure of egalitarian liberalism, as is often the case with enduring injustices. Here again, the corollary of such an ideology, Sanders argued, was more enduring injustice still: "And what is the right thing to do? Cut welfare. Cut food stamps and nutrition programs. Cut affordable housing. Cut health care. Cut education. Cut fuel assistance. [...] No. Increasing hunger, homelessness, and human misery is how we help the poor."[5] By holding utopia accountable,

---

[2] Sanders, *Where We Go from Here*, p. 5.

[3] Spinner-Halev, p. 81.

[4] Sanders, *Outsider in the White House*, p. 174.

[5] Id.

Bernie Sanders blamed liberalism for violations of its own principles, which, to many, was arguably unfair in a number of cases. For Jeff Spinner-Halev, for example, the fact that "liberal democracy offers us the ability to see these failures is important, but to look to liberalism as a solution for its own shortcomings is simply too tall an order."[6] Yet Sanders saw such an argument as an aberration with regard to American values and lamented the way the conservative Republican ideology had become culturally hegemonic.

What the Occupy Wall Street movement gave Bernie Sanders, as he explained in a 2011 interview, was a decisive argument for deciding who was actually responsible for the situation of everyday Americans:

> I think what the protesters are doing in New York and across the country is extremely important for two reasons. Number one, they are focusing attention on the most powerful entity in our country which is Wall Street, which is also the most secretive and I believe the most dangerous. Let's never forget, ever forget, that it was the greed and recklessness and illegal behavior of Wall Street which plunged us into this horrible recession, which resulted in millions of people losing their jobs, their homes, and their lifesavings. So we have got to continue to focus on the greed on Wall Street and we have got to bring about real reforms to end the kind of abusive behavior that is taking place there.[7]

Occupy Wall Street helped Bernie Sanders designate who was responsible for the wrongs done, but of course those who were responsible for the wrongs done could not be those in charge of alleviating the wrong. This was arguably the mistake made by Barack Obama when he appointed his economic team in November 2008, a team composed of people who could be regarded as being responsible for letting the Great Recession happen, if not for participating in causing it in the first place. In "Distributing Responsibilities," an article published in the *Journal of Political Philosophy* in 2001, David Miller argued that there are four principles for deciding who is responsible to repair a wrong: those who are causally responsible, those who are morally responsible, the people who have the capacity to do so, and those who share a moral or political community

---

[6] Spinner-Halev, p. 79.

[7] Sanders, "Senator Sanders on Occupy Wall Street," *The Guardian*, October 21, 2011, https://www.youtube.com/watch?v=9HSaZOSWfrU.

with those who have suffered the wrong.[8] In the case made by Bernie Sanders, the state had a political responsibility to repair injustices. In other words, directly or indirectly, the state was politically responsible for corporate greed. The role and responsibility of the state were essential. As Spinner-Halev pointed out, what is "wrong with the arguments of the advocates of repairing past injustice" is that they too often leave some enduring injustice "without an agent that is responsible to repair the injustice."[9] In *Outsider in the White House*, Sanders argued that American political institutions, the two-party system, had defaulted on that democratic responsibility:

> Now, the United States has a major trade deficit problem. In fact, the deficit is at record-breaking levels. For most Republicans, President Clinton and many Democrats, and the corporate media the trade deficit is no cause for alarm. We hear very little about proposals to eliminate that deficit. No one suggests that we hold corporate America responsible or demand that they rebuild the manufacturing base in this country rather than invest tens of billions of dollars in China, Mexico, or other impoverished Third World countries.[10]

In *Our Revolution*, Sanders claimed that the government's responsibility was not only political, not only democratic, but that the responsibility was also a moral one:

> I believe that the government has a moral responsibility to provide for the vulnerable—children, the elderly, the sick, and the disabled. But I do not believe that taxpayers should have to expend huge sums of money subsidizing profitable corporations owned by some of the wealthiest people in this country. That's absurd.[11]

Taxation, therefore, should function as compensation for the 99%, as a form of reparative, redistributive justice for resources that, Sanders

---

[8] David Miller, "Distributing responsibilities," *Journal of Political Philosophy*, vol. 9, n° 4, 2001, pp. 453–472. Spinner-Halev, p. 82.

[9] Ibid.

[10] Sanders, *Outsider in the White House*, p. 223.

[11] Id., *Our Revolution*, p. 224.

argued, had been diverted for ends other than social justice and the common good:

> Say Bill Gates was actually taxed $100 billion. We could end homelessness and provide safe drinking water to everyone in this country. Bill would still be a multibillionaire. Our message: the billionaire class cannot have it all when so many have so little.[12]

Hence, for example, the *CEO & Worker Pension Fairness Act*, a plan Sanders introduced with Senator Chris Van Hollen (D-Md.) on February 27, 2020, to raise taxes on executive retirement plans in order to bolster funding for 1.7 million American workers' pensions plans. The first line of Sanders's description of the *CEO & Worker Pension Fairness Act* read: "It is no secret that the country's wealthiest CEOs live by different rules than the other 99 percent."[13] While the bill was almost doomed in the first place in the context of a divided Congress, it was highly indicative of Sanders's thinking as he was campaigning for the presidency.

Taxation lies at the core of socialism as compared to capitalism. Under capitalism, the means of production are owned by private individuals, which means that the economy runs through individuals who own and operate private companies. Companies live by the motivation for profit and exist to make money. The goal of the corporation is to maximize shareholder wealth. Under socialism, the means of production are owned to some degree by the public, via the state. People work for wealth that is in turn redistributed to everyone, including among public institutions following decisions made by the government. There is a more limited free market and taxes are typically higher than in a capitalist system. Liberal democracies have a blended economic system that includes aspects of both capitalism and socialism but, with the ascendancy of neoliberalism, leftists argue, democracy was turned on its head with "socialism [i.e. state protection] for the rich" and "rugged individualism [i.e. capitalistic competition] for the poor."[14] Taxation appears

---

[12] Id., Twitter post, November 7, 2019, https://twitter.com/berniesanders/status/119 24784356937 80992.

[13] Id., "CEO & Worker Pension Fairness Act," U.S. Senator for Vermont website, February 27, 2020, https://www.sanders.senate.gov/download/ceo-tax-breaks-fact-sheet? id=BA69C607-1E52-4557-A723-BC9543B57613.

[14] See *supra*, p. 415.

as the logical tool for redistributive justice. American taxpayers largely overlap with the constituents of American society, which makes the state the logical agent of the people, therefore the responsible collective agent of the people. However, taxpayers consent to paying taxes in a democratic society because this is how the state is funded. If the state is said to have defaulted on its own democratic mission, and since the state is democratically responsible for redressing its own wrongs, Bernie Sanders's democratic socialism argued that planning to tax the 99% to redress the wrongs of the 1%, or extending tax cuts for the most wealthy, was morally wrong. As he took to the Senate floor in 2008 to oppose what he called the Wall Street bailout, Sanders roared that "if taxpayer money must be placed at risk, if we are going to bail out Wall Street, it should be those people who have caused the problem, those people who have benefited from President Bush's tax breaks for millionaires and billionaires, those people who have taken advantage of deregulation who should pick up the tab, not ordinary working people."[15]

Incidentally, the issue of whether taxpayers who have no causal responsibility should be held accountable through taxation has implications that reach far beyond the scope of this study. There are a number of debates as to whether the tax money of citizens who immigrated to the United States after the end of slavery and of segregation, for example, some of them possibly even of African ancestry, should be used in the case of reparations for the descendants of slaves. This raises the larger issue of what being part of a nation entails, in terms of rights and in terms of duties, and in terms of collective responsibilities. Bernie Sanders consistently sought to circumvent the slavery reparations issue and was sometimes blamed for it by opponents, by claiming that there were "better ways" to help people than "writing out a check."[16] This argument may sound curious in the discourse of one of the strongest proponents of the welfare state, especially as Martin Luther King Jr. himself had resorted to the same metaphor on the steps of the Lincoln Memorial on August 28, 1963:

[15] See *supra*, p. 551.

[16] John Haltiwanger, "Bernie Sanders When Asked About Reparations Says There Are 'Better Ways' to Help People Than 'Writing Out A Check,'" *Business Insider*, March 1, 2019, https://www.businessinsider.fr/us/bernie-sanders-reparations-better-ways-help-writing-check-2019-3.

In a sense we've come to our nation's capital to cash a check. When the architects of our republic wrote the magnificent words of the Constitution and the Declaration of Independence, they were signing a promissory note to which every American was to fall heir. This note was a promise that all men, yes, black men as well as white men, would be guaranteed the "unalienable Rights" of "Life, Liberty and the pursuit of Happiness." It is obvious today that America has defaulted on this promissory note, insofar as her citizens of color are concerned.[17]

Bernie Sanders, who presented himself as the heir to the policies and ideals of Franklin Roosevelt and Martin Luther King Jr.,[18] resorted to the metaphor to reframe the thorny racial issue in economic terms with a typical class perspective, to imply that it would take more than mere compensations or even reparations to relieve a community from enduring injustice:

I think we have to do everything that we can to end institutional racism in this country. It is not acceptable to me that the rate of childhood poverty among the African American community is over 30%, in this country. That is beyond belief, that, African Americans die from cancer at higher rates than whites.

So we are going to do everything we can, to put resources into distressed communities, and improve lives, for those people who have been hurt from the legacy of slavery. [...]

As a result of the legacy of slavery, you have massive levels of inequality. It has to be addressed and it has to be addressed now.[19]

11.2   Liberalism and Responsibility

The question of responsibility occurs even in a situation where there is no causal agent to be held responsible. In the case of terrible natural disasters, for example, such as hurricanes or earthquakes, countries that are able to help the victims often feel responsible to do so, even though they did not—and, for that matter, no one did—cause the disaster. Spinner-Halev

---

[17] King Jr., "I Have a Dream," op. cit., p. 147.

[18] Sanders, *Our Revolution*, op. cit., p. 198.

[19] Sanders, "Bernie Sanders On Reparations - Town Hall February 2019," CNN, February 26, 2019, https://www.youtube.com/watch?time_continue=74&v=ze7fKop9jeo.

underlined the fact that the poor are usually the victims of natural disasters more than the wealthy, since they have less protection from these disasters. The consequence is that even if natural disasters have no causal agent, their consequences are often heavily influenced by government policies. "Flood walls," Spinner-Halev wrote, "are often constructed where the wealthy live, leaving the poor more vulnerable when waters rise," and "mobile homes are more prone to being badly damaged during natural disasters than the houses of wealthier citizens."[20] Many people consider that wealthy countries do in fact owe aid to poorer countries, even when there is no responsibility whatsoever that the wealthy countries may have in the situation of poorer countries. "Instead of first finding the responsible party for an enduring injustice," Spinner-Halev suggested "we first look to see who is best able to repair the injustice." In fact, Spinner-Halev applied this reflection to the tensions between African Americans and the government of the United States:

> Sometimes these two views [the responsible party and who is best able to repair the injustice] will overlap. If trust is to be rebuilt between African Americans and the U.S. government, then the latter has some work to do; the argument from responsibility will also argue that the U.S. government must work to remedy enduring justices suffered by African Americans.[21]

The metaphor of the natural disaster used by Spinner-Halev is extremely telling and raises a number of additional questions in the perimeter of our reflection.

It appears, if we follow Spinner-Halev's argument, that, in the natural order, wealthy people are prone to assist other people—poor people, but not only—in the context of *accidental* natural disasters, such as floods, hurricanes, wildfires, or earthquakes. In the case of enduring problems, however, such as desertification, climate change, racism, war, or poverty, the response is quite different: people are much less willing to help. Should a crisis like the Great Recession be regarded as an *accidental* natural disaster that occurred in the liberal natural order of things, and, therefore, required immediate help in the form of bailouts? From that perspective, the neoliberal prism erases the link between cause and effect, as Bernie Sanders lamented in *Our Revolution*, explaining in what his

---

[20] Spinner-Halev, pp. 82–83.

[21] Ibid., p. 83.

own education in socialism helped him identify the seemingly natural but in reality highly ideological disconnect between causes and effect:

> While at the university, I became a member of the Young People's Socialist League (YPSL), the Student Peace Union (SPU), and the Congress of Racial Equality (CORE). Through these organizations, I learned to look at politics in a new way. It wasn't just that racism, war, poverty, and other social evils must be opposed. It was that there was a cause-and-effect dynamic and an interconnectedness between all aspects of society. Things didn't just happen by accident. There was a relationship between wealth, power, and the perpetuation of capitalism.[22]

If liberalism, the political philosophy conceived some five hundred years ago and put into effect at the birth of the United States two hundred and fifty years later, was to be defined as tantamount to the natural order and to natural rights, then, as Sanders put it, "[t]he political establishment became thoroughly dominated by people for whom unfettered and unstrained free market capitalism was virtually a religion."[23] In *Liberalism and the Limits of Justice*, Michael J. Sandel provided a definition of natural-rights liberalism, which he referred to as "deontological" liberalism:

> [S]ociety, being composed of a plurality of persons, each with his own aims, interests, and conceptions of the good, is best arranged when it is governed by principles that do not *themselves* presuppose any particular conception of the good; what justifies these regulative principles above all is not that they maximize the social welfare or otherwise promote the good, but rather that they conform to the concept of right, a moral category given prior to the good and independent of it.[24]

The consequence is that "principles of justice are justified in a way that does not depend on any particular vision of the good. To the contrary: given its independent status, the right constrains the good and sets its bounds."[25] Sanders's political philosophy differed from natural-rights

---

[22] Sanders, *Our Revolution*, p. 18.

[23] Ibid., p. 210.

[24] Michael J. Sandel, *Liberalism and the Limits of Justice*, Cambridge, Cambridge University Press, 1982. Rpt. 1998, p. 1.

[25] Ibid., p. 2.

liberalism thus defined, which provided for the ideal context of liberal capitalism, an ideology that does not set the constitutional intent of promoting "the general Welfare"[26] as a primary objective of government, and which, by imposing a permanent constraint on the good for the sake of the right, implements a determined economic and political environment. That brand of liberalism was the core target of Bernie Sanders's self-proclaimed revolution: "The economic establishment tells us that there is no alternative to this type of rapacious, cutthroat capitalism, that this is how the system and globalization works, and that there's no turning back. They are dead wrong."[27]

As a testimony to the significant connection between natural disasters and political responsibility, Bernie Sanders posted an invitation to read an article entitled "Hurricane Katrina and Bernie Sanders: From Neoliberal Disaster to 'Political Revolution'"[28] on his Facebook account on August 30, 2015.[29] The article was published on the occasion of the tenth anniversary of the devastation of New Orleans in the aftermath of Hurricane Katrina during the late summer of 2005. At the same time, other magazines, such as *U.S. News and World Report*, reminded their readers of how badly Hurricane Katrina damaged George W. Bush's presidency and reputation and argued that it started his undoing. Katrina illustrated the perils that presidents face when they fail to deal with such calamities in a timely and efficient way. When Katrina hit, Bush was and remained on vacation in his ranch in Crawford, Texas, and let himself become isolated from the country. On the way back, he had Air Force One fly over parts of the devastated area and caught a glimpse of the wreckage from the plane. Photographers were allowed to take photos of a grim-faced Bush looking out an Air Force One window. Many Americans saw the photo and received it as evidence that Bush was too distant from the misery

---

[26] U.S. Constitution, Preamble, op. cit., p. 61.

[27] Sanders, *Our Revolution*, p. 260.

[28] Adolph Reed Jr., Michael Francis, Steve Striffler, "Hurricane Katrina and Bernie Sanders: From Neoliberal Disaster to 'Political Revolution,'" *Common Dreams*, August 29, 2015, https://www.commondreams.org/views/2015/08/29/hurricane-katrina-and-bernie-sanders-neoliberal-disaster-political-revolution.

[29] Sanders, Facebook post, August 30, 2015, https://www.facebook.com/berniesanders/posts/must-read-hurricane-katrina-and-bernie-sanders-from-neoliberal-disaster-to-polit/891706100884395.

below.[30] The article published by Adolph Reed Jr., Michael Francis, and Steve Striffler, "Hurricane Katrina and Bernie Sanders: From Neoliberal Disaster to 'Political Revolution,'" took a totally different perspective. The article did not refer to George W. Bush but strove to link causes and effects to account for what had happened in New Orleans, to claim that, from a political point of view, Katrina was not only a "natural" disaster:

> The political arrangements that led to Katrina's disastrous aftermath were bipartisan and neoliberal. Democrats as well as Republicans, at local, state, and national levels, for decades bled the public sector, sold off or abandoned public goods, and mortgaged the environment—in south Louisiana in particular the wetlands that protected the New Orleans area from storm surge—to corporate interests, all justified with fairy tales about efficiency of the market or doing more with less. Assaults on the living standards of poor and working people persisted unabated without regard to whether Democrats or Republicans were in office.[31]

While "[c]alls to fix the levees and invest in infrastructure prior to Katrina went unheeded, as did warnings from scientists that climate change would lead to larger storms, and that the destruction of Louisiana wetlands had weakened the region's natural defenses,"[32] even the rescue efforts seemed to add disaster to the disaster:

> Dismantling the public sector has been the guiding mantra for those who have controlled the post-storm recovery. The chaos of Katrina not only provided cover for powerful interests to slash public services at a much faster rate but allowed them to pass off such policies as much needed "reform" (and then sell it as a "model" for the rest of the country).[33]

Bernie Sanders who was running for the 2016 Democratic nomination when the article was published, was viewed as the only "presidential candidate who ha[d] consistently fought for the kinds of policies that New Orleans so desperately required prior to and during Katrina, and that it

---

[30] Kenneth T. Walsh, "The Undoing of George W. Bush," *U.S. News and World Report*, August 28, 2015, https://www.usnews.com/news/the-report/articles/2015/08/28/hurricane-katrina-was-the-beginning-of-the-end-for-george-w-bush.

[31] Reed Jr., Francis, Striffler, op. cit, p. 208.

[32] Ibid.

[33] Ibid.

need[ed] now more than ever."[34] While the authors of the article were visibly sympathetic with Sanders,[35] the issues they exposed bore strong significance in the ongoing debate over state responsibility in the context of the deregulated neoliberal state.

Spinner-Halev's metaphor of the natural disaster, with wealthy people being prone to help other people in the context of *accidental* natural disasters is useful here again. When there is no causal agent to a crisis, such as a natural disaster, the best solution seems to identify who is best able to repair the injustice.[36] In practice, however, the example of Hurricane Katrina reveals that the state may be deemed accountable for not alleviating the suffering of the victims sufficiently or rapidly enough. Its responsibility can be engaged by the people even without it being the causal agent. However, deregulation, the absence of state control, may, as Sanders pleaded in a number of writings, turn the state into an implicit causal agent of social suffering by letting conditions unfavorable to the majority of Americans develop:

> Over the years, as a member of the House, I played an active role in fighting the deregulation of Wall Street and opposing corporate welfare and an unfair tax system. I was also on the picket lines against disastrous trade deals like the North American Free Trade Agreement (NAFTA) and Permanent Normal Trade Relations (PNTR) with China.[37] [...]
>
> I believe that the Democratic Party bears an enormous amount of responsibility for this sad state of affairs. Over the years, the party has closed its doors to ordinary Americans—working people, young people, minorities, and the poor, who once filled its ranks. As Democratic leadership became more dependent on corporate interests, it drifted further away from the hopes, needs, and participation of ordinary Americans. It became a top-down party, far removed from those struggling in our inner cities and rural counties.[38] [...]

[34] Ibid.

[35] Adolph Reed Jr. was a Professor Emeritus of Political Science at the University of Pennsylvania, Michael C. Francis, M.D. a native New Orleanian, practicing anesthesiology and pain medicine in the city, and Steve Striffler Director of the Labor Resource Center at the University of Massachusetts-Boston.

[36] See *supra*, p. 207.

[37] Sanders, *Our Revolution*, p. 43.

[38] Ibid., p. 159.

In 1993, President Clinton appointed [Robert Rubin] head of the National Economic Council, and in 1995 he became treasury secretary. While in government he spearheaded financial deregulation, including the repeal of Glass-Steagall. He also prevented the regulation of derivatives.[39] [...]

From the point of view of a democratic socialist like Bernie Sanders, even Adam Smith's "invisible hand" of the market, the hand that supposedly leads the rich "to make nearly the same distribution of the necessaries of life, which would have been made, had the earth been divided into equal portions among all its inhabitants,"[40] was not there.[41] In the case of the natural disaster, therefore, whether it be economic or climatic, the state is likely to be held accountable. In both instances, Bernie Sanders's democratic socialism appears as both a political platform and a demand for accountability.

The debate over reparations for slavery may cast light on significant perspectives. Can people be held accountable in the present for a crime, slavery, that was committed when the practice was legal? Our answer is that, of course, as a nation, people collectively owe reparations for past crimes and enduring injustices. However, let us suppose that future generations in developing countries suffering from climate change decide to hold their predecessors in developed countries accountable for climate injustice. Simon Caney tackled this issue in an article for *The Journal of Social Philosophy*:

Many discussions of historic injustice and reparations focus, reasonably enough, on slavery and colonialism. However, the question of how to respond to environmental injustices (ranging from the role developed

---

[39] Ibid., p. 299.

[40] Adam Smith, *The Theory of Moral Sentiments*, edited by D. D. Raphael, A. L. Macfie, Indianapolis, Ind., Liberty Fund, 1976, pp. 184–185.

[41] Joseph Stiglitz makes a similar point: "Adam Smith, the father of modern economics, is often cited as arguing for the 'invisible hand' and free markets: firms... But unlike his followers, Adam Smith was aware of some of the limitations of free markets, and research since then has further clarified why free markets, by themselves, often do not lead to what is best. ... [T]he reason that the invisible hand often seems invisible is that it is often not there." Daniel Altman, "Managing Globalization: Q & A with Joseph Stiglitz," *International Herald Tribune*, October 11, 2006, https://economistsview.typepad.com/economistsview/2006/10/joseph_stiglitz.html.

countries have played in the creation of global warming to the expropria-
tion of natural resources) has not been the subject of much philosophical
analysis. [...] The members of industrialized states, it is widely recog-
nized, have contributed greatly to the creation and acceleration of global
warming. In light of this, many argue that industrialized states owe reparations to the less developed countries. To use a term that is now gaining
considerable currency, some claim that currently wealthy countries owe an
"ecological debt."[42]

In typical fashion, Bernie Sanders's ambitious promise for a $16.3 trillion
Green New Deal revealed how he historicized the climate crisis, one that
he believed was caused by unfettered liberalism and corporate greed, and
envisioned it from an economic and class perspective, as he did with the
question of reparations to the descendants of slaves:

> The scope of the challenge ahead of us shares similarities with the crisis
> faced by President Franklin Delano Roosevelt in the 1940s. Battling a
> world war on two fronts—both in the East and the West—the United
> States came together, and within three short years restructured the entire
> economy in order to win the war and defeat fascism. As president, Bernie
> Sanders will boldly embrace the moral imperative of addressing the climate
> crisis and act immediately to mobilize millions of people across the country
> in support of the Green New Deal. [...]
> We need a president who has the courage, the vision, and the record to
> face down the greed of fossil fuel executives and the billionaire class who
> stand in the way of climate action. We need a president who welcomes
> their hatred. Bernie will lead our country to enact the Green New Deal
> and bring the world together to defeat the existential threat of climate
> change.[43]

Bernie Sanders presented democratic socialism as the intention to seek
and remove causal agents: "[E]nd the greed of the fossil fuel industry and
hold them accountable."[44] References to Franklin Roosevelt and to the
New Deal, for example via a reimagined and expanded Civilian Conserva-
tion Corp, were constantly introduced as subliminal messages to try and

---

[42] Simon Caney, "Environmental Degradation, Reparations, and the Moral Significance
of History," *Journal of Social Philosophy*, vol. 37, n° 3, 2006, p. 464.

[43] Sanders, "The Green New Deal," *Not me. Us.* (2020 campaign website), https://
berniesanders.com/issues/green-new-deal.

[44] Ibid.

convince mainstream voters that his plan was not a socialist makeover of the American economy in the name of addressing climate change, but one to make egalitarian liberalism accountable, including to future generations, and the United States a livable society for everyone.

11.3   THE AGE OF CORPORATE APOLOGIES

On June 6, 1966, as he was visiting South Africa, Robert F. Kennedy pronounced a speech given to National Union of South African Students[45] at the University of Cape Town, South Africa:

> I come here this evening because of my deep interest and affection for a land settled by the Dutch in the mid-seventeenth century, then taken over by the British, and at last independent; a land in which the native inhabitants were at first subdued, but relations with whom remain a problem to this day; a land which defined itself on a hostile frontier; a land which has tamed rich natural resources through the energetic application of modern technology; a land which was once the importer of slaves, and now must struggle to wipe out the last traces of that former bondage. I refer, of course, to the United States of America.[46]

The opening of Kennedy's "Day of Affirmation Address" that day was a daring one as it is uncommon, in diplomatic discourse, or for any elected official, to undermine the image and to expose the weaknesses of one's own country while speaking publicly in another country. The case of South Africa is significant because of the relation between capital and apartheid which was studied by several historians, such as Robert Davies, Christopher Saunders, Nicoli Nattrass, and more recently, Bonny Ibhawoh.[47] A radical school of thought holds that "segregation and

---

[45] The National Union of South African Students was an important force for liberalism and later radicalism in anti-apartheid movements.

[46] Robert F. Kennedy, Day of Affirmation Address, University of Cape Town, South Africa, June 6, 1966, John F. Kennedy Presidential Library, https://www.jfklibrary.org/learn/about-jfk/the-kennedy-family/robert-f-kennedy/robert-f-kennedy-speeches/day-of-affirmation-address-university-of-capetown-capetown-south-africa-june-6-1966.

[47] Robert Davies, *Capital, State and White Labour in South Africa, 1900-1960*, Brighton, Harvester Press, 1979; Christopher Saunders, *The Making of the South African Past: Major Historians on Race and Class*, Cape Town, David Philip, 1998; Nicoli Nattrass, "Controversies About Capitalism and Apartheid in South Africa: An Economic Perspective," *Journal of Southern African Studies*, vol. 17, n° 4 (1991), pp. 654–677; in

apartheid structured the process of class formation and underpinned corporate profitability by depressing black labor costs."[48] From that perspective, apartheid appears as a system of "racial capitalism" which created "an environment that was particularly conducive for privileged white business."[49] Bonny Ibhawoh showed how attention recently shifted to corporate responsibility and culpability for apartheid victimization. Local corporations benefited from the exploitation and repression of apartheid through the exploitation of black labor. As a consequence, transnational corporations continued to do business with the apartheid regime in defiance of international sanctions. They "rationalized their engagement with the apartheid regime in terms of the 'constructive engagement' argument that shaped Thatcherite and Reaganite policies toward apartheid South Africa."[50] From there, Ibhawoh studied the relatively unexplored issue of corporate apologies. Corporations rarely apologize, and their apologies are even more "uncommon and controversial" than state apologies, if only because apologies may create legal liabilities for the apologist.[51] While the post-World War II era marked the age of state apology, Ibhawoh argued, non-state actors like transnational corporations now wield unprecedented influence over the lives of people in the age of globalization, which suggests that corporate apologies may become as important as state apologies.[52] Ibhawoh was particularly interested in what he referred to as "the radical corporate apology" in the South African context, which arose "when gross human rights violations [were] involved," "when the acts or omissions for which a corporation apologize[d] [were] not merely about failure to meet industry standards and public expectations, but rather, about the systemic violation of the basic human rights of large groups of people."[53] In other words, radical

---

Bonny Ibhawoh, "Rethinking Corporate Apologies: Business and Apartheid Victimization in South Africa," *The Age of Apology: Facing Up to the Past*, edited by Mark Gibney, et al., Philadelphia, University of Pennsylvania Press, 2008, p. 274.

[48] Ibhawoh, p. 275. The liberal school, on the other hand, considers that apartheid was founded on state interventionism in all sectors of society and therefore that it conflicted with the basic tenets of free market capitalism. Ibid.

[49] Ibid., pp. 275, 277.

[50] Ibid., p. 271.

[51] Ibid., p. 272.

[52] Ibid.

[53] Ibid., p. 273.

corporate apologies are not about infringements on consumer rights, they are about violations of fundamental human rights. And, Ibhawoh argued, "[w]here companies have been accused of gross human rights violations, it is often because they have connections with a repressive government."[54]

Of course it is a bold step to compare the United States with South Africa, but this is what Robert F. Kennedy implicitly did in his 1966 address at the University of Cape Town. Beyond, thus magnified, and admittedly exaggerated, the parallel helps cast light on a number of characteristics of Bernie Sanders's democratic socialism. From the point of view of Bernie Sanders, the neoliberal regime is indeed a repressive government, and also a regime with connections to major business corporations regarded as "too big to fail," because their collapse would cause catastrophic damage to the economy: "[W]e must end, once and for all the scheme that is nothing more than a free insurance policy for Wall Street: the policy of 'too big to fail.'"[55] This was one of the core debates that surrounded the Great Recession, when corporations "too big to fail" were bailed out by the government:

> In 2010, Bank of America set up more than two hundred subsidiaries in the Caymans. Not only did it pay no federal income taxes that year, it received a tax refund for $1.9 billion. Apparently Bank of America thought stiffing the American treasury was the appropriate way to thank taxpayers for the more than $1.3 trillion it received through the bailout and the Federal Reserve.
> In 2013, JPMorgan Chase made a profit of more than $17 billion, but received a $1.3 billion tax refund, thanks in large part to its four subsidiaries incorporated in offshore tax havens. I guess JPMorgan Chase thought that was the right thing to do after receiving a bailout of more than $400 billion. [...]
> On and on it goes.[56]

The bailouts were a bipartisan measure, one typical of the rule of the market and unfettered free trade: "Corporate America spoke," Sanders

---

[54] Ibid., p. 274.

[55] Sanders, *Our Revolution*, p. 307.

[56] Ibid., p. 269.

wrote, "the leaders of both parties responded to their needs, and American people suffered."[57] The parallel with racial capitalism in South Africa as described by Bonny Ibhawoh is also significant in that it emphasizes a neoliberal pattern of economic exploitation beneath race relations in the United States. This is certainly a debatable issue,[58] particularly around the question of reparations to the descendants of slaves, but the perspective helps better understand how and why Bernie Sanders systematically reframed the slavery reparations issue as a distinctively economic, class issue,[59] the root cause being state-sanctioned corporate greed.

The issue at stake dates back at least to the end of the nineteenth century, when Scottish-born industrialist and philanthropist Andrew Carnegie, one of the titans of America's Gilded Age, wrote in *The North American Review* in 1899:

> The Socialist or Anarchist who seeks to overturn present conditions is to be regarded as attacking the foundation upon which civilization itself rests, for civilization took its start from the day that the capable, industrious workman said to his incompetent and lazy fellow, "If thou dost not sow, thou shalt not reap," and thus ended primitive Communism by separating the drones from the bees.[60]

Carnegie boldly articulated his view of the rich as mere "trustees" of their wealth who should live unostentatiously, provide moderately for their families, and use their fortunes to promote "the best good of the community in which and from which [they] had been acquired."[61] Carnegie went on to suggest some "best uses" to which the millionaire could devote his wealth, "the best fields for philanthropy," like universities, libraries, medical institutions, and public parks.[62] As a socialist,

---

[57] Ibid., p. 286.

[58] One argument sometimes leveled by opponents to slavery reparations is that African Americans are better off today in the contemporary United States than their enslaved ancestors and, therefore, that they are not confronted by historical or even enduring injustice.

[59] See *supra*, p. 206.

[60] Andrew Carnegie, *The Gospel of Wealth*, New York, Carnegie Corporation of New York, 2017, p. 4.

[61] Ibid., p. 19.

[62] Ibid., pp. 24, 25, 28, 29.

Bernie Sanders, like his model Eugene Debs before him, held a different view of "civilization," of who the "drones"—those who live on the labors of others—really are. In an article entitled "Andrew Carnegie on 'Best Fields for Philanthropy,'" Eugene Debs ironically debunked Carnegie's "Gospel of Wealth"[63]:

> In maintaining that the foregoing are "the best fields for philanthropy," Carnegie spreads himself like a green bay tree—and it is well enough to comment, briefly upon such subjects. Carnegie admits that great wealth, colossal fortunes, should be administered for the best good of the community *in which* and *from which* it had been acquired. Carnegie calls it "surplus wealth." In acquiring it from a "community" it had been taken from the people. What people? From workers who alone create wealth [...].[64]

"It is not a little amusing," Debs continued, "to note Carnegie's survey of 'the best fields for philanthropy.'"[65] Carnegie's philanthropy may be regarded as an early form of corporate self-exoneration, an early form of corporate apologies:

> It will be observed that Carnegie believes that it will be easier for him to get into heaven than for "a camel to go through the eye of a needle." But Carnegie ought to remember that Christ did not take his view of beggars—he did not denounce beggars, he took pity on them; they excited his sympathy, and he wrought miracles to feed them. Carnegie, in his "Gospel," takes no stock in beggars. "Of every $1,000 spent in so-called charity," Mr. Carnegie thought "$900 was unwisely spent" [...].[66]

In *Our Revolution*, Bernie Sanders exposed the activities of the Koch brothers, "the second-wealthiest family in America, with a net worth

---

[63] Andrew Carnegie, "Wealth," *North American Review*, vol. 148, n° 391, June 1889, pp. 653–665, June 1889. The article was later published as part 1 of *The Gospel of Wealth*. See: *The Gospel of Wealth*, The Carnegie Corporation of New York, https://www.carnegie.org/about/our-history/gospelofwealth.

[64] Debs, "Andrew Carnegie on 'Best Fields for Philanthropy,'" *Locomotive Firemen's Magazine*, vol. 14, n° 2, February 1890, pp. 104–106, E.V. Debs Internet Archive, https://www.marxists.org/archive/debs/works/1890/900200-debs-carnegieonphilanthropy.pdf.

[65] Ibid.

[66] Ibid.

of at least $82 billion" and, according to Sanders, "the leading force in the oligarchic movement,"[67] to show how philanthropy could be instrumentalized:

> In *Dark Money*,[68] her brilliant book on the Kochs, Jane Mayer writes that these billionaire brothers "subsidized networks of seemingly unconnected think tanks and academic programs and spawned advocacy groups to make their arguments in the national political debate. They hired lobbyists to push their interests in Congress and operatives to create synthetic grass-roots groups to give their movement political momentum on the ground. In addition, they financed legal groups and judicial junkets to press their cases in the courts. Eventually, they added to this a private political machine that rivaled, and threatened to subsume, the Republican Party. Much of this activism was cloaked in secrecy and presented as philanthropy, leaving almost no money trail that the public could trace. But cumulatively it formed, as one of their operatives boasted in 2015, a fully integrated network."[69]

Sanders demanded accountability and denounced philanthropy that could be regarded simply as a candid, indirect form of corporate apology. Corporate greed, he argued, must be held financially accountable: "We should not have a regressive tax system in which large, profitable corporations like Amazon pay nothing in federal income taxes."[70] Corporate apologies have become a common feature of corporate communication nowadays, one that is arguably designed to deflect responsibility and accountability. *Forbes* published an article entitled "10 Powerful Example of Corporate Apologies" in October 2018, citing apologies by KFC, PwC, O.B., Apple, Airbnb, JetBlue, Netflix, Sony, Toyota, and Domino.[71] In November 2018, CNBC published "Mark Zuckerberg

---

[67] Sanders, *Our Revolution*, p. 197.

[68] Jane Mayer, *Dark Money: The Hidden History of the Billionaires Behind the Rise of the Radical Right*, New York, Anchor Books, 2016.

[69] Sanders, *Our Revolution*, pp. 197–198.

[70] Id., "I'm Running for President," Bernie Sanders YouTube Channel, February 19, 2019, https://www.youtube.com/watch?time_continue=2&v=s7DRwz0cAt0.

[71] Blake Morgan, "10 Powerful Examples Of Corporate Apologies," *Forbes*, October 24, 2018, https://www.forbes.com/sites/blakemorgan/2018/10/24/10-powerful-examples-of-corporate-apologies/#6b25b6df40de.

has been talking and apologizing about privacy since 2003"[72] on its website, and in April 2019, the *Washington Post* released "14 years of Mark Zuckerberg saying sorry, not sorry."[73] As stated by the International Center for Transitional Justice, official apologies are not enough as reparation to victims of serious violations:

> While apologies have value in themselves and can address both moral and physical harm, they should be combined with material forms of reparation. In particular, care needs to be taken to ensure that a disproportionate emphasis on apologies does not diminish the likelihood that other reparative measures, such as restitution and medical care, will be implemented, to help limit the long-term harm caused to victims or address their physical needs.[74]

Democratic socialism applied the same argument to corporate apologies, as in Sanders's *Outsider in the White House*:

> Today, a national industrial policy is considered an anachronism by the apologists for corporate America, even though those same apologists never have any quarrel with massive government efforts to assist "free-market capitalism" or establish "free trade" as our industrial policy.[75]

The ideological argument to counter-democratic socialism was that socialism was a foreign-born ideology, an ideology of the past, an "anachronism" outside of mainstream politics.

---

[72] Sara Salinas, Anita Balakrishnan, "Mark Zuckerberg Has Been Talking and Apologizing About Privacy Since 2003," CNBC, December 19, 2018, https://www.cnbc.com/2018/12/19/facebook-ceo-mark-zuckerberg-privacy-apologies.html.

[73] Geoffrey A. Fowler, Chiqui Esteban, "14 Years of Mark Zuckerberg Saying Sorry, Not Sorry," *Washington Post*, April 9, 2018, https://www.washingtonpost.com/graphics/2018/business/facebook-zuckerberg-apologies.

[74] Ruben Carranza, Cristián Correa, Elena Naughton, "More Than Words: Apologies as a Form of Reparation," International Center for Transitional Justice, January 27, 2016, https://www.ictj.org/publication/more-than-words-apologies-form-reparation.

[75] Sanders, *Outsider in the White House*, p. 291.

References

Altman, Daniel. "Managing Globalization: Q & A with Joseph Stiglitz." *International Herald Tribune* (October 11, 2006), https://economistsview.typepad.com/economistsview/2006/10/joseph_stiglitz.html.

Caney, Simon. "Environmental Degradation, Reparations, and the Moral Significance of History" *Journal of Social Philosophy*, vol. 37, n° 3 (2006), pp. 464–482.

Carnegie, Andrew. "Wealth." *North American Review*, vol. 148, n° 391 (June 1889), pp. 653–665, June 1889.

———. *The Gospel of Wealth*. New York: Carnegie Corporation of New York, 2017.

Carranza, Ruben, Cristián Correa, Elena Naughton. "More Than Words: Apologies as a Form of Reparation." International Center for Transitional Justice (January 27, 2016), https://www.ictj.org/publication/more-than-words-apologies-form-reparation.

Davies, Robert. *Capital, State and White Labour in South Africa, 1900-1960*. Brighton: Harvester Press, 1979.

Debs, Eugene V. "Andrew Carnegie on 'Best Fields for Philanthropy.'" *Locomotive Firemen's Magazine*, vol. 14, n° 2 (February 1890), pp. 104–106, E.V. Debs Internet Archive, https://www.marxists.org/archive/debs/works/1890/900200-debs-carnegieonphilanthropy.pdf.

Fowler, Geoffrey A., Chiqui Esteban. "14 Years of Mark Zuckerberg Saying Sorry, Not Sorry." *Washington Post* (April 9, 2018), https://www.washingtonpost.com/graphics/2018/business/facebook-zuckerberg-apologies.

Haltiwanger, John. "Bernie Sanders When Asked About Reparations Says There Are 'Better Ways' to Help People Than 'Writing Out A Check.'" *Business Insider* (March 1, 2019), https://www.businessinsider.fr/us/bernie-sanders-reparations-better-ways-help-writing-check-2019-3.

Ibhawoh, Bonny. "Rethinking Corporate Apologies: Business and Apartheid Victimization in South Africa." *The Age of Apology: Facing Up to the Past*, edited by Mark Gibney, et al. Philadelphia: University of Pennsylvania Press, 2008, pp. 271–284.

Kennedy, Robert F. Day of Affirmation Address, University of Cape Town, South Africa (June 6, 1966), John F. Kennedy Presidential Library, https://www.jfklibrary.org/learn/about-jfk/the-kennedy-family/robert-f-kennedy/robert-f-kennedy-speeches/day-of-affirmation-address-university-of-capetown-capetown-south-africa-june-6-1966.

King, Martin Luther Jr. "I Have a Dream," Address delivered at the March on Washington for Jobs and Freedom (August 28, 1963). The Martin Luther King Jr. Research and Education Institute (Stanford University), https://kinginstitute.stanford.edu/king-papers/documents/i-have-dream-address-delivered-march-washington-jobs-and-freedom.

Mayer, Jane. *Dark Money: The Hidden History of the Billionaires Behind the Rise of the Radical Right.* New York: Anchor Books, 2016.

Miller, David. "Distributing Responsibilities." *Journal of Political Philosophy,* vol. 9, n° 4, (2001), pp. 453–472.

Morgan, Blake. "10 Powerful Examples of Corporate Apologies." *Forbes* (October 24, 2018), https://www.forbes.com/sites/blakemorgan/2018/10/24/10-powerful-examples-of-corporate-apologies/#6b25b6df40de.

Nattrass, Nicoli. "Controversies About Capitalism and Apartheid in South Africa: An Economic Perspective." *Journal of Southern African Studies,* vol. 17, n° 4 (1991), pp. 654–677.

Reed, Adolph Jr., Michael Francis, Steve Striffler. "Hurricane Katrina and Bernie Sanders: From Neoliberal Disaster to 'Political Revolution,'" *Common Dreams* (August 29, 2015), https://www.commondreams.org/views/2015/08/29/hurricane-katrina-and-bernie-sanders-neoliberal-disaster-political-revolution.

Salinas, Sara, Anita Balakrishnan. "Mark Zuckerberg Has Been Talking and Apologizing About Privacy Since 2003." CNBC (December 19, 2018), https://www.cnbc.com/2018/12/19/facebook-ceo-mark-zuckerberg-privacy-apologies.html.

Sandel, Michael J. *Liberalism and the Limits of Justice.* Cambridge: Cambridge University Press, 1982. Rpt. 1998.

Sanders, Bernard. with Huck Gutman. *Outsider in the House: A Political Autobiography.* New York: Verso, 1997. Rpt. *Outsider in the White House,* 2015.

———. *Our Revolution: A Future to Believe In.* New York: Thomas Dunne Books, 2016.

———. "Senator Sanders on Occupy Wall Street." *The Guardian* (October 21, 2011), https://www.youtube.com/watch?v=9HSaZOSWfrU.

———. *Bernie Speaks: Speeches by Bernie Sanders,* compiled by David Cane. CreateSpace Independent Publishing Platform: Greenbridge Publishing, 2017.

———. *Where We Go from Here: Two Years in the Resistance.* New York: Thomas Dunne Books, 2018.

Saunders, Christopher. *The Making of the South African Past: Major Historians on Race and Class.* Cape Town: David Philip, 1998.

Smith, Adam. *The Theory of Moral Sentiments,* edited by D. D. Raphael, A. L. Macfie. Indianapolis, Ind.: Liberty Fund, 1976.

Spinner-Halev, Jeff. *Enduring Injustice.* Cambridge: Cambridge University Press, 2012.

Walsh, Kenneth T. "The Undoing of George W. Bush." *U.S. News and World Report* (August 28, 2015), https://www.usnews.com/news/the-report/articles/2015/08/28/hurricane-katrina-was-the-beginning-of-the-end-for-george-w-bush.

CHAPTER 12

Democratic Socialism and the Mainstream

The popularity of Bernie Sanders and his meteoric rise during the 2016 and 2020 presidential campaigns raise two important questions. One is that as long as Bernie Sanders was on the campaign trail, his popularity seemed to grow among Democratic voters and democratic socialism became an everyday conversation topic. Second, considering his popularity, the fact that Sanders consistently placed his vision of society under the "S" word[1] (socialism) instead of aligning with the Democratic Party, which he did not do even while running for the Democratic nomination, seemed to forever hinder his electability. A President Sanders would have been the first commander-in-chief describing himself as a "democratic socialist," a most unlikely scenario in American politics.

12.1 Democratic Socialism

The political discourse surrounding Bernie Sanders was considerably locked by the reference to socialism, with socialism ultimately being more indicative of the motivations of whoever was using the term than of the factual reality of Sanders's platform. While Sanders kept repeating that

---

[1] The expression is borrowed from the title of John Nichols's, *The "S" Word: A Short History of an American Tradition...Socialism*, New York, Verso, 2011.

© The Author(s), under exclusive license to Springer Nature Switzerland AG 2021
N. Gachon, *Bernie Sanders's Democratic Socialism*,
https://doi.org/10.1007/978-3-030-69661-0_12

233

what he meant by "democratic socialism" had nothing to do with collectivizing the means of production in the United States,[2] and that he saw himself as the political heir of Franklin Roosevelt and Martin Luther King Jr.,[3] the reference to socialism made him an easy target for opponents who could assimilate him with Soviet communist dictatorships,[4] the nationalization of the economy by the federal government, and even a socialist takeover of America. The political discourse was locked in dichotomies of the past and in a position that questioned where the Democratic Party and the American political mainstream exactly stood: an icon of the Democratic Party, Roosevelt, was summoned by Sanders, a socialist candidate running for the nomination of the Democratic Party after being asked by the Democratic Party to sign a pledge that, as a socialist candidate, he formally pledged to be a Democrat.[5]

There was a distinctively reparative dimension to Bernie Sanders's socialism in that it vowed to repair democracy through a set of policy measures aiming to reverse what Sanders regarded as neoliberal violations of human rights: Medicare for all, free post-secondary education, progressive taxation, universal childcare, guaranteed employment at a living wage, a sustainable environment, and public housing. In political terms, the platform entailed a paradigm shift in that it redefined what the very nature of the economy should be to answer the democratically determined needs of the people. From that angle, Bernie Sanders could be regarded as a social democrat rather than a democratic socialist, i.e., as someone who proposed a reformist approach that would not do away with capitalism but instead regulate it, providing public services and substantial welfare within the frame of an essentially market-led economy. As a matter of fact, the fundamental difference between socialism and social democracy is precisely that socialism advocates for social ownership of the means of production, which Bernie Sanders did not suggest, and does not believe in reforms within capitalism, which Sanders did seem to believe in, but in a revolution of the whole system.

Due to a number of remarks and statements by Bernie Sanders, much was made of his fascination for Nordic countries. Markets Insider,

[2] Sanders, *Our Revolution*, op. cit., p. 20.

[3] See *supra*, p. 198.

[4] See *supra*, p. 54.

[5] See *supra*, p. 93.

for example, published an article entitled "Bernie Sanders and AOC support the 'Nordic model,' which features robust health and social-welfare systems—one that Finland's leader calls 'the American Dream'" in February 2020:

> Sen. Bernie Sanders and Rep. Alexandria Ocasio-Cortez of New York have supported modeling the United States after Nordic countries like Finland, Sweden and Norway—all of which feature cradle-to-grave benefits like government-run healthcare and a robust social welfare system.[6]

One typical statement made on the subject by Bernie Sanders is to be found in *Outsider in the White House*:

> The truth is that, very sadly, the corporate media ignores some of the huge accomplishments that have taken place in countries like Denmark, Finland, Sweden and Norway. [...] These countries, which have a long history of democratic socialist or labor governments, have excellent and universal health care systems, excellent educational systems and they have gone a long way toward eliminating poverty and creating a far more egalitarian society than we have. I think that there are economic and social models out there that we can learn a heck of a lot from, and that's something I would be talking about.[7]

While it is certainly true that social democracy was politically and socially appealing to Bernie Sanders, his vision of society was in reality always more radical, and arguably even more explicitly so in the wake of the Occupy Wall Street movement. In redefining what the very nature of the economy should be to answer the democratically determined needs of the people, Sanders did indeed propose a radical paradigm shift. Those needs were the needs of the 99% in an economy which, Sanders argued, prioritized answering to the needs of the 1%. That was a radical paradigm shift in that the aim was to reverse the neoliberal prism and to repair enduring injustice in the United States. "For the federal government to

[6] Joseph Zeballos-Roig, "Bernie Sanders and AOC Support the 'Nordic Model,' Which Features Robust Health and Social-Welfare Systems—One That Finland's Leader Calls 'the American Dream,'" Markets Insider, February 3, 2020, https://markets.businessinsider.com/news/stocks/bernie-sanders-nordic-model-finland-american-dream-sanna-marin-2020-2-1028868627.

[7] Sanders, *Outsider in the White House*, p. 342.

reach out and provide assistance to those in need is bad and harmful," Sanders wrote, "[t]he Republicans get away with this absurd argument, the Democrats collapse before it, and the American people swallow it because there is virtually no organized opposition."[8] Organized opposition may be what Sanders's democratic socialism was essentially about, the conscience that what had brought social programs and ultimately social democracy in those very countries he often praised, Nordic countries in particular, class warfare, militant labor and socialist movements were the forces that had initially achieved the paradigm shift. Social democracy, from that perspective, was not the work of moderates, was not born in the mainstream. That dimension had always been present in Sanders's political views, as testified by his veneration for Eugene Debs, but it was suddenly magnified by Occupy Wall Street, a movement credited by many[9] with making the case for "class warfare."

As a detonator of social discontent, Occupy launched Bernie Sanders's political ascension. Once class warfare had become an issue again, Sanders could defuse his own radicalism and plead, from a more mainstream posture, for a completion of Roosevelt's New Deal, and call for reparative justice on behalf of the 99%. To some extent, the strategy was rhetorical. As Sarah Brady Siff remarked, "[t]he term '99 percent' is technically nonsense, as the bottom 99 percent of households in America includes plenty of millionaires."[10] And even Paul Krugman, the liberal economist, insisted that Bernie Sanders was not a socialist but that "he play[ed] one on TV," and that it was exactly where the problem lay:

> The thing is, Bernie Sanders isn't actually a socialist in any normal sense of the term. He doesn't want to nationalize our major industries and replace markets with central planning; he has expressed admiration, not for Venezuela, but for Denmark. He's basically what Europeans would call a social democrat—and social democracies like Denmark are, in fact, quite nice places to live, with societies that are, if anything, freer than our own.[11]

---

[8] Ibid., p. 174.

[9] See, for example: Sarah Brady Siff, "From Karl Marx to Karl Rove: 'Class Warfare' in American Politics," *Origins*, vol. 5, n° 12, September 2012, http://origins.osu.edu/art icle/karl-marx-karl-rove-class-warfare-american-politics.

[10] Ibid.

[11] Krugman, "Bernie Sanders Isn't a Socialist," *New York Times*, February 13, 2020, https://www.nytimes.com/2020/02/13/opinion/bernie-sanders-socialism.html.

So why did Sanders call himself a socialist? "I'd say," Krugman proceeded, "that it [was] mainly about personal branding, with a dash of glee at shocking the bourgeoisie. And this self-indulgence did no harm as long as he was just a senator from a very liberal state."[12] Krugman's argument arguably took "democratic socialism" from the perspective of "social democracy," while Sanders arguably took it from the other end, from the perspective of "class warfare," i.e., of what had made social democracy possible in the first place. "Health care reform in America will not come without radical political change and the growth of a strong progressive movement," Sanders wrote in *Outsider in the House*.[13]

Bernie Sanders could not be regarded as a mere social liberal in 1970 when he released *Eugene V. Debs: Trade Unionist, Socialist, Revolutionary, 1855–1926* and quoted Eugene Debs's 1918 Canton, Ohio speech:

> In the middle ages the feudal lords and barons, the economic predecessors of the capitalists of our day, declared all wars. And their miserable serfs fought all the battles. The poor, ignorant serfs had been taught to revere their masters; to believe that when their masters declared war upon one another, it was their patriotic duty to fall upon each other and to cut one another's throats for the profit and glory of the lords and barons who held them in contempt. And that is war in a nutshell. It hasn't changed. The master class has always declared the wars; the subject class has always fought the battles. The master class has had all to gain and nothing to lose, while the subject class has had nothing to gain and all to lose-especially their lives.[14]

Sanders's democratic socialism was prospectively rooted in the agency that could come from organized opposition, from the power to envision alternative realities, from the belief that the course of capitalism could indeed be modified. The strategy was certainly more rhetorical than it was subversive, but it was radical in that it sought to invert the 1–99% power structure in the United States, therefore to recalibrate the political mainstream. Socialism, the specter of socialism, the "S" word, etc. were extremely significant labels in a country where the typical audience was always likely to equate socialism with communism, authoritarian regimes,

---

[12] Ibid.

[13] Sanders, *Outsider in the White House*, p. 222.

[14] Id., *Eugene Debs*, band 11, "The Speech That Sent Debs to Jail."

Stalinism, etc. By contrast, Bernie Sanders sought to put forward the "democratic" nature of his "socialism" and to inscribe it in the democratic mainstream. Occupy Wall Street had opened new perspectives. A majority of the American people, nurtured in the utopia of a classless society with limitless upward mobility, now suddenly agreed, as testified by the Pew Research Center in 2012, that there were "very strong" or "strong" conflicts between the rich and the poor.[15] The inscription into the political mainstream of bolder egalitarian measures under the banner of democratic socialism by a candidate who presented himself as the heir of Franklin Roosevelt carried collateral damage for the establishment of the Democratic Party. "The pundits and the establishment may not have thought so," Sanders wrote, "but I have always felt that the ideas I was espousing were not radical or fringe. They were mainstream, the views that millions held."[16] In democratic fashion, the collateral damage would be taken to the polls:

> [I]f poor people would utilize their leverage at the polls, they would realize the great principle that in a democratic society they, as much as anyone else, have the right to determine the future of this country and shape its social contract. That sense of empowerment, in itself, would transform the lives of millions of people and, ultimately, the entire nation.
>
> If poor people voted, the government would pay far more attention to economic injustice, health care, education, and other issues largely ignored today.[17]

12.2   DEMOCRATIC SOCIALISM AND THE DEMOCRATS

For the Democratic establishment, Bernie Sanders's two campaigns for the party's nomination brought back memories of 1972, not because Sanders ran unsuccessfully in the Vermont gubernatorial election that year but because 1972 was the year of George McGovern's landslide defeat to Richard Nixon in the presidential election. The 1972 reelection of Richard Nixon was no contest: Senator George McGovern (D-S.D.)

---

[15] Pew Research Center, "Rising Share of Americans See Conflict Between Rich and Poor," op. cit., p. 171.

[16] Sanders, *Our Revolution*, p. 91.

[17] Id., *Outsider in the White House*, p. 177.

lost 49 states (except Massachusetts) to Richard Nixon.[18] The ghost of George McGovern loomed over the Democratic Party ever after: conventional wisdom had it that he had gone too far left on the campaign trail and that voters eventually rejected his ideology. One consequence of George McGovern's cataclysmic defeat was that it pushed the Democratic Party to the center, a rightward move that was carried to completion during the political triangulations of the Clinton years, when the president proclaimed that "the era of big government" was "over,"[19] and that he had a plan to end welfare as Americans knew it: "For so long, government has failed us, and one of its worst failures has been welfare. I have a plan to end welfare as we know it, to break the cycle of welfare dependency."[20] For the left, that was often understood as a shift from the Democratic Party's principles of standing up for the working class and the oppressed. For those who compared Bernie Sanders to George McGovern, the lesson of 1972 was that if the Democratic Party was taken too far to the left, it was likely to suffer dramatic defeat. Such was arguably the case in 2016, with a highly contested Democratic National Convention, and even more so in 2020 with the specter of a Nixonian reelection for Donald Trump.

Bernie Sanders, for his part, hardly ever participated in this debate, hardly ever referred to George McGovern, and only with considerable—prudent—distance when he did, as in *Outsider in the White House*:

> 1972 was the year Richard Nixon won a landslide victory over George McGovern. During that campaign, the Liberty Union threw its support behind the presidential candidate of the People's Party, Dr. Benjamin Spock, the world-famous pediatrician. [...] As the Liberty Union candidate for governor, and the head of our ticket, I was given the responsibility of meeting Spock at the airport when he came to Vermont. I was broke at the time, and needed to borrow a few bucks to put gas into my old VW bug just to get there. At the airport, after convincing the Secret Service that I really was a candidate for governor, I was able to welcome Spock to Vermont.[21]

---

[18] See *supra*, p. 33.

[19] William. J. Clinton, op. cit., p. 508.

[20] Id., in "Bill Clinton in 1992 ad: 'A Plan to End Welfare as We Know It,'" *Washington Post*, August 30, 2016, https://www.washingtonpost.com/video/politics/bill-clinton-in-1992-ad-a-plan-to-end-welfare-as-we-know-it/2016/08/30/9e6350f8-6ee0-11e6-993f-73c693a89820_video.html.

[21] Sanders, *Outsider in the White House*, pp. 22–23.

In this passage, Sanders drew attention to the fact that he was a candidate for governor of Vermont that year, not yet even thinking of national
politics, and that the party he was running for—the Liberty Union—
supported Benjamin Spock of the People's Party. The People's Party was a
coalition of left-wing organizations whose platform "called for the immediate withdrawal of all American troops abroad; free medical care as a
right; an end to tax preference; an allowance of $6,500 for a family of
four; the legalization of abortion on demand and marijuana, and an end
to discrimination against women and homosexuals."[22] Sanders's distance
is also noticeable in that neither he nor the Liberty Union Party supported
Louis Fisher, the presidential candidate of the Socialist Labor Party of
America, although he did run on an anticapitalist platform.[23] Benjamin
Spock and the People's Party were even further to the left than George
McGovern was. As Steve Nisse, a delegate from Ann Arbor, Michigan,
said:

> The liberals imagine the Senator to be a lot more liberal than he really is.
> [McGovern] is perhaps better than most, but he's not much different. We
> want to fundamentally change the social structure. We're just beginning,
> but on the local level we can be effective.[24]

Benjamin Spock's rhetoric prefigured much of Sanders's own rhetoric:

> We are out to build an in dependent political movement. That means we
> are independent of both political parties. Both of them got us involved
> in Vietnam. Neither one got us out. Both are beholden to industry. Both
> bore new tax loopholes.[25]

For progressives, the argument that George McGovern went too far
left to be electable in 1972 is still open for debate. It seems, however, that
as the Democratic Party establishment moved to the center, i.e., to the

---

[22] Andrew H. Malcom, "Spock Nominated by People's Party," *New York Times*,
July 30, 1972, https://www.nytimes.com/1972/07/30/archives/spock-nominated-by-
peoples-party-convention-formally-names.html.

[23] Socialist Labor Party of America, "National Platform," April 11, 1972, http://www.
slp.org/pdf/platforms/plat1972.pdf.

[24] Malcom, op. cit., p. 227

[25] Ibid.

right, in the following decades, the progressive grassroots moved to the left, with dire consequences for the party. As Rahm Emanuel, the former Clinton adviser and Obama chief of staff, put it during an interview with Todd Purdum for *The Atlantic* in 2019, resentment against Bill Clinton and Barack Obama surpassed resentment against George W. Bush among progressives:

> Today's progressives are more angry at Clinton and Obama than they are at Bush 43. Whether it's Clinton's "small ideas" and welfare reform, or Obama's Affordable Care Act without a public option—those are the things where they feel like there were missed moments for big, bold ideas. Really? And that's what drives the energy. Yes, they're angry at Trump. Yes, they're angry at Bush. But a lot of the energy is directed at the fact that they don't love those two presidents—which I'd remind everybody are the only two Democrats to get reelected since Franklin Roosevelt.[26]

Bernie Sanders's strongest support was among young voters, among students or recent college graduates, among the millennials who had overtaken the Baby Boomers as the nation's largest living adult generation and consistently increased their voting rates and were now threatening to outvote older generations.[27] They could be regarded as the descendants of the McGovern generation in that they gravitated to the Democratic Party over social and environmental concerns and over moral outrage at the Vietnam War and later the American invasion of Iraq and more recently, in the wake of the Great Recession, over what they saw as the irresponsibility of Wall Street and the billionaire class.[28] In other words, what took place in 1972, and what George McGovern paid the electoral price for, was the first concrete manifestation of the collapse of the New Deal coalition. The landslide defeat was due to divisions among the Democratic Party at least as much as it was due to McGovern's left-wing campaign: Jimmy Carter, who would be elected to the White House in 1976, led the "Stop McGovern" movement at the 1972

[26] Todd S. Purdum, "Democrats of All Ages Agree on Nothing," *The Atlantic*, August 11, 2019, https://www.theatlantic.com/politics/archive/2019/08/how-democrats-view-obama/595837.

[27] Pew Research Center, "Gen Z, Millennials and Gen X Outvoted Older Generations in 2018 Midterms," May 29, 2019, https://www.pewresearch.org/fact-tank/2019/05/29/gen-z-millennials-and-gen-x-outvoted-older-generations-in-2018-midterms.

[28] Judis, p. 84.

Democratic Convention in Miami.[29] McGovern represented a revolt against a long line of successful Democratic presidents from Franklin Roosevelt through Lyndon Johnson, a revolt that divided Democratic voters and contributed to handing victory to Nixon. 2016 and 2020, from that angle, were almost like history repeating itself: here was Bernie Sanders, a candidate for the Democratic primary that embodied a revolt against two successful Democratic presidents, Bill Clinton and Barack Obama. Contrary to what Joe Scarborough claimed, however, Sanders's supporters were not only "pirates from outside the establishment."[30] They were interested in more than a hostile takeover of the Democratic Party, they were intent on winning the presidential election. Unlike Bernie Sanders, George McGovern never looked like he was going to beat Richard Nixon. The comparison between McGovern and Sanders can hardly go any further, therefore. McGovern arguably lost because he was facing a popular incumbent presiding over a booming economy more than because he was too far to the left.

Bernie Sanders's appeal to younger generations in the wake of the Occupy Wall Street movement built on the realization that the American promise would most likely not be fulfilled for them in the wake of the Great Recession, that there would be fewer opportunities on the job market but still more college debts to pay back. The Pew Research Center reported that a record 37% of young households had outstanding student loans in 2010, up from 22% in 2001 and 16% in 1989.[31] Socialism was no longer taboo among younger people. On January 27, 2016, the web-based market research and data analytics firm YouGov indicated that 43% of young adults under 30 had a very favorable (8%) or favorable (35%) opinion of socialism, as opposed to 26% who had a somewhat unfavorable (13%) or unfavorable (13%) opinion.[32] Unlike Lincoln Steffens in

---

[29] Bernard Ryan Jr., *Jimmy Carter: U.S. President and Humanitarian*, New York, Ferguson, 2006, p. 47.

[30] Scarborough, op. cit., p. 6.

[31] Pew Research Center, "Young Adults, Student Debt and Economic Well-Being," May 14, 2014, https://www.pewsocialtrends.org/2014/05/14/young-adults-student-debt-and-economic-well-being.

[32] YouGov, "Socialism and Bernie Sanders," January 27, 2015, https://d25d2506s fb94s.cloudfront.net/cumulus_uploads/document/467z1ta5ys/tabs_OP_Socialism_201 60127.pdf.

1919,[33] they could no longer envision a future that would work, no utopia that could hold a promise for the future or, even looking backward as Edward Bellamy had done,[34] make sense of the present. Bernie Sanders's self-proclamation as a democratic socialist, therefore, certainly came to be seen as an electoral handicap by the Democratic establishment but his anti-establishment message gave him an edge among younger voters in 2016, earning more of their votes than Hillary Clinton and Donald Trump combined.[35] Sanders did not so much promise a socialist utopia as much as he promised to hold the American utopia socially accountable. The United States was envisioned as an American utopia, the promise of a better world, "a more perfect Union,"[36] away from the divine rights of kings, one that would "promote the general Welfare."[37] Utopias are also forms of protest when they react to unsatisfactory conditions and point to positive alternative to these conditions. The appeal of Sanders's democratic socialism was boosted by the Great Recession, by the Occupy Wall Street movement, and also by the insufficient fulfillment of Barack Obama's promise to America. As Sally L. Kitch wrote, "America promises utopia, and its failure to realize that promise makes its sins seem much worse than bigger sins seem in other place. Where the promise is great, so too is the potential for disillusionment."[38] The Democratic grassroots had moved to the left as the Democratic establishment had moved to the center-right. Sanders confronted the Democrats with an insoluble equation, one that could not be triangulated. On March 4, 2020, in an interview with Bo Erickson of CBS News, Joe Biden tried to co-opt the grassroots in order to discredit claims by Bernie Sanders that the Democratic establishment was trying to defeat him: "The establishment are all those hardworking, middle class people, those

[33] Steffens, Letter to Marie Howe, op. cit., p. 68.

[34] Bellamy, op. cit., p. 46.

[35] Center for Information and Research on Civic Learning and Engagement (CIRCLE), "Youth Voting in the 2016 Primaries," July 27, 2016, https://circle.tufts.edu/latest-res earch/youth-voting-2016-primaries.

[36] U.S. Constitution, op. cit., p. 61.

[37] Ibid.

[38] Sally L. Kitch, *From Utopianism to Realism in American Feminist Thought and Theory*, Chicago, IL, University of Chicago Press, 2000, p. 72.

African Americans…they are the establishment!"[39] Sanders immediately tweeted his reply: "No, Joe. The 'establishment' are the 60 billionaires who are funding your campaign and the corporate-funded super PACs that are spending millions on negative ads attacking me."[40] The division within the Democratic Party, from that perspective, was McGovernesque indeed.

12.3   REDISTRIBUTIVE JUSTICE

Bernie Sanders's political message is strong on promising reparative justice for mainstream America. His 2020 campaign promise to make public colleges, universities, and trade schools tuition-free and to cancel all student debt within ten years, to expand Social Security and to increase benefits for low-income senior citizens and people with disabilities by more than $1,300 a year, to guarantee housing as a human right and to eliminate homelessness would have cost $2.5 trillion over the next decade. Guaranteeing, to guarantee universal childcare and pre-school to every family in America who needs would have cost $1.5 trillion. Sanders also promised to eliminate all of the $81 billion in past-due medical debt held by 79 million Americans, to fundamentally transform the U.S. energy system away from fossil fuel and toward energy efficiency and renewable energy (which should also create 20 million good-paying union jobs in the process), and to save over $450 billion in healthcare costs, and prevent 68,000 unnecessary deaths every year with Medicare for all.[41] Such promises were highly significant, so would have been the consequences of breaking or not fulfilling them had he been elected. Although his 2020 campaign website did provide a plan to finance his major proposals,[42] estimated at a staggering $60 trillion,[43] Sanders was

[39] Bo Erickson, Twitter post, March 4, 2020, https://twitter.com/BoKnowsNews/status/1235323686972018690.

[40] Sanders, Twitter post, March 4, 2020, https://twitter.com/berniesanders/status/1235335576288743427.

[41] Sanders, "How Does Bernie Pay for His Major Plans," Not me. Us (2020 campaign website), https://berniesanders.com/issues/how-does-bernie-pay-his-major-plans.

[42] Ibid.

[43] Ronald Brownstein, "The Cost of Sanders' Agenda—Possibly $60 Trillion—Would Set a Peacetime U.S. Record," CNN, January 18, 2020, https://edition.cnn.com/2020/01/14/politics/bernie-sanders-proposals-cost/index.html.

often at pains to explain in detail and with convincing precision how much his proposals would cost and what taxes he would raise to pay for them. He avoided the questions of Anderson Cooper on "60 Minutes" on February 24, 2020, shortly after his win in the Nevada caucuses:

> COOPER: But you say you don't know what the total price is, but you know how it's gonna be paid for. How do you know it's gonna be paid for if you don't know how much the price is?
> SANDERS: Well, I can't—you know, I can't rattle off to you ever nickel and every dime. But we have accounted for—you—you talked about Medicare for All. We have options out there that will pay for it.[44]

The next day, during a CNN town Hall in Charleston, South Carolina, Sanders handed the moderator, Chris Cuomo,[45] a document that he said cataloged the details of all his spending plans, including the taxes that he was proposing to pay for them, and that he promised to post on his website.[46] The challenge, for Sanders, was to produce a politically acceptable plan to fund his spending and his constant response, notably during the February 25, 2020, town hall, was "a modest tax on Wall Street speculation."[47] Many critics immediately answered that the numbers did not add up, that Sanders was minimizing the real cost of his plans and overstating the funds they would generate.[48] Beyond the figures, from Sanders's perspective, the debate was over reparative justice for the American people, justice to be implemented through taxation, through redistributive justice. The debate was ideological more than it was economic. As Ronald Brownstein noted, although Sanders's plan could not be precisely qualified, it would increase government spending far more than Franklin Roosevelt's New Deal,

[44] Sanders, "Bernie Sanders on Being the Democratic Front-Runner and Taking on Donald Trump," 60 Minutes, CBS News, February 24, 2020, https://www.cbsnews.com/news/bernie-sanders-democratic-presidential-front-runner-anderson-cooper-60-minutes.

[45] Id., "Bernie Sanders: I Thought This Question Might Come Up," CNN, February 24, 2020, https://www.youtube.com/watch?v=hYmlzB7AlWM&feature=emb_logo.

[46] Id., "How Does Bernie Pay for His Major Plans," op. cit., p. 231.

[47] Id., "Bernie Sanders: I Thought This Question Might Come Up," op. cit., p. 231.

[48] Ben Ritz, "Even with New Pay-Fors, Bernie's Agenda Still Has a $25 Trillion Hole," *Forbes*, February 25, 2020, https://www.forbes.com/sites/benritz/2020/02/25/even-with-new-pay-fors-bernies-agenda-still-has-a-25-trillion-hole/#599af64466c1.

Lyndon Johnson's Great Society, or even George McGovern's 1972 presidential platform. Sanders's plan, Brownstein continued, would also increase the size of government far more than any modern Republican president, including Ronald Reagan, had sought to cut it. Yet the source of Brownstein's argument was "a historical analysis shared with CNN by Larry Summers, the former chief White House economic adviser for Barack Obama and treasury secretary for Bill Clinton,"[49] in other words an analysis produced by a member of the Democratic establishment that had moved to the center-right and was trying to halt Sanders's momentum. Larry Summers was one of the members of Barack Obama's economic team whom Gerard Baker had dubbed "the Robert Rubin Memorial All Stars."[50] Summers had co-orchestrated the Wall Street bailout in 2008; for Sanders, reparative and redistributive justice were the sides of the same coin, they were a matter of accountability to mainstream America:

> The taxpayers of this country bailed out Wall Street in 2008; as I said earlier, now it's time for Wall Street to start helping the middle class of this country—by making public colleges and universities throughout the country tuition-free.[51]

After signing the *Tax Relief, Unemployment Insurance Reauthorization, and Job Creation Act* on December 17, 2010,[52] a compromise tax package with the Republicans in Congress that extended the Bush tax cuts for two years, Barack Obama unveiled plans to increase taxes for millionaires—people making more than $1 million a year—in September 2011, in the midst of the Occupy Wall Street movement. Obama called his plan the "Buffett Rule," the *Paying a Fair Share Act*, by its real name, to acknowledge billionaire investor Warren Buffett who had recently criticized the system that allowed the rich to pay a smaller portion of their income in taxes than middle- and working-class Americans whose wages were taxed at a higher rate than investment income:

---

[49] Brownstein, op. cit., p. 231.

[50] Gerard Baker, "Why Barack Obama Picked a Political Who's Who," op. cit., p. 150.

[51] Sanders, *Our Revolution*, p. 350.

[52] Tax Relief, Unemployment Insurance Reauthorization, and Job Creation Act, Pub.L. 111-312, December 17, 2010.

Last year my federal tax bill—the income tax I paid, as well as payroll taxes paid by me and on my behalf—was $6,938,744. That sounds like a lot of money. But what I paid was only 17.4 percent of my taxable income — and that's actually a lower percentage than was paid by any of the other 20 people in our office. Their tax burdens ranged from 33 percent to 41 percent and averaged 36 percent.

If you make money with money, as some of my super-rich friends do, your percentage may be a bit lower than mine. But if you earn money from a job, your percentage will surely exceed mine—most likely by a lot.[53]

Although Barack Obama's plan, later introduced as S. 2059[54] in February 2012, had little chance of being enacted without Republican support (it was eventually stopped by a Republican filibuster), the Republicans immediately reacted along robust ideological lines. Paul Ryan (R-Wis.), chairman of the House of Representatives Budget Committee, famously invoked class warfare on Fox News: "Class warfare may make for good politics but it makes for rotten economics."[55] Sanders, who had unsuccessfully filibustered the 2010 extension of the Bush tax cuts by the Obama administration,[56] supported the Buffet Rule and claimed that with a record-breaking $15 trillion national debt and a growing gap between the rich and everyone else, it was "absolutely absurd that the wealthiest people in the country [were] paying the lowest effective tax rate in decades."[57] In the context of the Occupy Wall Street movement, taxation, more than ever, stood out as the tool to implement social justice. The Marxist economist and professor emeritus at the University of Massachusetts, Amherst, Richard Wolff, published figures and arguments that comforted Sanders's more and more vocal demands for social

---

[53] Warren Buffett, "Stop Cuddling the Super-Rich," *New York Times*, August 14, 2011, https://www.nytimes.com/2011/08/15/opinion/stop-coddling-the-super-rich.html.

[54] S. 2059, A bill to reduce the deficit by imposing a minimum effective tax rate for high-income taxpayers, 112th Congress, 2nd Session, February 1, 2012, GovTrack.us, https://www.govtrack.us/congress/bills/112/s2059.

[55] "Republicans Criticize Tax on Millionaires Idea," Reuters, September 18, 2011, https://www.reuters.com/article/us-usa-debt-republicans/republicans-criticize-tax-on-millionaires-idea-idUSTRE78H19J20110918.

[56] Sanders, *The Speech*, op. cit., p. 167.

[57] Id., "The Buffett Rule," U.S. Senator for Vermont website, February 1, 2012, https://www.sanders.senate.gov/newsroom/recent-business/the-buffett-rule.

justice. In "The truth about 'class war' in America," Wolff contended that the Republican charge of class war was "Orwellian" and obtuse:

> First, at the end of the second world war, for every dollar Washington raised in taxes on individuals, it raised $1.50 in taxes on business profits. Today, that ratio is very different: for every dollar Washington gets in taxes on individuals, it takes 25 cents in taxes on business. In short, the last half century has seen a massive shift of the burden of federal taxation off business and onto individuals. Second, [...] over the same period, the federal income tax rate on the richest individuals fell from 91% to the current 35%.[58]

Figures published by the Tax Policy Center confirm that the corporate tax rates went down from 40% in 1945 to 21% in 2018,[59] and that the richest Americans lowered their marginal tax rate from 94% in 1945 to 37% in 2020.[60]

To finance his 2020 campaign promises, Sanders initially resorted to two main strategies to tax Wall Street. A tax of "a fraction of a percent" would be imposed "on Wall Street speculators who nearly destroyed the economy" a decade earlier in order to cancel all student debt and to offer tuition-free colleges.[61] The measure was almost presented as a form of restorative justice: "If Wall Street can be bailed out for several trillion dollars, 45 million Americans can and will be bailed out of the $1.6 trillion burden of student loan debt and we can provide free college for all."[62] The other measures were financed under one transversal—and highly symbolic—proposal that would ensure "that assets owned by the

[58] Richard D. Wolff, "The Truth About 'Class War' in America," *The Guardian*, September 19, 2011, https://www.theguardian.com/commentisfree/cifamerica/2011/sep/19/class-war-america-republicans-rich.

[59] Tax Policy Center, "Corporate Top Tax Rate and Bracket, 1909 to 2018," July 17, 2019, https://www.taxpolicycenter.org/statistics/corporate-top-tax-rate-and-bracket.

[60] Id., "Historical Highest Marginal Income Tax Rates, 1913 to 2020," February 4, 2020, https://www.taxpolicycenter.org/statistics/historical-highest-marginal-income-tax-rates.

[61] A 0.5% tax on stock trades (50 cents on every $100 of stock), a 0.1% fee on bond trades, and a 0.005% fee on derivative trade. Sanders, "College for All and Cancel All Student Debt," Not me. *Us* (2020 campaign website), https://berniesanders.com/issues/free-college-cancel-debt.

[62] Ibid.

top 0.1 percent are taxed the same way as much of the wealth owned by the middle-class is already taxed."[63] Later in the 2020 campaign for the Democratic nomination, Sanders released a new Income Inequality Tax Plan[64] specifically tailored to finance his plan to eliminate medical debt; the Income Inequality Tax Plan also aimed to send a message to corporate America: "stop paying your workers inadequate wages while CEOs make outrageous compensation packages."[65] Corporate taxes would increase according to how much more companies pay their top executives than their typical workers: +0.5% between 50 and 100 times; +1% between 100 and 200 times; +2% between 200 and 300 times; +3% between 300 and 400 times; +4% between 400 and 500 times; +5% over 500 times.[66] With the corporate top tax rate at 40% in 1945 and at 21% in 2020, while a 5% increase could indeed be regarded as a reparative measure, it was not perfectly restorative in itself in terms of social justice. But Sanders's Income Inequality Tax Plan was part of a larger, more comprehensive plan. The other significant component was a tax "on extreme wealth,"[67] which, to many opponents was no less than punitive. An annual tax would be imposed on the extreme wealth of the top 0.1 percent of American households (only to net worth of over $32 million) in order to raise an estimated $4.35 trillion over ten years and to "cut the wealth of billionaires in half over 15 years, which would substantially break up the concentration of wealth and power of this small privileged class."[68] In the words of Richard Rubin for the *Wall Street Journal*, Bernie Sanders's tax hikes amounted to "the biggest expansion of taxation since World War II,"[69] when the cost of fighting fascism prompted the federal government to extend the income tax to the middle class, roughly doubling the federal tax burden. While federal tax revenues amounted

---

[63] Id., "How Does Bernie Pay for His Major Plans," op. cit., p. 231.

[64] Id., "The Sanders Income Inequality Tax Plan," Not me. *Us* (2020 campaign website), https://berniesanders.com/issues/income-inequality-tax-plan.

[65] Id., "The Sanders Income Inequality Tax Plan," op. cit., p. 235.

[66] Ibid.

[67] Sanders, "Tax on Extreme Wealth," Not me. *Us* (2020 campaign website), https://berniesanders.com/issues/tax-extreme-wealth.

[68] Ibid.

[69] Richard Rubin, "Bernie Sanders's Tax Plan Would Be Biggest Expansion of Taxation Since World War II," *Wall Street Journal*, March 6, 2020, https://www.wsj.com/articles/sanders-plan-would-hoist-taxes-11583449105.

to 9.9% of gross domestic product in 1942, they had risen to 20.5% by 1944. Bernie Sanders's plan would raise the tax-revenue share of GDP by roughly the same amount, from a current average of 17.4% to a little more than 28% in ten years. Sanders's proposed tax increases topped $30 trillion over a decade, Rubin wrote, reaching more than 10% of GDP and at least a 60% increase in taxes. That would certainly entail a radical paradigm shift in a country like the United States. "Mr. Sanders's combination of taxes on wealth, income, financial transactions, corporate profits, payrolls, estates and capital gains would hit rich Americans from every direction," Rubin continued. "If Congress were to pass all his plans, the total U.S. tax burden—including federal, state and local taxes—would resemble Canada's or Germany's rather than being near the bottom of the pack of rich nations."[70]

If, as Jan-Werner Müller put it, "populists claim that they, and only they, represent the people,"[71] Bernie Sanders was a populist in that he claimed to represent the people. On the other hand, he was not really a populist if his 2020 slogan "Not me. Us" did mean that he did not claim that "he, and only he," represented the people:

Are the majority of people in our country deeply concerned about the grotesque level of income and wealth inequality that we are experiencing? You bet they are. Do they believe that our campaign finance system is corrupt and enables the rich to buy elections? Overwhelmingly, they do.

Do they want to raise the minimum wage to a living wage and provide pay equity for women? Yes, they do. Do they think the very rich and large corporations should pay more in taxes so that all of our kids can have free tuition at public colleges and universities? Yup. Do they believe that the United States should join every other major country and guarantee health care as a right? Yes, again. Do they believe climate change is real? You've got to be kidding. Are they tired of the United States of America, the wealthiest country in the history of the world, falling apart at the seams, with roads, bridges, water systems, wastewater plants, airports, rail, levees, and dams either failing or at risk of failing? Who isn't?[72]

To be sure, Bernie Sanders was a socialist. A democratic socialist.

---

[70] Ibid.

[71] Jan-Werner Müller, op. cit., p. 49.

[72] Sanders, *Where We Go from Here*, p. 3.

REFERENCES

Baker, Gerard. "Why Barack Obama Picked a Political Who's Who." *The Times* (December 5, 2008), https://www.thetimes.co.uk/article/why-bar ack-obama-picked-a-political-whos-who-mjc76tgzm6t.

Bellamy, Edward. *Looking Backward, 2000–1887.* Boston, MA: Houghton, Mifflin & Co., 1888. Rpt. Matthew Beaumont, ed. Oxford, New York: Oxford University Press, 2007.

Brownstein, Ronald. "The Cost of Sanders' Agenda—Possibly $60 Trillion— Would Set a Peacetime U.S. Record." CNN (January 18, 2020), https:// edition.cnn.com/2020/01/14/politics/bernie-sanders-proposals-cost/index. html.

Buffett, Warren. "Stop Cuddling the Super-Rich." *New York Times* (August 14, 2011), https://www.nytimes.com/2011/08/15/opinion/stop-coddling-the-super-rich.html.

Clinton, William J. In "Bill Clinton in 1992 ad: 'A Plan to End Welfare as We Know It.'" *Washington Post* (August 30, 2016), https://www.washingto npost.com/video/politics/bill-clinton-in-1992-ad-a-plan-to-end-welfare-as-we-know-it/2016/08/30/9e6350f8-6ee0-11e6-993f-73c693a89820_video. html.

———. Address Before a Joint Session of the Congress on the State of the Union (January 23, 1996). The American Presidency Project, https://www. presidency.ucsb.edu/node/223046.

Judis, John B. *The Populist Explosion: How the Great Recession Transformed American and European Politics.* New York: Columbia Global Reports, 2016.

Kitch, Sally L. *From Utopianism to Realism in American Feminist Thought and Theory.* Chicago, IL: University of Chicago Press, 2000.

Krugman, Paul. "Bernie Sanders Isn't a Socialist." *New York Times* (February 13, 2020), https://www.nytimes.com/2020/02/13/opinion/bernie-sanders-soc ialism.html.

Malcom, Andrew H. "Spock Nominated by People's Party." *New York Times* (July 30, 1972), https://www.nytimes.com/1972/07/30/archives/spock-nominated-by-peoples-party-convention-formally-names.html.

Müller, Jan-Werner. *What Is Populism?* Philadelphia: University of Pennsylvania Press, 2016.

Nichols, John. *The "S" Word: A Short History of an American Tradition…Socialism.* New York: Verso, 2011.

Purdum, Todd S. "Democrats of All Ages Agree on Nothing." *The Atlantic* (August 11, 2019), https://www.theatlantic.com/politics/archive/2019/ 08/how-democrats-view-obama/595837.

Ritz, Ben. "Even With New Pay-Fors, Bernie's Agenda Still Has A $25 Trillion Hole." *Forbes* (February 25, 2020), https://www.forbes.com/sites/benritz/ 2020/02/25/even-with-new-pay-fors-bernies-agenda-still-has-a-25-trillion-hole/#599af64466c1.

Rubin, Richard. "Bernie Sanders's Tax Plan Would Be Biggest Expansion of Taxation Since World War II." *Wall Street Journal* (March 6, 2020), https://www.wsj.com/articles/sanders-plan-would-hoist-taxes-11583449105.

Ryan, Bernard Jr. *Jimmy Carter: U.S. President and Humanitarian.* New York: Ferguson, 2006.

Sanders, Bernard. *Eugene V. Debs: Trade Unionist, Socialist, Revolutionary, 1855–1926.* New York: Folkways Records, 1979.

———, with Huck Gutman. *Outsider in the House: A Political Autobiography.* New York: Verso, 1997. Rpt. *Outsider in the White House,* 2015.

———. *The Speech: A Historic Filibuster on Corporate Greed and the Decline of Our Middle Class.* New York: Nation Books, 2011.

———. "The Buffett Rule." U.S. Senator for Vermont website (February 1, 2012), https://www.sanders.senate.gov/newsroom/recent-business/the-buffett-rule.

———. *Our Revolution: A Future to Believe in.* New York: Thomas Dunne Books, 2016.

———. Presidential Candidate Written Affirmation (March 5, 2019). NBC News, https://www.documentcloud.org/documents/5759487-Bernie-Sanders-signs-DNC-loyalty-pledge.html.

———. In "Bernie Sanders on Being the Democratic Front-Runner and Taking on Donald Trump." 60 Minutes, CBS News (February 24, 2020), https://www.cbsnews.com/news/bernie-sanders-democratic-presidential-front-runner-anderson-cooper-60-minutes.

———. "Bernie Sanders: I Thought This Question Might Come Up." CNN (February 24, 2020), https://www.youtube.com/watch?v=hYmlzB7AIWM&feature=emb_logo.

Scarborough, Joe. "Alexander Hamilton's Warning to 2016 Voters." *Washington Post* (May 22, 2016), https://www.washingtonpost.com/blogs/post-partisan/wp/2016/05/22/the-modern-populist-mutiny.

Siff, Sarah Brady. " "From Karl Marx to Karl Rove: "Class Warfare" in American Politics." *Origins*, vol. 5, n° 12 (September 2012), http://origins.osu.edu/article/karl-marx-karl-rove-class-warfare-american-politics.

Steffens, Lincoln J. *The Letters of Lincoln Steffens*, vol. 1, edited by Ella Winter and Granville Hicks. New York: Harcourt, Brace & Co., 1938.

Wolff, Richard D. "The Truth About 'Class War' in America." *The Guardian* (September 19, 2011), https://www.theguardian.com/commentisfree/cif america/2011/sep/19/class-war-america-republicans-rich.

Zeballos-Roig, Joseph. "Bernie Sanders and AOC Support the 'Nordic Model,' Which Features Robust Health and Social-Welfare Systems—One That Finland's Leader Calls 'the American Dream.'" Markets Insider (February 3, 2020), https://markets.businessinsider.com/news/stocks/bernie-sanders-nordic-model-finland-american-dream-sanna-marin-2020-2-1028868627.

EPILOGUE

There is no evidence of any specific connection between the Marxist historian Richard Wolff and Bernie Sanders, but Wolff, like Sanders, identified
the Occupy Wall Street movement as a moment to demand accountability.
"We shouldn't have private banks," he wrote in *Occupy the Economy:
Challenging Capitalism*. "We should have a public banking system that
helps communities, enterprises, and people, a publicly accountable system
that is open and transparent, so that we do not have the risk of them
waltzing us into such a crisis yet again."[1] Wolff's approach was "democratic" in that it did not want power "concentrated in a tiny number
of people, let alone one," seeing to make it "a larger number of people
that are accountable to one another and to the public."[2] In *Capitalism's
Crisis Deepens: Essays on the Global Economic Meltdown, 2010–2014*, he
explained that Occupy Wall Street was "the urgently needed, broad movement to reorganize our society, to make our institutions accountable to
the public will, and to establish both economic democracy and ecological sanity."[3] Accountability may be regarded as a way to circumvent the
tension that has always existed between the two basic dimensions of the

---

[1] Wolff, *Occupy the Economy: Challenging Capitalism*, San Francisco, CA, City Lights
Books, 2012, p. 150.

[2] Ibid., p. 158.

[3] Id., *Capitalism's Crisis Deepens: Essays on the Global Economic Meltdown, 2010–2014*,
Chicago, IL, Haymarket Books, 2016, p. 284.

American left. The American left, Wolff wrote in *Democracy at Work: A Cure for Capitalism*, needs and desires to be concrete and practical, with direct responses to people's immediate needs and solutions for current problems. But on the other hand it needs to project its utopian dimensions, its visions for what could solve not only current problems but also the underlying structural conditions that keep regenerating them. Utopian visions carry sets of alternative conditions that people believe could work and are therefore worth fighting for.[4] The tension in the American left, and what Wolff identified as "structural conditions" that keep generating social problems, is in fact what the conversation between Barack Obama and Bernie Sanders was all about, about what it meant to "tear down the system."[5] Utopia is a double-edged sword that is often instrumentalized in the political discourse.

"When a word as contentious as 'utopia' appears in a book's title," Barbara Goodwin and Keith Taylor wrote in *The Politics of Utopia: A Study in Theory and Practice*, "the first chapter is usually bristling with definitions and refutations of counter definitions."[6] A deliberate choice in the present volume was to start from an analysis of Bernie Sanders's political trajectory to understand how his democratic socialism could be said to hold utopia accountable. In the words of Goodwin and Taylor:

> To start with a stipulative definition of the term [...] would be self-defeating because, in dealing with the place of utopianism in political thought, we must consider theories which have been called utopian by their critics, perhaps erroneously, as well as works conforming to the traditional utopian form—a voyage to a lost island or into the future.[7]

Everyone has their own pre-conceived definition of utopia, ranging from the pejorative to the laudatory, from something "unrealizable because hopelessly idealistic" to something that connotes "an ideal, a real alternative."[8] Holding utopia accountable, from that angle, therefore, can

---

[4] Wolff, *Democracy at Work: A Cure for Capitalism*, Chicago, IL, Haymarket Books, 2012, p. 178.

[5] See *supra*, p. 31.

[6] Barbara Goodwin, Keith Taylor, *The Politics of Utopia: A Study in Theory and Practice*, London, Hutchinson & Co., 1982. Rpt. Bern, Peter Lang, 2009, p. 3.

[7] Ibid.

[8] Ibid.

be regarded has having two distinct, arguably opposite meanings. One was Barack Obama's argument to discredit Bernie Sanders's democratic socialism, claiming that "the average American doesn't think we have to completely tear down the system,"[9] or for what Democratic candidate Joe Biden called "pie in the sky" to qualify Sanders's proposals in March 2020.[10] The other was Sanders's answer to Obama: "[w]ell, it depends on what you mean by tear down the system."[11] For Sanders, holding utopia accountable meant actualizing the American promise for all Americans by effectively, radically, addressing what Richard Wolff called "the underlying structural conditions"[12] that keep generating inequality.

While the entire socialist project, both in thought and action, has always been predicated on hope for the future,[13] Occupy Wall Street was a movement that focused on social ills in the present, on what Martin Luther King Jr. called "the fierce urgency of now,"[14] and sought to occupy the very location of "the underlying structural conditions"[15] that keep generating inequality. In the wake of Occupy Wall Street, Sanders's utopian spirit stemmed from a realization that the future could no longer transcend the present, therefore that the present had to be changed so that the future could, possibly, surpass it. In *The End of Utopia: Politics and Culture in an Age of Apathy*, Russell Jacoby wrote about the perceived inevitability of present conditions:

> We are increasingly asked to choose between the status quo or something worse. Other alternatives do not seem to exist. We have entered the era of acquiescence, in which we build our lives, families and careers with little expectation that the future will diverge from the present.[16]

[9] Obama, quoted in Medina, Lerer, op. cit., p. 31.

[10] Zack Budryk, "Biden Steps Up Attacks on Sanders as Super Tuesday Approaches," The Hill, March 1, 2020, https://thehill.com/homenews/sunday-talk-shows/485365-biden-steps-up-attacks-on-sanders-as-super-tuesday-approaches.

[11] Sanders, quoted in Medina, Lerer, op. cit., p. 31.

[12] Wolff, *Democracy at Work*, op. cit., p. 239.

[13] Ruth Levitas, "Extended Review: Socialism and Utopia," *The Sociological Review*, vol. 33, n° 3, August 1985, p. 559.

[14] King, "I Have a Dream," op. cit., p. 147.

[15] Wolff, *Democracy at Work*, op. cit., p. 239.

[16] Russell Jacoby, *The End of Utopia: Politics and Culture in an Age of Apathy*, New York, Basic Books, 1999, p. xi.

Utopia, therefore, must be held accountable and actualized in the present according to Sanders. And the root causes that keep generating inequality were known to him: "The United States is the wealthiest country in the history of the world. But that reality means very little for most Americans, because so much of that wealth is owned and controlled by a tiny handful of individuals."[17] Those individuals, therefore, must be made accountable to the 99% of Americans, as the system they live by, in the words of Richard Wolff, is itself a "neoclassical" utopia of America:

> Neoclassical economists had always attacked the Keynesian economics associated with Roosevelt's New Deal for seriously distorting and slowing economic growth and promoting social conflict (sometimes dubbed "class war"). They sought to reinstitute the neoclassical utopia: private and competitive markets lifting the incomes of both labor and capital and thereby avoiding class conflicts by means of growth.[18]

When this system arguably failed the great majority of American people, Sanders asked for accountability. Bernie Sanders's democratic socialism started as a socialist utopia and evolved into the political mainstream as he sought to make it progressively accountable to the present of American democracy, to "the fierce urgency of now," suggesting an alternative system and demanding social reparations for the great majority of Americans:

> We cannot allow this to continue. I urge all of you to stand up, fight back, and get active in the political process.
> —Bernie Sanders.[19]

[17] Sanders, *Our Revolution*, p. 206.

[18] Wolff, *Capitalism Crisis Deepens*, p. 8.

[19] Sanders, *Where We Go from Here*, p. 138.

REFERENCES

Budryk, Zack. "Biden Steps Up Attacks on Sanders as Super Tuesday Approaches." *The Hill* (March 1, 2020), https://thehill.com/homenews/sunday-talk-shows/485365-biden-steps-up-attacks-on-sanders-as-super-tuesday-approaches.

Goodwin, Barbara, Keith Taylor. *The Politics of Utopia: A Study in Theory and Practice.* London: Hutchinson & Co., 1982. Rpt. Bern, Peter Lang, 2009.

Jacoby, Russell. *The End of Utopia: Politics and Culture in an Age of Apathy.* New York: Basic Books, 1999.

King, Martin Luther Jr. "I Have a Dream," Address delivered at the March on Washington for Jobs and Freedom (August 28, 1963). The Martin Luther King Jr. Research and Education Institute (Stanford University), https://kinginstitute.stanford.edu/king-papers/documents/i-have-dream-address-delivered-march-washington-jobs-and-freedom.

Levitas, Ruth. "Extended Review: Socialism and Utopia." *The Sociological Review*, vol. 33, n° 3 (August 1985), pp. 558–588.

Medina, Jennifer, Lisa Lerer. "Too Far Left? Some Democratic Candidates Don't Buy Obama's Argument." *New York Times* (November 22, 2019), https://www.nytimes.com/2019/11/16/us/obama-left-democrats-2020.html.

Sanders, Bernard. *Our Revolution: A Future to Believe in.* New York: Thomas Dunne Books, 2016.

———. *Where We Go from Here: Two Years in the Resistance.* New York: Thomas Dunne Books, 2018.

Wolff, Richard D. *Occupy the Economy: Challenging Capitalism.* San Francisco, CA: City Lights Books, 2012.

© The Editor(s) (if applicable) and The Author(s), under exclusive license to Springer Nature Switzerland AG 2021
N. Gachon, *Bernie Sanders's Democratic Socialism*,
https://doi.org/10.1007/978-3-030-69661-0

———. *Democracy at Work: A Cure for Capitalism.* Chicago, IL: Haymarket Books, 2012.

———. *Capitalism's Crisis Deepens: Essays on the Global Economic Meltdown, 2010–2014.* Chicago, IL: Haymarket Books, 2016.

INDEX

© The Editor(s) (if applicable) and The Author(s), under exclusive
license to Springer Nature Switzerland AG 2021
N. Gachon, *Bernie Sanders's Democratic Socialism*,
https://doi.org/10.1007/978-3-030-69661-0

Printed by Printforce, the Netherlands